Credits

Every effort has been made to contact copyright holders for permission to reproduce borrowed material where necessary. We apologize for any oversights and would be happy to rectify them in future printings.

Story, "Under the Mountain," used by permission of Bryce Stevens.

Story, "And They Lived Happily Ever After," by Hilda Avant, used by permission of Patsy Floyd.

Story, "A Little Girl's View: Persecution in the Pews," used by permission of Pam Petty.

Personal story, "Chainsaw Nightmare," used by permission of Roger Hyder.

Story, "Goldilocks and the What?" by Hilda Avant, used by permission of Patsy Floyd.

Personal story, "Kidnapped," used by permission of Gail Hyder.

Jake Bridgewater stories that appeared in *Once-Upon-A Times* used by permission of Joe Yukish, editor, *Once-Upon-A Times*.

Story, "Anna Joyce and Shelby," used by permission of author, Lynda Breeden, and editor, *Once-Upon-A Times,* Joe Yukish.

Story, "An Invented Spelling Experience," used by permission of author, Danielle Aspinwall, and editor, *Tennessee Reading Teacher*, Ed Dwyer.

Excerpt from *The War at Home* by Connie Jordan Green. New York: Margaret K. McElderry Books, 1989. Used by permission of the author.

"Romeo and Juliet Retelling" used by permission of author, Dustin L. Smith.

Illustration, "Freytag Pyramid," used by permission of Harcourt Brace.

Story about Bird Henson, used by permission of author, Charles Sherrill.

"The Story of Raven" used by permission of teller, Martha Sauceman.

Story, "The Trick That Worked," used by permission of author, M. Jane Crooks.

Story, "My Story" used by permission of author, Pam Petty.

Story, " And All This Junk Is a Truck?" used by permission of author, Boyd Ray.

Story, " Granny Ollie," used by permission of author, Jeff Huddleston.

Christopher-Gordon Publishers, Inc.
1502 Providence Highway, Suite #12
Norwood, MA 02062
Tel: 800-934-8322

Copyright 1998 by Christopher-Gordon Publishers, Inc.

Printed in the United States of America

10 9 8 7 6 5 4 3 2 1   02 01 00 99 98 97

ISBN: 0-926842-71-4

Teaching Through Stories:
Yours, Mine and Theirs

Teaching Through Stories: Yours, Mine and Theirs

Betty Roe,

Suellen Alfred, Sandy Smith

Christopher-Gordon Publishers, Inc.
Norwood, Massachusetts

Dedication

To Michael H. Roe, with thanks for his help and support throughout this project; to Dusty and Tyler Smith for their inspiration and cooperation; and in memory of Freeda Murray Alfred, a natural storyteller.

Acknowledgments

In working on this book we have had assistance from many people. We would like to acknowledge their help and express our sincere appreciation.

The book would never have come into being if Sue Canavan had not seen merit in our initial idea and supported us in its development. We are also appreciative of Laurie Maker's editorial assistance and the helpful comments of reviewers of the manuscript.

We particularly appreciate the stories provided to us by our families, friends, and students. We feel that the stories are the heart of the book. Therefore, we owe a particular debt of gratitude to Connie Jordan Green, Charles Sherrill, Bryce Stevens, Pam Petty, Gail and Roger Hyder, Martha Sauceman, Dusty Smith, Martha Albright, Jeff Huddleston, Jane Crooks, Lynda Walker Breeden, Danielle Aspinwall, Annika Garman, Lisa Morrison, and Boyd Ray. We are also indebted to Patsy Floyd for allowing us to use two stories written by the late Hilda Avant, a wonderful teacher and storyteller.

We also want to express appreciation to Mike Roe and Connie Green for their careful readings and insightful comments about the manuscript, and we want to thank Mike for his computer assistance and help with the task of permissions collections. Finally, we want to thank Ellen Wolfe for her assistance with the index.

Table of Contents

Preface

Overview

The idea for writing this book originally came from classroom teachers who heard us present sessions about storytelling and said, "We need a book with this kind of material. You should write a book." We took them at their word and this was the result.

Teaching Through Stories: Yours, Mine, and Theirs is designed to help teachers learn to use storytelling in the classroom to convey information, develop rapport, and provide pleasurable learning experiences. It describes uses for teachers' and children's own stories, as well as the stories from a multitude of outside sources.

This book provides information on the importance of using stories in classroom settings, how teachers and students can tell effective stories, and how to use stories in various curricular areas. It offers teachers a theoretical basis for the use of storytelling, gives them practical tips on storytelling techniques, and provides practical storytelling activities for use across the curriculum in kindergarten through high school. It shows teachers both how to learn and tell stories themselves and how to help students learn and tell stories. We have either personally classroom tested the activities that we describe in this book, or we have observed their successful use by others.

This book is appropriate for use in storytelling classes, in inservice training sessions, and as a resource for individual teachers who wish to use storytelling in their classrooms. Storytelling is a powerful tool for teachers who integrate instruction across the curriculum and for teachers in many separate content areas.

Approach

The book is written in a conversational style intermingled with story examples, but it is well documented with references to lead interested readers to source materials.

Each chapter opens with an appropriate story, which can serve as the basis for discussion of some chapter content. In most chapters, the story is concluded at the end of the chapter. Readers who do not want the suspense to extend throughout the chapters can turn to the ends of the chapters and read the stories' conclusions. Each chapter contains suggested practical activities applicable to the chapter focus and a bibliography. Activities and stories for use with grades K-12 are presented.

We have included personal stories and folktales in this book, as well as literary tales, and we show applications for teachers in middle school and high school settings, as well as in elementary schools. We feel that teachers in higher grades have frequently been overlooked. Stories can be a vehicle for working on many literacy and content skills and understandings. We address the use of storytelling in several different content areas.

Personal stories offer personal involvement in and ownership of the classroom activities in which they are featured, aspects that are important for effective instruction. The journals in the reading and language arts fields reflect the movement toward holistic teaching practices and thematic teaching in all grade levels, including secondary schools. Resources for middle and secondary school teachers do not appear to have kept pace with the need, and the interest in storytelling in elementary schools appears to be higher than ever before.

This book serves three functions. It shows teachers how to tell stories effectively, how to help students tell stories, and how to use stories for instructional purposes. It also encourages the use of stories that *belong* to the teacher and students in special ways, lessening the need for extensive access to anthologies.

Chapter 1 provides a brief overview of the subject to set the stage for the ensuing chapters and gives background about storytelling that some readers may lack. Chapter 2 offers information about how to tell stories and how to help children become tellers. Chapters 3-10 address the integration of storytelling into the curriculum in a number of content areas. Chapter 11 considers the topic of cultural diversity, and Chapter 12 addresses the use of storytelling to help understand oneself and others. Two appendixes provide suggested storytelling references and sources of stories for tellers.

Betty D. Roe
Suellen Alfred
Sandy Smith

Chapter 1
The Importance of Story

꧁꧂

Linda rousted us out before seven o'clock. Amidst our sleepy protests she announced, "It's my van, and I'm leaving. If you want to ride out of here, get up and pack."

"Linda, why are you so set on leaving right now?" I asked. "It's a beautiful morning."

"I just want to go. Now. I don't know why," she said.

Soon we were on the road. We all relaxed and enjoyed the scenery as we traveled the twenty-some miles of gravel forest service and logging roads from our campsite back to the highway. Tall trees and occasional small ponds lined most of the road, broken here and there by clearcuts which revealed panoramas of western Washington's mountain crests receding to the misty blue horizon.

When we reached the highway an hour later, we all piled out, thankful for a chance to stretch. Looking up, we saw a black cloud rolling in across the western sky. We were surprised to see a small airplane that seemed barely able to outrun the cloud's leading edge.

"I haven't seen a storm come in like that since I was a kid in Indiana," I remarked.

"Looks like we're really in for it," a friend agreed.

A rabbit darted out of the undergrowth into the highway, paused with a look of surprise and confusion, then leapt into the brush across the road. A flicker flew from a high limb to the brush as if in pursuit of the rabbit. A pea green forest service vehicle raced past us at breakneck speed.

"I wonder what his big hurry is," Linda said.

"I don't know," I said, "but that storm is nearly over us. We'd better get in the van or we're going to get soaked."

We were barely situated in the van when the storm hit. Solid chunks clattered against the roof and bounced off the road, accumulating to half an inch in under a minute. Linda's boyfriend Mike started the engine and pulled onto the highway, when the nature of the downpour abruptly changed. Large globules of mud suddenly coated everything, eliminating visibility. This lasted only a minute or so in real time; much longer in the confusion of the crisis, as Mike slowed to a crawl. He pulled at the washer fluid knob in an effort to keep the windshield clear enough to see through.

The mudfall ceased with the same suddenness that it started, and blackness enveloped us. We all rode in grim silence, unsure and disoriented by the unnatural phenomenon. I noticed that Linda's olive Native American complexion was nearly as pale as the rest of us were naturally. My wife Trinda's eyes were wide with wonder. Mike's muscles were taut, his knuckles white from gripping the steering wheel. We looked at one another with mute incomprehension. I felt a welling panic.

The black gloom thickened. Visibility with the headlights dropped to a scant yard. We began choking on fine dust that poured in through the weary joints of the aging Volkswagen.

"The volcano," Trinda murmured.

"I think we're in trouble," Linda said with a sigh.

Thoughts of Pompeii came to my mind. The volcano, of course. We had gone camping in hopes of seeing the steam plume St. Helens had been producing for several weeks. And now the mountain itself was raining down on us. I kept imagining those Pompeii victims, choked and fossilized in their efforts to escape that ancient eruption.

We spoke very little. Linda summed it up: "I'm scared. I want out of here."

The class members drank in Bryce Stevens' personal experience with rapt attention. Their absorption in the experience was complete.

Ash fell. We slowly pushed on. I realized that it must have been a shower of pumice pebbles that first fell on us, not hail. There was no way to guess how much ash might fall on us or how far we would manage to travel before it forced us to stop.

I suggested trying to get to a twenty-four hour restaurant in Randle, about six miles down the road. "At least we'll be with other people, and they'll try to dig out a place like that before they go after isolated vehicles like ours," I said.

The others readily agreed. Having a goal that was within reach lifted our spirits. Unless the showering ash increased dramatically, we would be able to reach Randle before the highway became impassable.

*To fight against the choking, stinging ash, Trinda collected every-
one's bandanas. She opened the ice chest, soaked the bandanas in the
melt water and passed them around. Tying them over our mouths and
noses helped our breathing, but could not keep the scratchy grit from
our eyes.*

*Our progress was reduced by now to about three miles an hour.
The roadway had disappeared under a thick layer of ash. The only
way Mike could find our path was to feel for the gentle bumps of the
road turtles marking the highway lanes. He frequently lost the reas-
suring thump of the markers, the crunch of gravel warning him that
he had strayed too far to the left or right. Mike had always seemed
carefree, content to let others worry about responsibilities. But now,
groping for a safe path out of the oblivion, his apparent calm as he
finessed his way down the highway was belied by the iron determination that sculpted his face.*

Bryce's story told of history being made, but it also told of a very intense
personal involvement in the making. These involved listeners would not soon
forget Bryce's graphic descriptions.

What Is Story?

In the example above, we see story at work, but what exactly is story?
Livo and Rietz (1986, p. 2) say, "'Story' is...a way of thinking, a primary
organizer of information and ideas, the soul of a culture, and the mythic and
metaphoric consciousness of a people. It is a prehistoric and historic thread of
human awareness, a way in which we can know, remember, and understand."
A story is a restructured experience that has information arranged in a way
that allows it to be saved and retrieved. Everyday experiences can be restructured into the story shapes, sometimes being somewhat transformed by the
process (Livo & Rietz, 1986). This definition fits our envisionment of story
quite well. We also believe, as do Trousdale, Woestehoff, and Schwartz
(1994) that through these restructurings we define ourselves and our places in
the order of things. Indeed, we understand our pasts and picture our futures
through the stories that we tell and that we hear others tell. Through his story,
Bryce came to realize the significance of the events that he had experienced
and was able to structure these events into a form that would allow him to
retrieve them for reflection in the future.

Some people hesitate to tell stories about real happenings because they
are afraid that they will not remember every detail exactly, or perhaps they do
not wish to share all of the details. A personal experience story can be effective, however, even if every detail is not told exactly as it happened, as long

as the overall telling is true to the point being made. For example, in his story about Mount St. Helens, Bryce includes dialogue, even though those present at the event probably didn't speak those exact words. Sometimes the story-teller may even exaggerate an element of an event to emphasize its significance, but the story is true to the spirit of the event.

Producing oral accounts of experiences is different from producing written ones. Oral stories contain noises, vocal inflections, facial expressions, and body language that may not lend themselves well to written language. Thus, since oral language lacks the permanence of written language, these oral accounts must be repeated again and again to endure (Livo & Rietz, 1986).

A story needs a beginning that draws the audience into the story, a logical sequence, and a definite ending that brings the action to a close. Crafting these parts for personal stories is somewhat more difficult than simply telling a folktale or a story that someone else has written because the responsibility for *framing* the story is left up to the teller. Tellers must include sensory information to make the story come alive—sights, sounds, smells, tastes, and sensations of touch all help to paint the word picture. (Bryce told the group about *large globules of mud that suddenly coated everything, solid chunks that clattered against the roof, and choking on the fine dust,* among other sensory details that brought the story alive in the chapter-opening story.)

In actuality, an oral story is a fresh event every time it is retold. Like jazz, it has an ethereal quality because it captures a series of events in a unique way and then is gone, leaving only a memory. Repeated tellings of a story will result in smoothing of and modifications to it, but it will never be completely formed. It will always be "in process," and no two tellings will ever be the same. Even though it is constantly changing, a personal story is rarely forgotten because the teller has lived through the experience, leaving him or her with a more vivid impression of it than would be likely with a story from a printed source.

A story emerges from a particular telling differently from other tellings because of the dynamic context in which it is told, including the particular audience and setting. The audience enters into the story with the teller and affects its construction (Hillman, 1979; Livo & Rietz, 1986). For example, students may establish connections with classmates by sharing personal stories, and teachers may relieve tension and build a sense of community with fellow teachers by sharing stories about significant teaching experiences. Likewise, family members strengthen bonds as they share family history, problems, and triumphs. For these reasons, putting personal experiences into story form is important for a person's psychological well-being. Storytelling acts as a therapeutic release for the teller and a revelation for the listener in situations of stress and tension.

The following story is one that Hilda Avant's fellow teachers could easily relate to:

And They Lived Happily Ever After
By Hilda Avant

Storytelling was always one of my favorite classroom activities. Being a "ham" by nature, I took pride in being able to transport children from their daily routines into a fantasyland—allowing them to crawl inside the skins of their favorite storybook characters. Even after I left the classroom and assumed the role of supervisor, I often asked teachers to allow me the privilege of borrowing their classes for the storytelling hour.

One day, my assistant and I were visiting a parochial school where, apparently, the students had been denied the privilege of meeting the classic storybook characters. I was telling the story of The Gingerbread Boy, *and I capitalized on the naive interest of the children by giving my best dramatic delivery, complete with props which included a real gingerbread man. I used my voice to imply the excitement as the gingerbread boy arrived at the river and was met by the sly old fox.*

The children listened intently as I described the danger to the gingerbread boy when he climbed aboard the fox's tail, then moved upward to his back and finally onto the fox's head as the water grew deeper.

The air was tense as the anxious eyes of the six year olds silently pleaded with me for the safety of their hero. Carrying my audience further into the mystery, I embroidered the facts and extended the climax of the story. I described how the gingerbread boy finally climbed upon the nose of the greedy fox in order to escape the rising tide. "Then," I added in a voice of deep concern, "the fox took one big gulp, and what do you suppose happened?"

"I know! I know!" squealed one entranced little boy on the front row. "A big ole alligator come up from outta that water and he 'et up that mean old fox!"

I know when I've lost my audience. We all agreed that, indeed, an alligator could have rescued the gingerbread boy; and, since it was a make-believe story, it might as well have a happy ending (Avant, 1983, pp. 37-38).

This next story is one that Pam Petty's family members can enjoy and cherish as a part of family history:

❧❧❧

A Little Girl's View: Persecution in the Pews
By Pam Petty

From the time I was born until I was five years old and started first grade, my life revolved around the rhythm of that little country farm. We really didn't even need a calendar on the farm where I grew up. If you were working on the farm, it was somewhere between Monday and Friday. If you went to town to buy groceries, it was Saturday. And you could always tell when Sunday got there because that's when you went to church.

I don't know if this is true of most people, but as a child I equated church with...torture. It wasn't the religion, or even the going to church that bothered me. I liked that. It was the physical discomfort that went with it.

It started with being much cleaner than I generally liked to be. Intrusive types of clean, like ears, fingernails, and the occasional bruise that my mother did her best to scrub away. And me without the vocabulary to explain to her the dangers of aggravating an internal hematoma. I had to resort to saying the same three words over and over again, each time with increasing urgency: "You're killing me; you're killing me; you're killing me!" Which didn't slow her down one bit, but added a degree of drama to the entire episode.

Even after passing inspection umpteen dozen times, I still recall having to endure spit-baths in the parking lot of the church. The people who make those premoistened towelettes have saved children years of humiliation and motherly germs.

After I had achieved a tolerable level of cleanliness, there was the matter of being properly attired, so as to look like all the other little girls in Sunday school. I don't know who was in charge of the fashion industry for little girls in the 1950's, but whoever it was must have either (A) not ever known a real, live little girl or (B) known little girls but just not liked them very much.

First, there was the can-can slip to put on. A can-can slip starts out just like a regular slip—smooth, silky, nylon—but then just below the waist it takes a nasty turn. Layers and layers of netting are sewn onto the bodice to give dresses a flared-out effect. Now, if you have never tried to sit on a split-rail church pew for lengthy periods of time in a can-can slip, it is very much like sitting on wadded up chicken wire—covered with ants. You cannot make friends with a can-can slip. Every human rights organization of our time would be protesting in the streets if we tried to make convicted felons wear can-can slips. But in the 1950's it was perfectly acceptable, even expected, for a little girl to wear this uncomfortable garment in her "misery ensemble"—and that's not all!

Another part of the ensemble was a frilly dress with lace to tick-le tender places like around your neck, just below your elbow, and just above your knees. Which would have been tolerable if it hadn't been for the sash, which would have been tolerable if it hadn't been for the bow—and the dreaded "knot." Imagine with me, if you will, taking a golf ball and lodging it between your 18th and 19th verte-brae. Every breath you take helps lodge it further into your torso. No contortion of your spine will make it go away. And while it made you want to flop around on that pew like a bass on a river bank, there was a grandmother on one side and a mother on the other side that would pinch a plug out of you if you moved so as to draw attention to your-self. By the time you got to the car to go home, you were certain that that knot had grown to the size of a softball and you expected serious bruising had occurred.

I never entered that little country church without a tear in my eye. It wasn't that my religion and the conviction in my soul brought out deep, moving emotions. It was the unmerciful attacks on my hair each and every Sunday morning. God blessed/cursed me with naturally curly hair. If you don't know what being blessed/cursed is, you don't have naturally curly hair. Naturally curly-headed babies should not be born to straight-haired mothers. It is an anomaly of nature for this to happen. People suffer needlessly. Not understanding the unpre-dictable nature of my hair, my mother made it a lifetime goal to bat-tle it into submission. She would roll it on these little, tiny, pink sponge rollers. When these rollers had produced tight, cylindrical springs all over my head, she would determine it was time to "brush it out." To me, "brush it out" loosely translated into "pull it out." She would brush until her arms ached. And still it would spring back at her. She would limit her attack to one side of my head at a time, brush until she had it smooth, then move on to the next side, only to find that the first side had assumed its original springy structure. Frustrated and exhausted, she would resort to hair-holding implements—bar-rettes, rubber bands, bobby pins—lots of them. I'm sure I have brain lesions today from improperly applied barrettes that my mother real-ly wanted to hold that hair in place. There should be warning labels on those things: Jabbing this barrette directly into your child's scalp may cause permanent scarring and lots of screaming. And if it was raining or the humidity was high, well, let's just say that the rising and falling of tides, the constant changing of the seasons, and the twirling of naturally curly hair are in God's hands alone. My younger sister was the one who was really blessed. With her long straight hair, she did not have to endure the torture of the curly-headed. She often brushed her own hair in the car on the way to church. Talk about salt in an open wound!

And then, no little girl torture suit is complete without black, patent leather shoes. Now these particular implements of pain came in many shapes and styles, but they all served the same purpose: to overshadow the agony of the slip, the knot, and the hair-pulling devices. When I was a child, "A" was the only letter of the alphabet dedicated to the width of a black, patent leather shoe. Your foot simply did not have the "B, C, or W" option. Everyone was an "A". It was only after I became an adult and read about the practice of eastern civilizations' binding of women's feet that I realized the concept wasn't invented by the people who made patent leather shoes, but I suspect they looked to those foot binding people for advice.

Except for the possible brain lesions detectable only with sophisticated CAT Scan equipment, there are no visible signs of the little girl's pew persecution I suffered as a child. Remarkably, though, there are precious memories of that country church and my family members who sat on that pew with me each Sunday. And I feel proud, and very blessed, that people loved me enough to torture me that much, each and every Sunday (Petty, 1996).

Why Is Storytelling Important?

Storytelling has been important to individuals since the early days of civilization, and personal stories serve many of the same functions now that they did then. In those early days, storytelling included the tales of hunting recounted by the hunter and the tales of war recounted by the warrior. The listeners vicariously experienced the excitement of the hunt or the battle. As the people gathered around campfires, the stories told ranged from those designed to transmit information to those told strictly for entertainment. Both personal and historical stories were likely among the stories passed along at these times. Opportunities to brag about personal exploits, pay homage to ancestors, and pass along customs and rituals presented themselves at such times (Chambers, 1977; Maguire, 1985). Today we still tell stories of our adventures and everyday activities, and these stories continue to pass along messages or instructions to the listeners, issue warnings to them, and entertain them (Stone, 1988). Teachers, librarians, religious leaders, camp counselors, and public speakers of many types use stories as a flexible tool to inform and entertain their listeners.

Gradually, in the early days, some people emerged as better tellers and were chosen to learn and tell the stories of the group as a whole. At this time, the storyteller often became important enough to the tribe or village to be relieved of other duties in order to concentrate on preservation of the stories. This elevation of the teller is a strong testimony to the power of storytelling. Because of superior communication ability, the person who performed this duty eventually came to function in such roles as historian, spokesperson for the group in encounters with other groups, and mediator between the group and its deities. This person passed along stories that formed the basic beliefs of the people's religion; hero tales, which had their roots in truth, but had imaginative elaborations; other historical stories and genealogies of the tribe, village, or country; and fables, tales that taught morals or lessons. Because of the common attributes of humans, similar tales were passed down in various cultures, but the characteristics of the particular culture were evident in the variations (Sawyer, 1962; Tooze, 1959). Chapter 11 describes this situation in detail. In a way, these tales from a person's culture are also a part of that individual's personal stories, because they show the factors that have shaped his or her customs and beliefs.

Over the years before the language was so "frozen in print" as a result of the printing press, travelers carried stories from country to country. They spread the stories of one group to other groups as they made their way on their journeys—nomads, gypsies, traders, pilgrims, and crusaders all added to the mix of stories with common roots in different cultures. In some places there were people who devoted themselves to storytelling, many depending upon sponsorship of rich benefactors, but some simply traveling from place to place, bartering their stories for lodging and food (Chambers, 1977; Sawyer, 1962). Storytellers of the Lenapé (Delaware) tribe "traveled from village to village during the winter, telling stories. Upon entering a village, a Storyteller would be invited to tell his stories, gifts would be given, and food and shelter provided for him. Storytellers were regarded as bringers of good luck" (Hitakonanu'laxk, 1994, p. 42). And, throughout the ages, there have been people sitting in their houses or on their front porches, telling stories about themselves and their families.

Even today, there are some people who keep the tradition of learning the oral history of their culture, even though the stories can be committed to print. Paula Underwood (1996) is a fifth-generation Keeper of the Old Things for her Iroquois family. Such History Keepers are chosen young for their needed abilities, such as memory, concentration, attention, and comprehension, and are invited to embrace the calling. They are allowed to decide whether they want to invest a major part of their lives in learning and recalling the ancient tellings of their people. The Iroquois do not require passing along the history word-for-word as is true with Maori genealogies and the Community Histories of African griots, but they do expect the History Keeper to find ways to allow the community to re-experience the events. They are expected to retell the stories in contemporary ways, to reach the people who listen. They know a story so well that they can "stand in the middle of that memory and look around, trying once more to learn something new from an ancient and valuable Keeping" (Underwood, 1996, p. 21).

Although we now have vast collections of stories in print and many volumes of historical material available, there is still the need for sharing of personal stories. Storytelling establishes connections with others. It keeps alive events and understandings that are not likely to be committed to the printed page. Family members' trials, successes, and strange antics may pass into oblivion if no one bothers to learn and share these tales. We lose a part of our valued heritage each time an ancestor dies without passing along his or her stories.

Storytelling remains a way to teach subtle points and make elusive abstractions concrete. It can illustrate the human dimension of otherwise dry facts in history, geography, and science classes, and it serves parents well as they try to pass along family customs and values.

Finally, we should not overlook the pure joy and recreation that storytelling can provide. We are all treasure chests of personal and family stories. As Baker and Greene (1987) point out, storytelling is a gift that should be given to others.

Bryce Stevens continued telling his story to a room full of intent listeners.

Suddenly our whole field of vision opened when a thick rope of lightning exploded across the highway at tree-top level. We gasped in horror as an ancient fir burst into flame, almost immediately extinguished by the heavy ashfall. For the next hour this freakish staccato accompanied our trek. In the limited range of our headlights a bird dropped dead on the road. We saw the death dances of bees and insects etched upon the ash. The suffocating atmosphere, choking out fire and life, became my greatest concern as we struggled ahead in grim silence. Was it the thick ash, or was it a lack of oxygen due to volcanic gases that allowed nothing to survive but the frightening, sulfurous bolts of lightning? I studied my companions. Other than their pallor, which I attributed to awe and fear, they seemed fine. Everyone's eyes were wide open and alert; no signs of drowsiness or disorientation. It must have been the thick ash outside the van, and not the air itself, causing the bizarre events we were witnessing.

After two hours of work, no less grueling for us three passengers

than for our driver, we felt, more than saw, an openness around us.
The hellish bolts ceased. The black seemed less pressing.

"It's not as bad here," Linda observed.

"I think we may be in Randle," I said. "Watch for a big driveway;
that should be the restaurant."

"I think you're right," Mike told us. "We've come almost seven
miles."

"Is that a sign post?" asked Linda, pointing to a dim silhouette
that looked like a telephone pole set in a low rectangular planter.

"Let's find out," said Mike.

He pulled into a broad paved area and crept across it at a right
angle from the highway. A brick wall materialized before us. We per-
ceived a dim, steady light showing through a window.

"Let's see if they're open," Linda and Trinda cried out together.

We all piled out of the old van and felt along the wall until we
located the door. To our relief, it opened. Entering, we noticed only
two customers, gray with ash, and a waitress seated behind the
counter. Two kerosene lanterns provided illumination.

"Come on in," the waitress called cheerfully, "and close the
door. We're trying our best to keep the dust out of here." She drew four
glasses of fresh cold water and hurried toward us with them.

"Here you go. You'll want to wash that dust out of your throats.
The washrooms are right over there. Get yourselves cleaned up and
come join our party."

We glanced at each other and broke into laughter. Largely it was
the release from hours of stress and uncertainty that fueled our
laughs. But the sight of ourselves uniformly dressed in gray ash from
head to toe was compelling. Linda's thick black braids and Trinda's
golden curls were identically gray. The only colors distinguishable
were in our eyes, which were lattices of red and white from the irri-
tating ash, surrounding the colors of our irises. The other two patrons
wore the same gray fashion we did, but they enjoyed the luxury of
clean hands and faces.

We headed for the restrooms, eager to wash off the grime. Cool
water never felt so good, stripping the tiny, glassy bits of ash off our
skin and out of our eyes. We grabbed handfuls of tissue and blew more
ash from our noses.

When we reassembled in the dining room, the waitress told us she
could make cold sandwiches, but no hot food, explaining that the
restaurant had lost its power during the first earthquake accompanying St. Helens' explosive eruption. Now that we were seated in a less
mobile environment, we noticed the mild shaking of the continuing
earthquakes. Thanks to Linda's uncanny sensitivity we had been trav-

eling gravel roads when the eruption occurred, and we did not feel it. Nor had we heard the explosion. We learned later that the blast had been heard scores of miles away. Although we were fairly close to the event, we were in a valley over which the sound had skipped, as if in an eddy unaffected by the currents of a wild river.

We left the restaurant a couple of hours later, when the ashfall had nearly stopped in our area. The black cloud still let no sunlight through. With the failed electrical system the land was strangely dark. Our headlights were effective now, and we made good time. We were astonished by the number of birds and insects lying dead in the road.

Some twenty miles down the road the cloud lightened to the same gray that shrouded the fields and buildings we passed. Soon we emerged from it into a brilliant landscape of blue and green. Here the state police had set up a roadblock. As they inquired about conditions along the highway, we learned that we were the first people to emerge from the devastation.

Having satisfied their curiosity, we found a place to park. We joined a crowd of people standing in clusters in a field and watched the continuing eruption. Watching the tremendous column of ash boiling from the mountain, we noticed that we, too, were a subject of curious glances and comments. Fully aware of our good fortune in escaping from under the mountain, we agreed that we all felt a thrill of pride in having been in there and survived (Stevens, 1995).

  Suggested Activities for the Teacher

1. Reread Bryce Stevens' story (located in italics at the beginning and end of the chapter). Analyze it for sensory details—sights, sounds, smells, tastes, and sensations of touch. Think about how each of the examples you found enhanced the effectiveness of the story. Visualize the experience described by the story, using the details that you located.

2. Think of a significant event in your past. Tape yourself telling it as if you were sharing the event with a friend. Analyze your telling for sensory details, sequence, interesting beginning, and effective ending.

Suggested Activities for Use with Students

1. Have your students brainstorm types of personal experiences that would make interesting stories to share as someone lists them on the board. These experiences may include funny, sad, embarrassing, and exciting events as some possibilities. Students also may mention trips, experiences with important people, and favorite leisure activities. Let each one study the categories and make a personal list of possible stories from his or her own background. Model this activity for them by placing your own list on the chalkboard. Choose one of your options and share it with the class, including as much detail as needed to make the experience vivid for them.

2. Follow Activity 1 by having each student choose one of these experiences to share. Divide the class into small groups of four or five students each and have the students in each group share their experiences with the other members of their group. Encourage them to include enough details to allow the other students to picture the events in their minds.

3. Have each student ask someone to tell him or her a story about a significant event in his or her life. Have the students tape the stories with permission from the tellers. The results may not be in story form, so the students may need to structure a strong beginning, sequence events properly, and develop a satisfying ending to form a tellable story. After they have done this, let students who have the permission of the original tellers share the stories that they have collected on tape with partners or small groups within the class. This practice in shaping stories will be helpful to them with later assignments in which they collect stories.

References

Avant, H. (1983). "And they lived happily ever after." In Hilda Avant, *To chase a dream* (pp. 37-38). Collegedale, TN: The College Press.

Baker, A., & Greene, E. (1987). *Storytelling: Art and technique*. New York: R. R. Bowker.

Chambers, D. W. (1977). *The oral tradition: Storytelling and creative drama*. Dubuque, IA: Wm. C. Brown.

Gillard, M. (1996). *Storyteller, storyteacher*. York, ME: Stenhouse.

Hillman, J. (1979). A note on story. *Parabola, 4*, 43-45.

Hitakonanu'laxk. (1994). *The grandfathers speak: Native american folk tales of the Lenapé people*. New York: Interlink Books.

Livo, N. J., & Rietz, S. A. (1986). *Storytelling: Process and practice*. Littleton, CO: Libraries Unlimited.

Maguire, J. (1985). *Creative storytelling*. Cambridge, MA: Yellow Moon Press.

Petty, P. (1996). A little girl's view: Persecution in the pews. Unpublished story.

Sawyer, R. (1986). *The way of the storyteller*. New York: Viking.

Stevens, B. (1995). Under the mountain. Unpublished story.

Stone, E. (1988). *Black sheep and kissing cousins: How our family stories shape us*. New York: Penguin.

Tooze, R. (1959). *Storytelling*. Englewood Cliffs, NJ: Prentice-Hall.

Trousdale, A. M., Woestehoff, S. A., & Schwartz, M. (Eds.). (1994). *Give a listen: Stories of storytelling in school*. Urbana, IL: National Council of Teachers of English.

Underwood, P. (1996). Standing in the middle of a memory. *Storytelling Magazine, 8* (May), 18-21.

Chapter 2
Tips about the Storytelling Process

July 11, 1995, started out as most days had this summer. My daughter Tiffany and I loaded our saws and other supplies into our log truck and headed to the tornado-stricken area near City Lake. We were in good spirits as we traveled to our job site for a day of cutting trees that had been blown down by the tornado. We stopped at the service station to get gas for the truck and also to get our daily ration of beef jerky and cold drinks.

We got to the woods, and I began to cut trees into logs, while Tiffany began to drag the trees to the log yard. We were having a good time talking and working together, as we always do. I was cutting a tree that had a lot of pressure on it because it had been blown down. The limbs were kicking back as I cut them off, but I had everything under control—or so I thought.

Suddenly a limb that I was sawing broke loose, and it jerked my saw out of my hands. The limb came back, and I thought it hit my knee. When I looked down, my pants were ripped from the knee to the ankle. It was then that I realized the limb was not what had hit me. It was the chainsaw that had cut me while it was running wide open. The cut started on my knee cap and went to the back of my leg.

Roger Hyder, the storyteller, had started out a bit hesitantly, but his voice gained strength as he plunged into the familiar story. As was true with most of the class, telling a personal experience story freed him to tell the story forcefully because it didn't add the stress of trying to remember the plot. The plot was all too familiar. The students listened intently, anticipating the crisis to come, because the story was structured to cue the impending action.

Teachers and librarians need to know how to tell stories effectively to captivate their listeners in order to accomplish curricular goals. Students need to know how to tell stories well in order to enhance their communication skills, particularly listening skills and speaking skills, although reading and writing skills can be advanced through storytelling as well. Storytelling also bolsters self-esteem and establishes bonds between tellers and listeners.

Why Tell Stories?

Teachers and librarians often want to tell stories to students for a number of reasons, such as the following:
- to entertain them.
- to expose them to various types of literature.
- to help them develop a love of language.
- to provide background or motivation for an area of study.
- to provide opportunities for them to practice listening skills. (Note: Listening to stories for particular purposes should also help to advance the parallel reading skills in your curriculum; for example, listening to evaluate a character's solution of a problem will generally help students read more effectively to perform the same task.)
- to encourage students to reflect on issues such as interpersonal relations, ethics, justice, and compassion.
- to build a personal connection to students.

Students generally have some different goals for their storytelling, although the desire to entertain others is probably paramount. Other student objectives may include a desire:
- to share life experiences with their classmates.
- to share stories that are pertinent to classroom activities.
- to gain status in the group.
- to demonstrate their creative abilities by crafting interesting tales.
- to return to stories that they have enjoyed in the past to savor them again.
- to share "special" stories with others who will appreciate them.
- to take on the roles of familiar and unfamiliar characters to experience activities vicariously.

How Does a Teller Choose Stories to Tell?

No matter whether the teller is a teacher, librarian or student, the following considerations are important in deciding what stories to tell:

1. Choose stories that meet your objectives.

   A teacher might use an Anansi story

   > in an introduction to a study of Africa,
   >
   > as an example of a folktale, or
   >
   > in a comparison of stories from Africa with stories common in the southern United States.

   A first grader might choose the story "The Little Red Hen" because it is an old favorite,

   > he/she feels it is a "special" story that a friend would like,
   >
   > it fits in with the discussion of planting crops that is taking place in social studies, or
   >
   > he/she wants to play the parts of the industrious hen and the lazy animals.

   A fifth grader might choose to tell the episode from *The Best Christmas Pageant Ever* (Robinson, 1972) in which the cat is brought to Show and Tell

   > to make his/her classmates laugh or
   >
   > to demonstrate his/her oral language and
   >
   > presentation skills through a story that is a favorite.

   An eighth grader might choose to tell a myth, such as "King Midas and the Golden Touch," because it fits in with a study of mythology.

   A high school senior might choose to tell an episode from one of the many books on Harriet Tubman

   > to enhance a study of American History or
   >
   > to fit with a study of biographies in English class.

2. Choose stories that you enjoy and want to share.

   If you as a teller do not like a story, you will not be likely to tell it well. No matter how well the story fits your objectives, your lack of personal engagement with the story is likely to result in inattention, disinterest, or dislike on the part of the listeners. Tellers transmit their enthusiasm and love for the stories that they tell to listeners. They also can transmit their boredom with and distaste for stories. Using a story that you don't like just to achieve an objective nearly always misfires, leaving teller and listener alike unfulfilled.

The students must have the freedom to choose stories that speak to them, that they can enjoy, and that they feel comfortable sharing. Of course, this admonition means that teachers should avoid assigning specific stories for students to tell. Some students may initially need help in choosing stories, but the final choice should be theirs. In order to allow students to choose appropriately, there should be many story resources in the classroom and/or library from which they can choose appropriate stories. Personal stories and original fictional accounts may also be used by students in some situations.

3. Choose stories that are right for your audience.

No matter how well you love the stories or how well they fit the topic, they will not work with an audience that is not mature enough or has no interest in the material. Some audiences are willing, and sometimes eager, to listen to stories that have a great deal of descriptive detail; others prefer stories that contain much dialogue, conflict, and continuous action. Some audiences will savor exotic vocabulary and visualize meanings in their heads; others will turn the story off when it smacks of the unfamiliar.

Primary grade children enjoy stories that are simple and straightforward, with a clear, uncomplicated plot line. They enjoy stories that have rhythm, rhyme, and repetition, and they love to join in on the repeated parts. They also often love stories that allow them to participate physically, by clapping, stomping, providing hand gestures and facial expressions, and providing sound effects, sometimes with rhythm instruments. Nursery rhymes, stories that involve familiar situations, and simple folktales and fairy tales are enjoyed by these children. They delight in predictable story parts that are often due to the rhyme and repetition. They claim to like scary stories, but many are frightened by more than the mild surprise, *got you* types of stories.

Intermediate grade children like more complex folktales, tall tales, legends, and some myths. They can deal with stories that involve less familiar situations. They also like to pick up on clues in the stories and predict outcomes. They enjoy discovering different variants of the same story, and they are ready to do comparisons and contrasts of similar stories from different cultures with understanding of how the culture affected the story. Many of them do like scary stories, having become accustomed to the television variety, but some are still disturbed by these stories.

Junior and senior high students begin to appreciate complex fairy tales, mythology, and romantic stories. They like human interest stories about famous historical figures or little known events related to significant historical ones. They may enjoy stories about how authors came to write their books. Problem stories involving young adults may appeal to them. They can understand more than the surface story, making stories with more depth of meaning usable. They also enjoy family and community stories.

Tellers get material from many sources. Some write original stories or have personal stories to tell. Some, who Denman (1991) calls "traditionalists," tell stories they have heard others tell. Others glean stories from printed sources. Appendix B contains some good sources of published stories.

How Can You Prepare a Story For Telling?

There are probably as many ways to prepare a story for telling as there are tellers. Nevertheless, over the years a number of techniques have been useful to many tellers. Every storyteller approaches the task in a different way. The following is one procedure for learning a story from a print source or tape that we have found to be effective over the years. Following that procedure are variations that would apply for learning a story from a live teller.

General Procedure

1. Read or listen to the story several times. The first time, read or listen to it just for pleasure. The second time, read or listen to the story to pay particular attention to each character—his or her physical characteristics, speech patterns, actions, and thoughts. "Watch" each character in your mind in action and "listen" to him or her talk to you. During the third reading or listening, picture the scenes in your mind. Note the order and the connections between scenes. During a final reading or listening, pay close attention to the beginning and ending events. These will be vital parts of the telling.

2. With a pencil, map or sketch the story to clarify the events and their order. The map may be very simple in form, as shown in Figure 2.1.

Figure 2.1 Map for "Three Little Pigs"

| Pigs leave mother | → | 1st Pig buys straw | → | 2nd Pig buys sticks | → | 3rd Pig buys bricks | → | Wolf visits 1st Pig, blows down house, eats pig (or pig escapes) | → | Wolf visits 2nd Pig, blows down house, eats pig (or pig escapes) | → | Wolf visits 3rd Pig, can't blow down house, ends up in pot of boiling water after sliding down chimney |

3. Try to tell the story aloud, to yourself, as you picture the characters and the scenes. Doing this is something like watching a movie of the action in your head and telling the listeners about it. Move through to the end, even though you realize that you have not included everything that you intended to include. Use your own words to tell the story, rather than the words that were in the printed copy or recording, except for those key expressions that give the flavor of the characters or the times, special chants or rhymes that were included, or striking details that are more vivid with the original language. You should have the story internalized, not memorized, and you should tell it as if sharing it with a friend.

4. Go back to the printed copy or tape and check your performance, especially any parts that caused you problems. Reread parts or listen again to parts, as needed.

   Work hard to develop good beginnings and endings. Plan the wording for your beginning to draw the audience into the story. Consider beginning by making them curious about what is going to happen and eager to hear it unfold. Sometimes just the old "Once upon a time..." formula transports children into the world of story. Endings should carry a feeling of completion. Don't just let your voice trail off and quit. If there is any doubt about the ending having been reached, use an expression of finality to confirm the matter. Jackie Torrence, a professional storyteller worthy of emulation, often ends a story with "and that was the end of that."

5. Audiotape yourself telling the story. Play the tape back and check your inflections, choice and flow of words, and enunciation. Repeat the process, as needed.

   Also consider the pace at which you tell your story. Don't rush headlong through the story, leaving your audience breathless, or dawdle needlessly, leading to boredom. Slow down for sad and serious parts or parts with beautiful language to be savored. In order to build suspense, you may wish to slow down as the climax is approached. Speed up for happy parts and action scenes. Change your pace for different characters, who naturally would not all speak at the same rate. Use pauses to build suspense and to emphasize important points.

6. Practice telling the story in front of a mirror, or videotape yourself telling it, so that you can check out your gestures and facial expressions.

   Remember to stay relatively still when you tell your story. Excess body movement, such as rocking or pacing, diverts attention from the story. Use only gestures that help to advance the story, and plan them carefully. Flailing arms are major distracters.

7. Practice telling to a person. A spouse, child, or friend who is sympathetic to your cause will do fine. This practice will help you improve your eye contact and timing.

Remember to be flexible when telling your story. If you forget a bit of it, improvise. Slow down and elaborate on details that you remember. As you do this, you may find that the missing material comes back to you. If not, most of the time no one will notice, except you. If you forget something that is vital to the story early and then remember it just before it is needed, simply say, "Oh, I forgot to tell you..." and proceed to tell them what they need know. Storytelling audiences are forgiving. Relax and enjoy the experience.

You know that your preparation is complete when you are comfortable with the story. It is a part of you. You tell it as if you are sharing a personal experience with a friend, because it is personal now, and it wants to be told.

(Note: If you are an extremely auditory learner, you may want to read a story that is available in print into a tape recorder and learn it from listening. If you are an extremely visual learner, you may want to transcribe a story available on a tape before beginning to learn it.)

Variation of the General Procedure When Learning a Story That You Have Heard Someone Tell, But Do Not Have In Print Or On Tape

1. Take notes on the important points of the story—include essential phrases, sequence of events, character names, and so on—as soon as possible after the telling, or maybe even during the telling. You may wish to map or sketch the story action at this time.

2. Tell the story aloud to yourself as soon as possible after hearing it. If you cannot tell it aloud immediately, go over it silently as often as possible until you can. Follow suggestions in General Procedure Step 3.

3. If you have trouble remembering details for which you do not have notes, try asking the teller or another listener for clarification.

4. Now follow Steps 5 through 7 in the General Procedure.

None of these techniques is foolproof. Each has its strengths for some people and its weaknesses for other people. Some of us "go wooden" before mirrors and don't exhibit even a semblance of the expression that we have before audiences.

Busy teachers and librarians may say, "There are too many steps." Maybe there are for them or for you. Try eliminating steps that don't help you particularly. Experiment until you find what works for you. Our experience has been that the most important steps involve telling the story aloud to yourself and practicing on another person.

What About Using Props?

Good storytellers often use props to enhance their telling, but props are not necessary. If you tell a story from the heart, listeners hear the sounds and see the scenes that you describe without assistance. Jay O'Callahan, an outstanding professional storyteller, often tells about how audiences "see" a giant bubble when he tells a tale that involves such a bubble, but he does not use a bubble as a prop; he simply uses effective vocal inflection and hand gestures. He has trouble convincing the audience that the bubble was not there, attesting to his storytelling artistry.

Nevertheless, many storytellers use musical instruments, flannelboards, transparencies, objects from the story, and puppets in their sessions. If you play an instrument, you may use it to accompany a song in the story or provide background sound that helps to set the stage for the story. However, be sure to practice with the instrument before you share the story in this way, so you will be able to work out the mechanics of the presentation. Use of flannelboards and transparencies may help to focus attention on story events for some and also lead to retelling activities later. Flannelboards and transparencies take the students' focus away from the teller, however, and they often cause the teller to lose vital eye contact with listeners. Objects from the story, such as articles of clothing and replicas of items, may help to ground the story in reality for children who are not acquainted with the artifacts displayed. Even these objects can be distracting though, causing students' attention to wander from the story itself. Artifacts should probably be placed out of sight during the story sessions.

Young children relate to puppet characters, and they may pay closer attention to the story if puppets are involved. They also may be more motivated to try to retell the story with the puppets. Still, many teachers struggle to use puppets and do a less effective job of telling the story when they have to worry about manipulating the puppets.

If you want to use any of these "extra enhancements" to your storytelling, be sure to practice with them extensively before using them in front of a group. If the use of the aids is not automatic, disaster is sure to strike.

How Can You Help Students Become Tellers?

If you want students to become storytellers in your classroom or library, you must make the atmosphere nonthreatening and the experience rewarding. That means you must accept offerings that are less than perfect without shattering criticism and you must bestow praise for participation, story selection, and technique when warranted. On the other hand, you must avoid false praise; students are quick to discern that ploy and do not feel encouraged by it. An honest "Thank you for sharing your story" is much more affirming than "What a wonderful story" for a story that was not delivered particularly well, but was an effort to contribute to the class activities.

One of the best ways to help children to become tellers is to point out the good points of each telling that they do. They will have a positive experience, and they will have specific information about what they did right. Just saying, "Good job" is not adequate. You need to say something like "Your use of dialogue was excellent. I could tell who was speaking each time because you gave each character his or her own voice." Students need to be prompted to tell one another specific good points of each telling. They become quite adept at this with practice, but you must model it for them extensively at first, so that they know what you expect.

An effective way to address storytelling weaknesses in older students is to say to an individual privately, "If you want to strengthen your storytelling skills, I have written down three suggestions for improvement. You may want to consider them as you prepare your next story." Such "targets for improvement" are much more effective than negative statements. For example, it is much more encouraging to say, "Next time, try to speak a little louder," than it is to say, "You did not speak loudly enough."

Primary students' first forays into storytelling may well be retellings of predictable stories that you have presented in class. These retellings may be supported by allowing the children to use flannelboard pieces to prompt their memory of the story. In a program where kindergarten through second grade students were exposed to daily storytelling for a seven-week period, Betty Roe (1988) found that students at all three grade levels quickly learned to retell stories such as "The Old Woman and Her Pig" and "The House that Jack Built," using flannelboard pieces to prompt their memories of the stories.

In helping fifth graders learn how to tell a story to second grade partners, Betty Roe (1992) had the children listen to the story several times. Then the class discussed the story extensively and, as a group, generated a story map that was drawn on the board and copied on their papers by the individual students. Next, the students practiced the story to themselves, first using the map as a prompt, and then trying to tell the story without a prompt. Finally, pairs of fifth graders practiced telling the story to each other, before visiting the second grade to tell the story to their second grade partners. The fifth graders exhibited a pride in presentation, and their partners had a chance to feel special, having older students learn a story just to tell to them.

An activity for secondary school students needs to be high interest. A study of *migratory tales*, or *urban legends*, can grab the interest of secondary students and start them on the road to telling. These stories are told all across the country as if they happened in each place; they appear to be plausible; and they are told as being true, but they have always come from an indirect source and cannot be proven. Here is an example of how you can use this genre to lure your students into storytelling:

Tell your students that you are going to tell them a story about something that someone told you happened to a friend. Tell them to listen carefully for similarities of this occurrence to situations that they have heard about before. Then tell the story "The Choking Doberman." A brief summary of the story is as follows:

A woman returns to her house to find her Doberman choking and having difficulty breathing. She rushes him to the veterinarian, who suggests that she leave the dog overnight for treatment. She returns home to find her telephone ringing insistently. When she answers, the veterinarian's voice tells her to get out of the house immediately, go to a nearby phone and call him back. She leaves rapidly, goes to a neighbor's house, and calls him. He tells her that he found three fingers stuck in the dog's throat and feared that an intruder might be in her house. About then, the police, having been called by the veterinarian, drive up to her house. They search the house and find a bleeding robber crouched in a closet in a state of shock.

Ask the students if they have heard of anything like this happening. Several will have probably heard variations of the story. If they have, let them recount their versions. (If they haven't, tell another urban legend, such as "The Elevator Incident," in which a man whose appearance is frightening to the other occupants of an elevator tells his dog to sit and all of the human occupants sit on the floor. Then continue the procedure with this story.) Record the major points of each telling on the board. Note the similarities and differences in such details as location, breed of dog, number of fingers, instructions from the vet, and method of apprehending the robber. You may want to make a chart to compare and contrast the stories. Ask the students how it would be possible for all of these to be true. At this point, define urban legend for the students.

Have the students learn the story, "The Choking Doberman." Divide them into small groups, have them outline the story, and have each member of the group try to tell the story from the outline first and then again without the outline.

Have the students go home and tell the story to parents, siblings, and/or friends. Have them record any variations that these people have already heard.

In class the next day, discuss the variations that the students have collected. Then let them tell you other urban legends that they have heard. Let small groups of students learn and search for variations of each of these stories and report back to the class. The class may even want to collect the legends in an urban legend anthology, to be placed in the library.

Appendix B includes several good sources for urban legends. Your experience is likely to provide even more.

If you want to turn students in your class into storytellers, you must give them opportunities to hear stories told, to discuss storytelling and decide what makes it enjoyable to hear, and to practice telling with feedback. Discussions about what makes storytelling experiences enjoyable may result in a chart of things that storytellers should attempt to do. The chart will have different types of items on it depending upon the age level of the students. Primary grade students may include "Speak loudly enough to be heard" and "Look at your audience, not at the floor." Secondary students may say, "Enunciate clearly" or "Make sure every detail relates directly to the elements of the story." The guidelines and the words need to come from and belong to the students if they are to benefit from trying to abide by them.

Having planned practice in storytelling with partners or in small groups is important. Everyone can be involved in telling and listening at once. Tellers may be asked to use lower voices as they tell; but, although the room is noisy, the students generally focus well on the stories to which they are listening. Gillard (1996) suggests having the students form two concentric circles, facing each other, and letting each student tell his/her story to the person he/she is facing. Then the students step to the side, get new partners, and practice again. With this activity, students can try different versions of their stories with different listeners, including changing voices for characters, using different gestures, and so on.

Hilda Avant (1983) shared a story about letting children tell stories that you should be able to appreciate:

Goldilocks and the What?

By Hilda Avant

When television made its debut in my home town, I was concerned about the children's viewing habits. I initiated a study with the children of those programs which were produced for children. My concern did not go unnoticed. The Superintendent of Schools proudly escorted the program director of the local T.V. station to my classroom, and I was invited to bring my students to the studio and to have them televise a part of their learnings to share with other students and parents.

The parents of my students volunteered to drive us downtown to the television station. Then, because space was so limited at the studio, the parents were to go to my apartment, which was nearby, and to watch the program on T.V. I had made careful preparation for the trip—or so I thought. However, I neglected one minor detail: a revolving door. The only entrance to the grand new T.V. station was a revolving door. There I stood on a sidewalk in front of a twelve-story building with 38 excited six year olds and five minutes to reach the eleventh floor. I gently placed a child in each compartment of the door—and turned it. But the children thought it was a game, and they kept riding around and around, returning to me on the sidewalk. Some amused spectators watched as I became more and more frustrated. At last, a few brave souls realized my predicament, and they assisted by riding through and plucking children from the door as it rotated.

Upstairs, the television crew was ready for us. I decided it was time to give Bobby his assignment. I wanted him to tell the story of The Three Bears, *as other children dressed in paper bag masks acted it out. I deliberately had not told Bobby of his responsibility before this time because I knew how well Bobby could tell stories, and I feared that, if his mother knew about the assignment, she would rehearse him until the creativity and spontaneity were diminished. Bobby was equal to the challenge! He agreed to tell the story for the young actors to perform.

"Now, Bobby," I cautioned, "I want you to tell the story your way. It doesn't have to be just like the book tells it. You make a good story about* The Three Bears."

Bobby nodded his agreement; and, in a flash, we were "on the air." Bobby took me at my word. No sooner had the cameras begun to roll than Bobby began to weave an extraordinary tale. According to Bobby, it wasn't Goldilocks who visited the vacant home of the bears but rather the uninvited bears who invaded Goldilocks' home. In his story, Baby Bear was delighted with running water in the bathtub; and, when the phone rang and the voice asked for the number, Baby Bear answered "Three" because there were three in his family. The children appeared perfectly relaxed, and they dramatized Bobby's wonderful story with a fair degree of realism.

I was seated just out of camera range, completely absorbed with the original story. "Ma'am," whispered the cameraman, "how long is the story going to last? We only have two minutes until sign off." "I don't know," I shushed him, "I've never heard this story before."

"But, Ma'am!"—Now it was the director pointing to his watch, "How can we wind this up!?" (I guess the T.V. crew was not as impressed as I was with Bobby's story.) Just at that moment, Wayne solved the problem for us. Wayne was the tiny little redhead who was playing Baby Bear. Apparently, the story was getting a bit much for his limited acting ability. Wayne lifted the paper bag mask which disguised him as Baby Bear and pleaded, "Bobby, for gosh sakes! Nobody in Chattanooga ever heard the Three Bears told that way before!"

The cameras clicked, and we were off the air!

The mothers were late picking us up after the program. I understand Bobby's mother fainted after the first chapter of her son's story. I'm just glad she never met that cameraman! But, as for me, I thought Bobby made a delightful storyteller for his first (and last) television appearance (Avant, 1983, pp. 39-41).

Surely Hilda's students were learning how to become true storytellers.

You should encourage students to use procedures similar to the ones that you use in learning stories, when they are trying to do so. Share your procedures with the students. Explain that some steps help some people more than others, and that they should experiment with procedures until they find what works best for them. Work with them on mapping and sketching stories that they are learning, because that procedure may not be familiar to many of them. Primary grade students like to do a series of sketches that illustrate the events in the story. Older students may find that a story map, with words, instead of pictures, helps them more.

Helping students become storytellers is a rewarding experience. They acquire a skill that will help them throughout their lives.

Roger Hyder continued the story of his chainsaw encounter:

Just as I realized that my leg was cut, Tiffany saw what had happened and went for the truck to take me to the hospital. I did not know how fast I would lose blood and was afraid I might pass out. We could not tell how deep the saw had gone into my leg. All we could tell was that it had hit my kneecap. The cut was gaping open, and blood was

running down my leg and into my boot. While Tiffany was getting the truck, which was parked several hundred yards from the log yard, I dragged myself to the log yard so she would have a place to turn around. She was 15-years-old, and didn't have her license to drive. Before that day, she hadn't driven a big truck anyplace but in a field.

Tiffany came through the woods like a professional truck driver and helped me get in the truck. We headed to the hospital, which was about twenty minutes away. She had to drive through heavy traffic while I sat beside her bleeding and moaning and complaining about the slow traffic. She pulled up to the emergency entrance at the hospital and got a nurse to bring a wheel chair to take me into the emergency room.

Tiffany called my wife, Gail, and told her that there had been a slight accident and that we would be home in a little while. She assured Gail that she did not need to worry, that it was only a minor cut, because she didn't want to worry her mother until she actually knew the extent of the accident.

The doctor checked my cut and told us that I would need a bone specialist to repair the damage to my knee. He ordered x-rays because he could not tell if the bone was broken or how severe the damage to my knee was. He could feel saw toothmarks in the bone. After the x-rays had been developed, a bone specialist checked the x-rays and came in and looked at my cut. She seemed to be in a good mood and told me that I was lucky that there were no broken bones or any permanent damage to my tendons or ligaments. She said that I should not lose much use of my leg, and announced that she would be back at 4:00 P.M. to sew it up. It was 11:00 A.M., and I was thinking that I would bleed to death by then.

The bleeding had stopped, so I was admitted to the hospital and given some very strong pain medication because the feeling was beginning to come back. The pain medicine helped a little; and with my daughter encouraging me and telling me stories, I was able to rest until it was time for the doctor to sew up my leg.

When I was in the operating room and the surgeon sat down and started to hum, I knew that I was in good hands. The next thing I knew, I was in the recovery room, and Gail and Tiffany were there to greet me. The surgeon had told Gail that it would be a slow healing process because she had to remove some of the skin and flesh that the saw had damaged too badly for her to repair. The surgeon was optimistic about my recovery, saying that, although I would be in a great deal of pain for a few days, I would be up and around soon.

The next day, Gail loaded me up, equipped with crutches, and we headed for home. That was the longest trip I have ever made.

Every bump felt like a knife sticking into my leg, and I was not a happy traveler.

The next eight days I spent in the house, not able to bend my leg or put any weight on it. The ninth day, I went back to the doctor, and she examined my leg and told me to bend it as much as possible so it would not form too much scar tissue. She also told me to quit using my crutches and walk as much as possible. I was able to go home and take a walk with my family to the end of the driveway. After that, my recovery was much faster, thanks to a good doctor and much help from my wife and daughter.

My knee is still numb, and it feels really weird when something touches it. When I go up or down steps or stand for a long period of time, it swells and hurts. Like a person who has arthritis, I can tell when the weather is going to change because my leg hurts. But I am thankful for a daughter who stayed cool during a crisis and a leg that is still attached to my body which enables me to take walks with my family (Hyder, 1995).

 Suggested Activities for the Teacher

1. Make a list of all of the purposes that storytelling can serve in your class room. Beside each item on the list, write at least one story that could help you attain that purpose. For example, if you want to teach the concept of justice through story, you might use the story "The Baker's Smell."

2. Audiotape yourself telling a story. Listen to the story to check the pace, the intonations, the volume, and your enunciation, as well as the story sequence.

3. Have someone videotape you telling a story. Watch the tape to check your facial expressions, posture, movements, and gestures, as well as the other aspects of the story. Be particularly vigilant for distracting move ments or mannerisms.

Suggested Activities for Use with Students

1. Have students list stories that they enjoyed hearing others read or tell, or even ones that they read for themselves and enjoyed, when they were younger. Have them discuss what they liked about these stories. Then ask each one to choose an "old favorite" to practice and tell to his/her classmates or to students in a lower grade.

2. After students have tried several techniques that you have suggested and demonstrated, let students construct their own steps in learning a new story.

References

Avant, H. (1983). Goldilocks and the what? In Hilda Avant, *To chase a dream* (pp. 39-41). Collegedale, TN: The College Press.

Baker, A., & Greene, E. (1987). *Storytelling: Art & technique*. New York: R. R. Bowker.

Denman, G. A. (1991). *Sit tight, and I'll swing you a tail*. Portsmouth, NH: Heinemann.

Farrell, C. (1991). *Storytelling: A guide for teachers*. New York: Scholastic.

Gillard, M. (1996). *Storyteller, storyteacher*. York, ME: Stenhouse.

Hyder, R. (1995). Chainsaw nightmare. Unpublished story.

Jeffers, H. (1997). A test for tellers: Where does your tale end? *Storytelling World*, 12-13.

MacDonald, M. R. (1993). *The storyteller's start-up book*. Little Rock, AR: August House.

Maguire, J. (1985) *Creative storytelling*. Cambridge, MA: Yellow Moon Press.

Robinson, B. (1972). *The best Christmas pageant ever*. New York: Avon.

Roe, B. D. (1992). Cross-grade pairing to promote learning, *Tennessee Reading Teacher, 20,* 1, 3-9.

Roe, B. D. (1988). Extending learning and knowledge through storytelling, *Educators' Forum*, 10, 15.

Ross, R. (1980). *Storyteller*. Columbus, OH: Charles E. Merrill.

Sawyer, R. (1970). *The way of the storyteller*. New York: Viking Press.

Chapter 3
Using Storytelling To Teach Language Skills—Part 1

June 6, 1966, is a day that will always be deeply engraved in my memory. I was ten years old and living in Cedar Bluff Subdivision in Knoxville with my parents and eight-year-old brother, Mark. It was a beautiful, sunny morning. Mark and I were excited, both because it was the first day of summer vacation and because this morning we were going to go to Bible School. My parents were in the kitchen paying some bills and counting the money my father would need for the business trip he was leaving on that morning. Mark came running into the house, frightened because he thought he had heard someone or something in the garage. I pretended to be brave, went outside, and walked into the garage to see what was the matter. I noticed the bicycle had overturned and decided that must have been the noise Mark had heard. Just as I walked toward the back of the garage to pick up the bicycle, I heard a car horn. It was our ride to Bible School, so I quickly turned and ran back into the house with Mark to tell our parents good-bye.

Bible School was as wonderful as we had anticipated that it would be, and Mark and I thought we would burst before we could tell our mother about our morning. Our ride dropped us off about 11:00 a.m., and we ran quickly to the house, flung open the door, and yelled for Mom. She didn't have a car and was always home to greet us with open arms when we arrived from school. But something was strange. She didn't answer.

I noticed the kitchen light was on and ran inside. The bills my parents had been working on were still spread all over the kitchen table. The bread, bologna, and mayonnaise were left open on the counter. How many times had Mom told me to put the mayonnaise right up because it would spoil?

The strange feeling that I had experienced when Mom didn't answer us was now more intense. As I left the kitchen, I could see that the bathroom light was on upstairs. Slowly I ascended the stairway, Mark at my side. Again we yelled for Mom, but there was no answer.

The tension in the room was strong. Knowing that Gail Hyder was telling a true personal experience, the listeners hung on every word.

When I entered the bathroom, I noticed something strange lying on the bathroom counter beside my Dad's electric razor. I walked over and carefully picked it up. It was coarse, jet black hair. I had never seen anything like that before and wasn't sure how it had gotten there. Mark was trembling, and I knew I had to be brave and try not to frighten him. Hand-in-hand we walked into our parents' bedroom. There in the middle of the floor was some strange clothing. I did not dare pick it up, but I could see that the torn, bloody pants and shirt were definitely not my father's. I decided it would be best for Mark and me to leave the house quickly.

I did my best to reassure Mark that everything was okay, even though inside I knew something was terribly wrong. Mark and I went from house to house asking each neighbor if anyone had seen our mother. But everywhere we went, we got the same response—no one had seen her. We finally decided to just sit on the curb in front of the house and wait. It seemed like an eternity, and I remember only too well the confused, frightened feelings I was experiencing.

At lunch time, our good neighbor Peggy sent over her husband who worked for the F.B.I. to look around the house. I took him from room to room showing him the "evidence," such as the black hair in the bathroom and the torn, bloody clothes in the bedroom. He didn't seem too concerned and said that Mom had probably just gone shopping with a friend. I felt so helpless I could have screamed! I knew our mother would never go anywhere without telling us, and going back into the house to show him the strange hair and clothing only served to intensify my fears.

Again Mark and I waited on the curb in front of the house. But for what? For Mom to drive up with a friend or to hear that something terrible had happened to her? I began to pray inside harder than I had ever prayed in my life. I could sense that Mark was doing the same thing as we sat there silently.

By late afternoon there was still no sign of Mom, and we had no idea where Dad had gone on his trip to get in touch with him. Peggy came over and asked if we had any relatives she could help us call.

The closest relatives were my aunt and uncle in Oak Ridge. We called and explained that Mom had disappeared.

What Language Skills Do Students Need?

Students in all grade levels—kindergarten through grade 12—need to develop skills in five areas—listening, speaking, reading, writing, and thinking. The first four areas are sometimes referred to as the language arts. Thinking skills are used in all four language areas. These skills allow people to recognize, understand, analyze, synthesize, evaluate, and apply ideas that they encounter in oral or written form.

Students need to listen for a variety of reasons—to comprehend oral language, to analyze and evaluate oral language, and to derive pleasure from oral language. They need to learn to express themselves orally and in writing to communicate with others, to create new ways to express ideas, and to provide pleasure to listeners. They need to learn to read for literal and interpretive understanding, for critical interpretation, for creative application, and for appreciation of written language.

How Can Storytelling Enhance the Teaching and Learning of These Skills?

Storytelling can be a tool for teaching language arts skills in an authentic and purposeful setting. All of the skills can be easily integrated into a storytelling program.

We will point out some of the advantages revealed by a storytelling program in which language skills were purposefully integrated, and then we will look at each language area for special applications to that area.

Integration of Language Arts

Listening to stories does many positive things for students when they receive adequate preparation for the telling and have language-related follow-ups that include speaking, reading, writing, and thinking. Students learn the meanings of new words as they listen to these words used in context; and, therefore, they expand their listening vocabularies through storytelling. They increase their ability to use such thinking skills as recognizing story sequence and cause-and-effect relationships, determining likenesses and differences among characters and other story elements, and distinguishing attributes of characters. They learn to analyze characters' actions and make judgments about these actions. They also learn much about story structure when they listen to many stories.

Studies by Betty Roe (1985, 1986, 1987, 1988) showed that primary-grade students (kindergarten through grade two) increased their vocabularies when they were exposed to daily one-hour storytelling and storyreading sessions with language follow-ups for a 7-week period. They gained in language fluency, using more total words in the stories that they told, and in speaking vocabulary, using more different words and more multisyllabic words in their stories at the end of the storytelling programs. These students also increased their knowledge of story structure, using more standard story elements in their stories after the 7-week storytelling periods. There were no overt lessons on story structure, but the students appeared to absorb an understanding of structure from the stories that were presented during the program.

All of the sessions included from one to three stories that were told or read to the children, and some sessions included songs and poems. Betty and her graduate assistant, John Pigg, planned the sessions, and either Betty, John, or the classroom teacher conducted each session. Every story, song, or poem used had some introductory or follow-up activity related to vocabulary. Either before or after the story, song, or poem, the presenter and the class talked about the meanings of important words, gave examples of these meanings, made sentences with the words, showed concrete or vicarious representations of the words, and/or talked about where they had heard or seen these words before. Misunderstandings that the children had about some words were cleared up, and they were excited about the new words. In some cases, words that they had used previously were explained to them for the first time. For example, one class of first graders had memorized and sung the song, "The Old Woman Who Swallowed a Fly," previously for an assembly program. They knew the words to the song well and sang it well, so Betty opened the first session with them singing that song with her. Then the group discussed vocabulary. The children did not know the meaning of the word "absurd," even though they had been singing "how absurd, to swallow a bird" repeatedly. The meaning was discussed, and each child then told the class something else that was absurd. If someone gave an incorrect example, the class discussed why that particular thing was not absurd. By the end of the lesson, everyone had given a correct example. In a later session, when John Pigg read *Horton Hatches the Egg* (Dr. Seuss, 1940), the children responded to the word "absurd" with "We know that. Dr. Roe told us that." And then they proceeded to tell him what it meant.

Vocabulary activities received much attention in this program because of the impact of vocabulary knowledge on learning in all subject areas, but many other related activities were used. For example, the students illustrated events from stories and dictated sentences to describe their pictures. The instructors wrote the dictated sentences on the pictures, or the students labeled the pictures, using invented spelling. These pictures were collected into booklets that the children read again and again. The pictures revealed how well the children comprehended the story; dictating the sentences provided the children with experience in using spoken language; and seeing their sentences written down from dictation was helpful in adding to the words that they recognized in reading.

Probably the favorite follow-up activity of the children was creative dramatics. The instructor told the story several times, following each telling with a discussion of setting, character traits, dialogue, or story sequence. Only after the students had internalized the story thoroughly through listening and discussion did the teacher assign cast members and allow the students to play the story, without direction, written scripts, props, or costumes. This activity allowed for much use of oral expression, use of the new vocabulary in a purposeful setting, physical interpretation of the language of the story, cooperation in a social situation, use of listening skills, and attention to details and sequence. The part of the class that was not cast in this initial performance acted as the audience. After the play was completed, the audience told the cast members what they did that was good, and the cast members told how they would change the performance, if they were to repeat it. The instructor then assigned a new cast for the dramatization, including the students who formed the audience for the initial presentation. This group performed the story, and another discussion/evaluation period followed. The story was performed until all class members had a chance to participate or until class members no longer had new ideas about how the dramatization should be changed for improvement.

Notice how thinking skills are involved throughout a creative dramatization. The students must recognize the important ideas to be presented in the dramatization, understand the ideas in order to respond appropriately to other characters in improvised dialogue, analyze what they hear in order to evaluate its accuracy and appropriateness, synthesize ideas gained from discussion in order to improve the next playing, and apply what was heard during the dramatization and discussion to the next dramatization.

Sometimes the follow-up was in the form of reconstructing the story in some way other than creative dramatics. For one story, Betty had cards with pictures of items that a character named Jack encountered, and the children came up and showed her what Jack did next by choosing the correct card. For many other stories, told using a flannelboard, the children were allowed to retell parts of the story in sequence, by putting the pieces on the flannelboard in sequence and telling those portions of the stories related to the pieces that they placed. These two activities and the creative dramatics all worked on the skill of sequencing, which had been identified by teachers as a problem area on the statewide standardized test that students were required to take each year. The methods met with much success. For example, one child, who had had little success earlier in the year with remembering either details or sequences in stories, successfully constructed in sequence much of the story of "The Old Woman and Her Pig" (one version is *The Old Woman and Her Pig*, Paul Galdone, 1960). He also successfully used the new vocabulary words, "stile" and "quench," appropriately.

Some of the follow-up sessions involved creative writing. After a presentation of the story "The House That Jack Built" (one version is *The House That Jack Built*, 1983), the children wrote a story with the same pattern that was called "The School That Crossville Built" in one of the schools involved in the program. The book *I Love Ladybugs* (Roach Van Allen, 1985) was used to provide a pattern for the children to use in writing a class book, with each child doing two pages that followed the pattern. The class book was read repeatedly throughout the rest of the year.

Other sessions involved discussions of the stories, with questioning to bring out the children's grasp of cause-and-effect relationships, attitudes of the characters in the stories, relationships between the events and/or feelings in the stories with the children's own experiences, and analyses of likenesses and differences among the characters and stories. The children improved steadily in their ability to participate in such discussions. In a follow-up discussion of some stories about things that grow, children contributed the usual responses of "grass," "vegetables," "hair," and "people," when one little boy from an extremely disadvantaged home environment offered the amazingly appropriate suggestion that our education grows. One day when discussing *Alexander and the Terrible, Horrible, No Good, Very Bad Day* (Judith Viorst, 1973) and "Soap, Soap, Soap" (*Grandfather Tales*, Richard Chase, 1948), a boy who was known as a "problem child" came up with the correct analysis that both main characters in the stories had had bad days. Also, in comparing the main characters in *Alexander and the Terrible, Horrible, No Good, Very Bad Day* and "Cheese, Peas, and Chocolate Pudding" (Betty Van Witson in *Storytelling with the Flannelboard*, Paul S. Anderson, 1970), a little girl, who was usually very quiet, insightfully pointed out that both boys had bad attitudes. We believe she was alerted to look for the characters' attitudes because of a discussion in an earlier lesson of *The Little Engine That Could* (Watty Piper, 1961).

The kindergarten students showed that they were capable of telling the difference between real and make believe during discussions of the story "Why Dogs Chase Cats" (one version is "Why Dogs Hate Cats" in *Parents and Children Together*, 1990).

Some of the follow-up activities were designed to give the children expanded experiences. The children had gingerbread boys to eat when the story of "The Gingerbread Boy" (one version is *The Gingerbread Boy*, Paul Galdone, Clarion, 1979) was told, and they had johnnycake when a story about it was presented. They planted beans and watched them grow when the stories about growing were being presented and discussed. They saw what a hundred beans and a thousand beans looked like when they heard the story *Millions of Cats* (Wanda Gag, 1928), and they speculated about the space that would be taken up by a hundred or a thousand cats, rather than beans. Because many songs have delightful stories in them and others reflect folk customs, Betty brought her guitar and banjo on different days when music was being incorporated into the lessons, and the children were delighted. For many, it was the first time they had been so close to these instruments, and they were given a chance to touch and strum to enhance the experience.

Even though the students were young, they were very attentive during the hour-long sessions, partially because they were so absorbed in the stories and partially because there were often changes of activity—short stories, poems, and songs, followed by the other language activities. Even students who were often disruptive of other activities gave no problems during story-time.

Listening

It isn't difficult to see how storytelling can be used to enhance listening skills. Students are eager to hear stories and want to understand them. Because of this motivation, they tend to concentrate on stories better than they would on standard classroom expository lectures or discussions. Their natural tendency to enjoy stories can be enhanced by telling the students that they will have the opportunity to discuss the stories, retell them, act them out, or write about them after the telling. Of course, personal narratives like that of Gail Hyder in the opening story in this chapter and her husband Roger's story in the opener for Chapter 2 offer internal motivation because of interest in the adventures of those we know and interest in situations in which people face peril.

The teacher should be specific about the purposes for which students are listening. They may be listening in order to recreate the story through creative dramatics, as described in the last section, for example. This activity would involve listening for unique beginnings and endings, setting, story sequence, dialogue, and character traits. The teacher would tell the story several times, with students listening first for enjoyment of the story and then for one or more of the topics listed above.

Listening is very important during the dramatizations also. The players in these dramatizations must listen carefully in order to respond to the other characters and move the plot along. This need for careful listening is particularly urgent because there is no written script, and the speech by each character must be processed for understanding and responded to appropriately by other characters.

The audience members also have good reasons to listen. They may be taking these parts later, and they need to see what the dialogue might be, get the sequence of events firmly in mind, and develop ideas about other ways to play the parts. In deciding how they will play the parts differently they are listening creatively. They also have the responsibility of discussing the good points of the dramatization after the play is finished, so they must listen analytically in order to contribute.

The purpose for listening may be to retell the story individually, either orally or in writing. Once again the students would listen for setting, sequence, dialogue, and character traits. They might also be particularly concerned with how the story begins and ends, since in telling a story, or in writing a story, the beginning is the part that draws the listener or reader into the story and the ending is the part that ties up the loose ends and indicates finality. Students who expect to be telling the story orally may listen for the storyteller's voice inflections and the vocal characteristics given to different characters, as well as to the pacing of the story and the voice volume needed for different parts of the story.

Of course, the purpose for listening to a story may be purely for appreciation of the literature or the experience being shared. This is a valid purpose and should not be overlooked. When listening for appreciation, students may be encouraged to listen to the way the sounds of the language contribute to the pleasure of the experience, the way that certain words evoke images effectively, and so on. But much listening for appreciation may take place with no formal preparation other than the statement: "Here is a story that I think you will enjoy." The purpose of enjoyment becomes explicit, and the pressure of listening to use the information in some way is removed. Students can relax and find pleasure in the spoken word. This relaxed situation provides the teacher with an opportunity to present students with good literature in a variety of genres that they would likely not choose to read for themselves and to expose them to many events and people outside their own circumstances. Such experiences provide the students with background knowledge about literature, events, and people that will serve them well in their later studies and in everyday life activities.

To provide a good listening environment for storytelling, you should remove distractions from the setting. Sitting in a circle around the teacher is a good arrangement for young children because it takes them away from the distractions of things on their desks. A semicircular arrangement of chairs, without desks, is beneficial for sessions with older students. If students do remain at their desks, the desks should be cleared of extraneous materials. Be sure the room temperature is at a comfortable level and the lighting is appropriate. The lights may be lowered for spooky stories, such as "The Monkey's Paw," for example.

Remind students that good listeners look at the speaker, refrain from interrupting the speaker, refrain from activities that could distract other listeners, and think about what they are hearing. Your listening program's goals of producing attentive, courteous, active listeners will be met if the students embrace these activities. Modeling attentive and courteous listening behaviors for the students is a powerful way to accomplish your listening instruction goals.

Speaking

Development of speaking skills also provides a natural tie-in for storytelling. Storytelling by students is an outstanding way to develop many speaking skills in a purposeful and pleasurable manner.

Teachers hope to improve students' speaking vocabularies, their voice control (use of pitch, tempo, volume, and pauses), and their ability to adjust the register of their speech to the situation. *Pitch* refers to the highness or lowness of sound, *tempo* to the rate of speech, *volume* to the loudness or softness of sound, and *pauses* to the breaks in speech that signal the ends of thoughts or stress the importance of adjacent words. *Register* refers to the style of speech used in different situations. This style may vary according to the subject of the discourse, the occasion, the location, the audience, and the purpose for speaking. Speech registers vary from extremely formal to intimate (Brown, 1987).

Speech instruction also often involves an understanding and appreciation of regional dialects. We discuss this factor in Chapter 4.

The telling of stories by students advances all of these goals of a speaking program. Students put new vocabulary into practice as they choose the words that fit the story. They learn to vary their pitch, tempo, volume, and pauses to convey the story to the audience. Pitch, tempo, and volume of characters' speech can be used to differentiate among the characters. These elements are also used to set the mood and indicate the action of the story. Pauses help to emphasize important words and phrases and build suspense. The speech register and dialect used for each character also help to show something about the characters, as well as to distinguish one from the other. Teachers can work with students as suggested in Chapter 2 to help them increase their speaking skills through storytelling.

If it is done well, storytelling by the teacher provides a speech model for the students. Many students who do not speak standard English at home may be first introduced to it through a teacher's storytelling. This modeling is a good way to develop "ear training" for the sounds of standard English, and modeling is a much better way to lead students to try this style of discourse than is exhortation to do so.

Of course, as has been mentioned before, discussion as a story follow-up is effective in helping the students to understand the story. It also offers a prime opportunity to work on the students' discussion skills. Discussion skills are practiced during creative dramatics sessions as well.

Reading

Students who wish to tell stories will be drawn to books for sources. They may find anthologies of stories from different lands or on specific topics to be particularly fertile ground, but they may also find picture books and episodes from chapter books and novels to be valuable. Younger students have found episodes from *Freckle Juice* (Judy Blume, 1971) to be fun to tell, whereas older students often enjoy the fence whitewashing scene from *Tom Sawyer* (Mark Twain, 1981), for example. The picture book *Why Mosquitoes Buzz in People's Ears* (Verna Aardema, 1975) is also a popular source.

Students who are preparing to tell a story may also want to read many different versions of the story to choose the one that they prefer, or they may wish to form their own version from several others. This reading is analytical/critical reading of the highest order when students judge the merits of the different versions. It is creative reading when they form their own versions through synthesis of the existing ones.

Having students prepare stories to read to the class orally with expression is also a worthy activity. It allows the students opportunities to experiment with vocal expression without the pressure of having to remember the story as well. It is often the first faltering step that a student takes toward storytelling, as he/she feels the power of the voice in conveying meaning and holding an audience's interest.

Storytelling by the teacher can offer students an invitation to books. Showing the book from which a story was drawn is an extremely effective technique. After a storytelling session, students often swamp the librarian with requests for books that contain stories that were presented.

Writing

Developing a story to tell is an act of composition, even if it is never put on paper. Still, students who are forming their own stories to tell will naturally do quite a bit of writing. They will want to record the story as they form it so that they won't forget what they have created. They will work to develop good beginnings that will grab the listeners' attention; well-developed, logically sequenced plots; and endings that bring the story to a definite, satisfying close. As they do this writing, they may experiment with vocabulary and sentence structure, dialogue, and effective descriptions, all of which will strengthen their writing skills.

As has been pointed out, writing activities make good follow-up activities to storytelling presentations. Among other types of activities, students can write reactions to the outcomes of the stories; other episodes for the stories, using the same characters; new stories of the same genres; letters to the characters; and letters to the authors.

Gillard (1996) mentions having students keep learning logs when they were preparing stories to tell. In these logs the students wrote their thoughts about choosing, preparing, and rehearsing their stories. She posed questions to them, and students responded to some or all of the questions in their logs. Her purpose was to encourage the students to think through the choice and preparation of their stories, but this process almost surely increased the ability of the students to do expository writing.

What Else Should You Know About Using Storytelling in Language Classes?

Because there are more implications for using storytelling in the language program than in any other part of the curriculum, we have divided the language information into two chapters. Any division of this material is necessarily arbitrary, but we believe that dealing with everything in this one chapter would have resulted in overload. Therefore, we have approached the next chapter as an extension of this one.

Gail continued her story to an audience that was held by the suspense she had generated.

It was about 5:00 p.m. before Uncle Curtis arrived, and again I gave a tour through the house pointing out the "evidence" along the way. But this time, my pleas that something had happened were finally heard. Uncle Curtis sent Mark and me out of the house while he contacted the sheriff.

The sheriff confirmed our suspicions. There had been a manhunt in our subdivision the night before for an escaped convict. He was wanted for kidnapping and robbery and was armed and considered very dangerous. The sheriff suspected he might have kidnapped my mother in order to escape. Again all we could do was wait.

A few hours later my parents called to say that they had in fact been kidnapped at gunpoint but had escaped and were unharmed. Our prayers had been answered.

The next few hours our house swarmed with newspaper and television reporters, fingerprinting crews, and neighbors we never even knew existed. Mark and I were on the front page of the Knoxville News-Sentinel *the next morning and on the Six O'clock News. We had become celebrities in the eyes of many. But nothing mattered except that my parents would be home soon.*

The convict, Sammy Lee Harper, had forced his way into the house and held my parents at gunpoint. He told them he did not mind killing them both because he had killed before. He had cleaned up,

*shaved, and changed into one of my father's best suits. My parents
were forced to drive him to Cincinnati, Ohio, where my father finally
persuaded Harper to let them go so he could get away faster. He
wrecked my father's new car in a high speed chase and was later
apprehended in Indiana. As far as I know, Sammy Lee Harper is now
serving a life prison term in a federal prison in Atlanta on charges of
kidnapping, armed robbery, and murder. As for my parents, they are
alive, well and living in Cookeville* (Hyder, 1995).

 Suggested Activities for the Teacher

1. Make a list of stories that would be good to use with creative dramatizations as a follow-up. Consider stories with limited settings, numerous characters, and much action.

2. Take a story that you particularly like to tell and make a list of the different ways you could use writing as a follow-up activity for this story.

3. Make a list of discussion questions that can be used following the telling of a specific story. Be sure to keep the questions open-ended, so that the students can apply their higher order thinking skills to the discussion.

4. Make a list of books that students might like to read as a follow-up to a story that you have just told. You may include books of the same genre, by the same author, or on the same topic, for example.

Suggested Activities for Use with Students

1. Teach the following lesson based on the story, "The Day It Snowed Tortillas," which is summarized below. A good source for the entire story is *The Day It Snowed Tortillas*, a collection of stories by Joe Hayes. Hayes also has this story on an audiotape of the same name.
    Story in Brief: Woodcutter cuts wood; he finds robber's hidden gold; he brings gold home; wife sends him for flour; wife hides gold; he brings flour to wife and takes a nap, while the wife cooks tortillas; wife puts tortillas on yard; he wakes up and wonders what has happened; wife tells him it has snowed tortillas and sends him to school when he says he never heard of it; he is put in first grade and embarrassed when he doesn't know the answers, so he goes back to cutting wood; robbers come for gold; wife denies knowing anything about it; robbers wait for woodcut-

ter; he says wife hid it the day before it snowed tortillas and his wife sent him to first grade; robbers think he is crazy and leave, never to return.

a. Present the story to the students several times, focusing on a different story element each time: characters, setting, and plot. Then have the children "try on" the characters in the story, practicing their vocal characteristics, dialogue, and actions. Let them locate places in the classroom for each major setting: Forest, Woodcutter's House, School, Town.

Then cast a group of students as the woodcutter, wife, robbers, store clerk, townspeople, schoolteacher, and school children. Let them act out the story with spontaneous dialogue and no props. The rest of the class can be the audience. After the story has been played, let the actors tell how they could have improved the performance if they repeated it. Also let the audience tell the actors what they did best.

Cast the parts again and let the children who were in the audience try their interpretations of the story. Follow this playing with both evaluation and a discussion in which the ways that different students portrayed the same character are compared and contrasted.

b. Have each student draw a story map that includes setting, characters, and plot. Let the students share their maps in small groups, making modifications as they see the need. Finally, let one child from each group share a map with the whole class. Students may continue to modify their maps as they gain ideas from the sharing. Students can decide during a whole-class discussion which of the maps have all of the necessary elements. One or more of these maps may be chosen by the students for display on the board or for transfer to a large poster.

c. Have each student choose a character and list as many descriptive words as possible to describe that character. Let students who chose the same character meet in a group and discuss the characteristics of that character. Let one person for each group report to the whole class about the conclusions the group formed about the character.

d. Find a recipe for tortillas. Duplicate it and let the students read it. Let them estimate how long it would really take to make one hundred pounds of flour into tortillas. Also let them decide how much of other ingredients would be needed to make these tortillas.

2. Plan to use the following set of activities as a follow-up to telling "Old One-Eye" from the book *Grandfather Tales* to encourage higher-order thinking skills for students.

    a. Divide the class members into sets of partners or small groups.

    b. Distribute the following instructions to the partners or groups: With a partner, discuss the answers to the following questions. Record the answer that you agree is correct. Share your responses with the rest of the class after all partners have finished answering the questions.

       (1) What caused the rogues to decide to rob the old lady?

       (2) What caused the first rogue to conclude that the old lady was a witch?

       (3) What caused the second rogue to conclude that the old lady was a witch?

       (4) What caused the third rogue to run away?

       (5) Did the old lady know that the rogues were there? Why do you think that?

       (6) Was the woman wise to keep her money where she kept it? Why, or why not?

    c. Have the small groups of students brainstorm answers to the following questions. Ask one person in each group to write all of the answers for his/her group. Then share the answers with the whole class.

       (1) What other places might the old woman have used to put her money?

       (2) If the old woman were determined to keep her money on the fireboard, what ways might she have protected it?

    d. Have each student choose one of the answers that was suggested for the question about how the woman might have protected her money and rewrite the story as it would have occurred if she had used that method of protecting her money. Have the students revise their stories and make copies to turn in to the teacher or have them share the stories orally with their classmates. Ask each of them to consider whether the original story or his/her revised story was funnier or more interesting and why.

    e. Have the students write an answer to the following question in their learning logs: What place do you think would have been best for the old lady to put her money? Why do you think so?

References

Aardema, V. (1975). *Why mosquitoes buzz in people's ears*. New York: Dial.

Allen, R. V. (1985). *I love ladybugs*. Allen, TX: DLM Teaching Resources.

Anderson, P. S. (1970). *Storytelling with the flannelboard: Book two*. Minneapolis, MN: T. S. Denison.

Barton, B., & Booth, D. (1990). *Stories in the classroom*. Portsmouth, NH: Heinemann.

Blume J. (1971). *Freckle juice*. New York: Dial

Brown, H. D. (1987). *Principles of language learning and teaching*. (2nd ed.). Englewood Cliffs, NJ: Prentice-Hall.

Chambers, D. (1970). *Storytelling and creative drama*. Dubuque, IA: Wm. C. Brown.

Chase, R. (1948). *Grandfather tales*. Boston: Houghton Mifflin.

Denman, G. A. (1991). *Sit tight and I'll swing you a tail*. Portsmouth, NH: Heinemann.

Gag, W. (1928). *Millions of cats*. New York: Coward, McCann, & Geoghegan.

Galdone, P. (1960). *The old woman and her pig*. New York: McGraw-Hill.

Galdone, P. (1979). *The gingerbread boy*. New York: Clarion.

Gillard, M. (1996). *Storyteller, storyteacher*. York, ME: Stenhouse.

Hayes, J. (1985). *The day it snowed tortillas*. Sante Fe, NM: Mariposa.

Hyder, G. (1995). Kidnapped. Unpublished story.

Livo, N. J., & Rietz, S. A. (1986). *Storytelling: Process & practice*. Littleton, CO: Libraries Unlimited.

Piper, W. (1961). *The little engine that could*. New York: Platt & Monk.

Roe, B. D. (1985). Use of storytelling/storyreading in conjunction with follow-up language activities to improve oral communication of rural first-grade students: Phase I. Cookeville, TN: Rural Education Consortium, Spring.

Roe, B. D. (1986). Use of storytelling/storyreading in conjunction with follow-up language activities to improve oral communication of rural first-grade students: Phase II. Cookeville, TN: Rural Education Consortium.

Roe, B. D. (1987). Use of storytelling/storyreading in conjunction with follow-up language activities to improve comprehension skills of rural primary-grade students. Cookeville, TN: Rural Education Consortium, Winter-Spring.

Roe, B. D. (1988). Extending learning and knowledge through storytelling. *Educators' Forum*, 10, 15.

Sawyer, R. (1970). *The way of the storyteller*. New York: Viking.

Seuss, Dr. (1940). *Horton hatches the egg*. New York: Random House.

Shermis, M. (1990). *Parents and children together*. Bloomington, IN: ERIC/RCS.

Stevens, J., illustrator. (1983). *The house that Jack built*. New York: Greenwillow.

Twain, M. (1981). *Tom Sawyer*. New York: Putnam.

Viorst, J. (1973). *Alexander and the terrible, horrible, no good, very bad day*. New York: Atheneum.

Wagner, J. A. (1970). *Children's literature through storytelling*. Dubuque, IA: Wm. C. Brown.

Witson, B. V. (1970). Cheese, peas, and chocolate pudding. In P. S. Anderson, pp. 75-79, *Storytelling with the flannelboard: Book two*. Minneapolis, MN: T. S. Denison.

Chapter 4
Using Storytelling to Teach Language Skills—Part 2

꧁꧂

They were lost, these northerners from Ohio who had come to East Tennessee where the fishing was so good. They drove for a number of miles before they saw the first sign of a house. Then they saw the small ragged country store, with the rusting gasoline pump and the ancient dog sleeping by the door. One of the men got out of the van to go ask for directions. The young woman behind the counter said, "Go out of the parking lot and turn right," pronouncing the word "right" with that flat "i" that we hear all over East Tennessee.

"Raht?" mocked the Ohio man, with amused derision in his voice. "How do you spell that, "R-I-T-E?" he asked.

The young woman leveled her gaze at him with a self-assurance that matched his own. With only the slightest smile she spoke in a thick Appalachian accent. "No wonder you're lost," she said. "You can't even spell."

꧁꧂

Certainly the natives of the Southern Appalachians have endured more than their share of teasing from people in other parts of the country. And they are not alone. Speakers of any dialect or any accent that falls outside the range of what most people regard as "standard" pronunciation, or usage, are often put on the defensive when others make fun of the way they talk.

We would do well to learn how to parry such insensitive comments from people who make fun of the way we speak. However, students are not usually quick enough nor self-assured enough to come up with such a response that blunts the insult. It is up to their teachers to help them appreciate the dialect with which they were reared and to use it to their own advantage in the classroom. After all, it is in the rhythms and cadences of our own speech that authentic "languaging" begins. That language can be a powerful resource for the teaching of English/language arts.

Why Use Personal Stories?

As shown in Chapter 3, the sources for storytelling are abundant. However, although the sources for good storytelling can be found in many places, from ancient Greek myths to contemporary urban legends, we must not overlook one of the richest sources at the students' disposal: their personal experiences. The story that opened this chapter is just such a story, told to Suellen by her late uncle, Matthew Gardner Nunnelley, who heard the store clerk's retort. It has now become a favorite story among the members of a family whose roots are deep in Southern Appalachian soil.

Personal and family stories address another very important issue as students strive to become more proficient in language usage; they encourage students to believe that they come to school already prepared in their unique way to use language effectively. That language may not be standard English, but it is generally a very useful vehicle for communicating with their family and friends. If students feel that the teacher respects their ability to communicate in their own dialects or primary languages, they will be more likely to approach their study of English/language arts with a positive attitude.

How Can You Develop A Supportive Environment?

One of the best ways to encourage students to grow in their ability to express themselves well is to adopt a "bidialectalist" approach in which a teacher respects and acknowledges students' dialects while encouraging them to learn the use of standard English as well. Teachers who resist respecting students' authentic language run the risk of alienating their students (Lucas & Borders, 1987). As Delaine, and others (1985, p. 171) state, "...teachers need to appreciate differences in communication strategies in order to foster an environment in the classroom that capitalizes on the strengths of all children." Such an approach creates a supportive learning environment. Delpit (1988) confirms the importance of such an environment when she states that students most easily learn an alternate form of language, not so much from rule-based instruction and correction, but through exposure, comfort level, motivation, familiarity, and practice in authentic assignments that connect with their own lives. In both learning new language and learning standard English, "The less stress attached to the process, the more easily it is accomplished" (Delpit, 1988, p. 249).

To establish such a supportive environment, you can start where the students are. You can give them legitimate opportunities to write and speak in their own dialects and thus affirm their richness and value. If in this approach students can be successful, the acquisition of standard usage will be less painful, because they will have developed a sense of accomplishment in their way of expressing themselves. When they are comfortable with their own language, students find it easier to write with a real sense of voice and to produce written work that sounds and feels authentic.

How Should You Deal with Dialect?

How can you help students use their own dialects as they develop their speaking and listening skills? Fortunately, a number of excellent works are available to show students the value of using their own voices as they learn how to use English/language arts effectively. Many excellent books and tapes in which professional storytellers recount their stories are available. For a list of useful books see Appendix B, which contains titles that are excellent examples of good stories to tell. Students may want to read some of them to gain a sense of cadence and style. A look at them shows the value of using authentic speaking patterns to create an entertaining oral presentation. Carson (1990) uses such patterns in *Stories I Ain't Told Nobody Yet*, a collection of performance pieces that use the Appalachian dialect with facility and grace. The pieces in this collection are numbered, not titled. Number 4, about George getting sick (p. 9); Number 9, about "brother Estes" (p. 17); and Number 16, about the stereotype of mountain people (p. 28) are excellent examples. As Carson (1992) once said, "If it doesn't feel right on my tongue, it won't feel right in your ear." Reading Carson's stories can give students some ideas about using authentic voices in telling their own stories.

Another excellent example is Ray Hicks' story, "The Day the Cow Ate My Britches" (Hicks, 1991, pp. 132-134). It is a very funny personal story about the misadventures of a young boy who gets snowed in at his sweetheart's house in Western North Carolina and the embarrassing events that befall him as he tries to stay warm in a drafty log cabin. Nikki Giovanni's poem, "Legacies," about a grandmother's puzzlement as to why her grandchild does not want to learn to bake biscuits is another good source to read for its authentic voice and its poignant example of miscommunication between two loved ones (Giovanni, 1985, p. 153). It can elicit a number of personal family stories. Actually encouraging students to gather and present family stories or stories from their cultural background requires creativity and careful planning.

How Can You Gather Personal Stories?

One way to encourage students to get in touch with and recreate family stories is to have them interview and audiotape members of their families.

However, sometimes it is difficult for people to begin telling family stories immediately after microphones are stuck in their faces. Abruptly beginning to record a person's stories without any warm-up or introduction usually results in a disappointing session. Thus, for a series of interviews, it is a good idea to ask students to use props such as photographs or personal belongings to stimulate memory and reflection. At the end of this chapter you will find three "Suggested Activities to Use With Students" that will help interviewers prompt the memories for stories of the people they interview.

Here are two stories that resulted from an assignment very similar to the ones at the end of the chapter. These stories came from students in a senior English class in a small East Tennessee town. Their instructions were to interview and/or tape a family member telling a personal story. The students worked on this project enthusiastically.

On the appointed day, the students came to class with some genuinely entertaining stories based not only on their family lore, but also on the community lore about some very well-known characters in the town. Even though the students had been asked to bring family stories to the class, a number of them brought stories about a town character whose antics had captured their imagination and that of their parents. The stories were not complex or extensive. In fact, some would even call them mere anecdotes; but they were very structured narratives that showed a conflict being solved or that revealed something very important about the main character. "Listen" to this one about Jake Bridgewater (not his real name).

❧❧❧

Jake Bridgewater was an infamous schemer who had a farm in the community during the early part of the 20th century. He compensated for his lack of formal education by using clever, problem-solving common sense. He was also a skinflint of mythological proportions who hated to spend money as much as he liked to make it.

One day Jake had to go to court over a property dispute about a boundary line. The judge took only a few minutes to rule in Jake's favor. As Jake and his lawyer were leaving the courthouse Jake said, "Well, now, how much do I owe you for helping me out?"

"Fifty dollars," said the lawyer, with self-assurance.

"Fifty dollars?!" Jake exclaimed, astonished. "Fer just ten minutes?"

"Jake, you're not payin' me for what I did. You're payin' me for what I know," said the lawyer in his well-pressed three-piece suit. So Jake paid the lawyer with great reluctance, in cash, as Jake never used a bank account; and they both went on their way.

A few weeks later, Jake met the lawyer on a back country road trying to persuade an uncooperative cow to cross a small bridge that spanned a noisy stream. "Jake, I can't seem to get this cow to cross this bridge. I'll pay you a little somethin' if you'll help me out," the lawyer said.

Without a word, Jake picked up a feed sack out of his wagon, placed it over the cow's head, and led her across that bridge as pretty as you please. The lawyer was visibly impressed and very relieved. "Well, thank you Jake," he said. "I never would've thought about using a feed sack. Now, how much do I owe you for helping me out?" (Anybody with a grain of imagination can predict the ensuing conversation, but for those who are still reading on the literal level, here is the rest of the story.)

"Fifty dollars," said Jake.

"Fifty dollars?!" exclaimed the lawyer, astonished. "For leading a cow across a bridge?"

"Mr. Lawyer, you ain't payin' me for what I did. You're payin' me for what I know," said Jake, in his rumpled overalls.

So the lawyer reluctantly paid Jake the fifty dollars, in cash, as Jake never used a bank account; and they both went on their way (Alfred, 1993, p.1).

Even though many of the students in the class had heard this story from their parents or grandparents, they listened with delight, nodding their heads in affirmation as their classmate recounted this familiar story with surprising skill. When the teller of the "cow story" had finished, another student said, "That reminds me of another Jake Bridgewater story"; and, with just the slightest encouragement, she was off on another tale. The class then became a kind of Jake Bridgewater storytelling festival, to the obvious delight of everyone. The teacher was delighted with the stories and with her students, not only "for what they did, but for what they knew" about the lore of the town, about the way to tell a story, and about how to interact with humor and good will with those around them. Not a bad way to spend some time in the classroom.

A testimony to the value of interviewing family members came a few weeks after the unit was finished. One student who had taped her frail and elderly grandfather told the teacher she would not have done so if she had not needed to interview him for an assignment. She said she was very glad she did, because not long after she taped him her grandfather died. That audiotape no doubt has become a priceless family treasure.

Here's another Jake story just for fun.

Jake Bridgewater was an uneducated man who hated to spend money as much as he loved to make it. Jake was always looking for a way to hang on to his cash; and, the truth be told, he had quite a lot of it stashed away in an old iron safe in a warehouse. If he couldn't weasel out of paying for something, he would barter his way out of it.

One day the town doctor came to Jake's farm to buy some hay. After Jake and the doctor got the hay loaded on the wagon, the doctor said to Jake, "Now, Jake, how much do I owe you for this hay?"

Jake acted like he had not heard the doctor's question. Jake scratched his head in concentration. "Doc, how much do I owe you down at the office?" he asked, with an innocent expression. (We know, of course, that there wasn't anything innocent about this horse trader's question.)

"Oh, I believe that bill is thirty-six dollars and seventeen cents," the doctor replied, in frustration. (As you can tell by the doctor's memory for the exact amount, Jake wasn't the only one of that pair who understood the value of a dollar.) "Now, how much do I owe you for this hay?" he asked again, impatiently. (And of course you can predict the rest of the story.)

"Well," said Jake, stretching out the vowel sound to its fullest extent, "I believe it comes to right at thirty-six dollars and seventeen cents. Did ye ever see anythang come out so even?"

And so, the doctor didn't give Jake a cent, but he went straight to his office and marked Jake Bridgewater's bill for thirty-six dollars and seventeen cents "Paid in Full." The horse trader had won again (Alfred, 1993, p. 3).

One of the most amusing stories resulting from this assignment is the one told by Lynda Walker Breeden.

Anna Joyce and Shelby
Copyright by Lynda Walker Breeden

Anna Joyce and Shelby was always a orderin' somethin' from the catalog and George would have to pay for it. They'd order foolish stuff. Stuff they couldn't even use. Why, one time they ordered a gui-tar or a banjer [banjo], one, I can't remember now. And neither one of 'em could play a lick. George would come across the railroad tracks just a cussin'. "Them girls has ordered another damn pack-age!" But he'd always pay for the stuff. Never would send it back.

Them two girls was mean! One time they brought an ole goat in the house. Put it in the bedroom. That thang was up on the bed, looked over in the glass of the chiffenrobe [chiffoniere—a high nar-row chest of drawers] and seen itself in the mirror. Thought it was another goat and kicked the glass all to pieces. Then it chewed up Hattie's curtains.

It ain't no wonder them girls got locked in the closet sometimes. They come by it honest, though. George wun't nothing but an ole drunk. And Hattie was mean as a black snake, too. She even shot George one time in the leg. Says she don't want to be buried by him, but I bet them girls put her there just for spite. Then, they won't have to go to two different places to decorate.

This story has a clear voice and a clear point of view. The effect of the story would be different if it were told in standard English. It would be inter-esting to have students listen to the story, then read it, noticing the phrases that indicate nonstandard usage. Then have students "translate" the story into stan-dard English and discuss the difference such a translation has on the voice and character of the story. Is it as amusing in one version as it is in the other? Does the standard usage capture the character of the narrator?

Isn't This Just for Fun?

Most students have a good time with the assignments and activities described in this chapter; nevertheless, more than fun is involved in these activities. Three very important points should be made about the academic value of these assignments. First, students are using their own language and seeing it validated in a school setting, a place where they are traditionally told how language *should be* used. Such validation leads to a sense of confidence in their ability to use language effectively and, thus, makes them more amenable to instruction in standard English. Second, students are talking in their own voices with each other in small and large groups, using authentic language to recount their personal and family experiences. They have an opportunity to become more facile in the use of oral language that "fits in their mouths," as Carson (1992) would say. Finally, without realizing it, they are practicing the narrative and dramatic arts, using point of view, voice, plot structure, and interaction of characters. (More extended discussions of these ideas are found in Chapters 5, 6, and 7.)

The activities found at the end of this chapter can bring a great deal of enjoyment to students and to teachers alike. Remember, it is important to keep a light heart about the whole process. Too much emphasis on the correct use of language can dampen students' enthusiasm. Certainly there is a place and time for polishing one's delivery and learning to use standard English, but these assignments are the beginning of that process, not the end. Polishing and standardizing must come after initial efforts have given students the confidence and the motivation to continue. Teachers who want to move from these informal uses of the language into an emphasis on more standard usage can use these student stories as a springboard for such assignments. Having students write the stories, translating them into formal English, can be a powerful way of illustrating the difference between dialect and standard usage. It can also show them the effect that various forms of usage can have on the tone and spirit of a story. In any event, family stories are an effective and enjoyable way to help students develop language arts skills.

On the next few pages you will find a list of "Suggested Activities to Use With Students." As an example of the "Walking and Wondering" assignment found below, here is a true personal story that Suellen thinks of every time she thinks of Carthage, Tennessee.

⚜

An Invented Spelling Experience

Annika was seven years old, precocious and persistent, energetic, amusing, and inventive. On a sunny Saturday in February, we went for a walk with Annika. "Tell me some words you want me to spell," Annika said. Annika was insatiable. Conversation was halted and incoherent, peppered with isolated words pronounced precisely by the adults, and with their spellings intoned by Annika. She showed no signs of fatigue with such a clever game.

Soon we were running out of words, but Annika was not running out of steam. She remained insistent. "Annika, that's enough, now," said Danielle, her mother.

"Give me another word." It was the chorus that answered all other elements of conversation.

At one point we rounded a bend and found a barking dog. With the hope that she could break the cycle of Annika's intractable spelling obsession, Suellen said, "Okay, now Annika, listen to that dog barking. Spell what that dog says." At that point, of course, the dog stopped barking. Annika leaned toward the animal with a determined look on her face.

*"Bark again!" she demanded. The dog complied and barked
again. Annika listened intently.*

*"A-R-F!" said Annika, inventively, and looked up in triumph at
her mother and her friend. A smile of accomplishment spread across
her upturned, shining face. And on we walked, spelling our way back
home* (Alfred & Garman, 1992).

No doubt, if Annika and her mother walked that same route again, they
would tell that story to each other. It would be interesting to hear the story told
by each of the three participants to hear their variations of it. For example,
Annika might disagree that she was insatiable; her mother might want to add
more description about her own frustration with Annika's persistence.

 Suggested Activities for the Teacher

1. Before assigning some of the activities below to your students, try them
    for yourself in order to gain firsthand experience of them.

2. Look for storytelling gatherings or festivals in your area and attend one
    of them so that you can experience firsthand the joy of listening to well-
    told stories.

Suggested Activities for Use with the Students

The activities below are appropriate for any time of the year, but they
often work best when used around a holiday when families traditionally get
together: Thanksgiving, Hanukkah, Christmas, Easter, Passover.

1. Give your students these instructions:

ONE PICTURE IS WORTH A THOUSAND WORDS, BUT I WANT YOU TO SAY THE WORDS ANYWAY

Almost all families have personal stories that they tell over and over
every time they get together. Usually these stories are very amusing.
Think of a story that your own family tells. Ask one of those family
members to tell that story to you again. You may want to tape record the
story as your relative tells it. Be sure to ask permission before you do the
taping. Also, assure your relative that you will not play any part of the
tape in class without his or her approval. If you don't have a tape
recorder, simply take good notes as the story is being told. Actually, you

have probably heard the story so many times that you could tell it your-self without any help. Often it is difficult to persuade a family member simply to launch into telling a story. Sometimes that person needs a prop or a prompt. Old family photographs are an effective way to get started.

Find a box or an album of family photographs. Ask your relative to look through the pictures and just have a conversation about some of her or his favorites. If you have a tape recorder, quietly turn it on and tape the conversation. More than likely, a photograph will stir a memory which will stir a story.

After you have heard the story and either taped it or taken notes on it, practice telling the story yourself. *Do not write it down.* This is a "telling" assignment, not a writing one. Come to class ready to tell your story initially to a partner. As you and your partner listen to each other's stories, share with each other questions you may have about the plot or the characters or the background and suggestions for improvement.

Using the same kind of language or dialect that was used by the orig-inal teller, tell your story to the rest of the class. Don't worry about stan-dard English usage in this assignment. Rather, try to use the voice of the original teller. However, you should avoid using socially unacceptable language or revealing family secrets that are best kept at home.

2.   A variation of "One Picture is Worth a Thousand Words But I Want You to Say the Words Anyway" involves the use of imagination and freewrit-ing. Give the students the instructions below. Speak slowly in a low, gentle voice so that not only your instructions, but also your demeanor, will encourage the students to relax.

WHAT I HEAR IN MY HEAD: A FREEWRITE

Settle down in your seat and relax. Close your eyes and breathe deeply for a few seconds. As you breathe, listen to the sounds around you. In front of your eyes draw a gray wall. Breath slowly and deeply. Look at the gray wall. Now, call up a memory of an event in your fami-ly or among your friends that everyone remembers and retells every time a group of you gets together. Project on the gray wall the scene as it plays out in your mind. Listen to the voice of the one who usually tells the story. Listen to the tone of voice, unusual vocabulary, usage, and phras-ing. Listen to the story all the way through. If you cannot recall a story, use this time to make up a unique story.

Spend about 6 or 7 minutes looking at and listening to the "video tape" as you project it on the gray wall.

Now, open your eyes and stretch. Please remain silent. Quietly take out several sheets of paper and pencil and freewrite for 10 minutes the narrative of the story that you just heard in your head. Do not worry about spelling, punctuation, sentence structure, unity, or coherence. Do not worry about standard usage. Instead, use the language you heard. If your storyteller talks like someone from the hills, use that language. If he or she talks like someone from the inner city, use that language. Once you begin writing, don't stop. Keep writing. If you get stuck, simply write the very last word you thought of until something else comes to you. Write with the idea that you will use this freewrite as a beginning of a polished story that you will *tell* (not *read*) in class. Thus, be sure that you keep in your story only those things about yourself, your family, and your friends that you and they would willingly share with others.

After your freewrite, find a partner who will listen to your story and who will tell his or hers to you. Spend some time making suggestions to each other about how the story can be strengthened.

Later, after you have worked on it, *tell*, don't read, your story to the class with as much energy and expression as you can.

(Note: This assignment has been a successful one in the past, but you may want to caution the students that their cooperation is important. Sometimes students can get the giggles when asked to do something like this that seems strange to them. Such active imagination cannot work in a group unless everyone respects the need for silence. You also want to be sensitive to students who come from such dysfunctional homes that they have few pleasant memories and find it difficult to produce stories that they would feel free to tell. That's why it is important to let them write stories or dialogues based on their interactions with their friends or to make up stories.)

3. Have students perform the following activity:

WALKING AND WONDERING

If you have one, use a battery operated, portable tape recorder for this assignment. If you do not have one, take a thick notebook and a good pen to take notes. Ask someone in your family to take a walk with you. Follow a route that is very familiar to the family, a route that reminds you and others of family memories. For example, this place may be where little Annie had a bicycle wreck and scared everyone half to death. It may be where your mother and daddy kissed each other for the first time. Tell your family member to walk this "memory trail" with you and tell the stories that come up as the two of you walk along. Be sure that the volume of the tape recorder is up enough to capture the storyteller's voice and to compensate for traffic noise. Also, be sure the route is not too long, too tiring, or too noisy.

After you have taken the walk, return to the place where you began and ask your storyteller if he or she remembers any other stories that took place along the route where you just walked.

When you have finished your recording, choose one of the stories that your storyteller shared and work on telling it in the same style and voice that your storyteller used.

4.   Have students try this activity:

WHEN WERE YOU THE MOST...

Ask a parent or a grandparent, aunt or uncle to tell you a specific experience he or she had as a child. To help him or her get started, ask "When were you the most _____ [afraid, or amused, or surprised, or delighted]?" You can fill in the blank. Using a key adjective in your question can work better than simply asking someone to tell you a childhood story.

5.   Try giving this assignment that requires multiple tellings from several points of view:

EVERYBODY'S SIDE OF THE STORY

Make an appointment with a number of your family members and ask them all to gather around the kitchen table. Put your tape recorder in the middle of the table and turn it on. Bring out an object or a photograph, or come up with a phrase or joke that causes everyone to remember a certain event in the family. For example, you may have in your family a cracked cup that has not been thrown away because the circumstances under which it became cracked are a valued family story. Show everyone the item and then ask everyone to tell the story that surrounds that object or photo or joke. The story will be more interesting if everyone has a slightly different version, depending on his or her point of view. More than likely, after the first person tells the story, another person will eagerly chime in and say, "No, that's not the way it happened." Once you hear that sentence, you are on to an interesting variation of the story you just heard.
(Note: This assignment can give students a very good lesson in the powerful influence that point of view can have on how a sequence of events develops in a narrative. What gets told depends a great deal on who does the telling.)

Some form of the assignments above have been used successfully with students in college, in high school, and in upper elementary grades.

References

Alfred, S. (1993). Using stories to connect with community lore. *Once-Upon-A Times*, 1.

Alfred, S. (1993). Jake Bridgewater and the doctor. *Once-Upon-A Times*, 3.

Alfred, S., & Garman, D. A. (1992). An invented spelling experience. *Tennessee Reading Teacher, 20* (Spring), 19.

Breeden, L. W. (1993). Anna Joyce and Shelby. *Once-Upon-A Times*, 3-4.

Carson, J. (1990). *Stories I ain't told nobody yet*. New York: Orchard Books.

Carson, J. (1992). Personal conversation. Knoxville, TN. December 7.

Delain, M. T., et al. (1985). Reading comprehension and creativity in black language use: You stand to gain by playing the sounding game. *American Educational Research Journal, 22*, 155-173.

Delpit, L. (1988). Language diversity and learning. In Susan Hynds & David Rubin (Eds.), *Perspectives on talk and learning* (pp. 247-266). Urbana, IL: National Council of Teachers of English.

Giovanni, N. (1985). Legacies. In Edmund J. Farrell, Ouida H. Clapp, & Karen J. Kuehner (Eds.), *Patterns in literature* (p. 153). Glenview, IL: Scott Foresman.

Hicks, R. (1991). The day the cow ate my britches. In *Best-loved stories told at the National Storytelling Festival* (pp. 132-134). 20th Anniversary Edition. Jonesborough, TN: National Storytelling Press.

Lucas, C., & Borders, D. (1987). Language diversity and classroom discourse. *American Educational Research Journal, 24*, (Spring), 119-141.

Chapter 5
Using Storytelling to Enhance Learning In and Through Literature—Part 1

Saturday was Mattie's favorite day of the week. While she rubbed polishing oil into the radio cabinet, she listened to Let's Pretend. *One of her favorite stories was on, the tale of Bluebeard who wouldn't allow his wife to go into one room, which he kept locked. Bluebeard's wife was turning the key in the lock when Virgil, carrying a bucket of coal for the stove, burst in.*

"That your last chore, Mattie? I'm all done now, and I'm going exploring. Wanta come?"

Mattie frowned at him, shook her head, and leaned closer to the radio.

Just then Janie Mae came in from the bedroom, where she'd been playing with paper dolls. "Can I go with you, Virgil?" she asked.

"Sure," Virgil said. "You can show me what's in those woods behind the house. Don't you wanta go, too, Mattie?"

Mattie snapped off the radio switch. "I might as well," she said. He'd made her miss her favorite part of the story, the moment when the wife looks into the room and sees the weapons Bluebeard used to kill his other wives. Besides, she didn't think it would be fair for Janie Mae to have to put up with Virgil all by herself.

Mother looked at them from the kitchen table, where she sat writing a letter. "Wear your sweaters," she said. "Remember, it's just barely spring."...

Mother didn't look up again as they left.

The sun shone warmly, something that didn't happen very often in Oak Ridge, it seemed to Mattie. Puddles still stood in the red clay soil, and Mattie remembered the day last summer when they'd moved into the house. Janie Mae had washed her dolls' clothes in a muddy pool, and the pastel dresses had picked up the color from the red clay so that even now they were antique-looking, like old lace stored for a long time in a trunk.

Mother had been too busy unpacking boxes to get mad at Janie Mae; but later, as she tried to get the stain out of the clothing without using bleach on the delicate fabrics, she had fussed at Janie Mae. "These were dresses you and Mattie wore when you were babies, and now look at them," she said.

Janie Mae's lip quivered at Mother's words, and Mattie put a protective arm around her. "She didn't mean to ruin them. She just thought she'd wash them like we used to in the creek."

Mother looked at Mattie sharply. "I know that, Mattie," she'd said. "But Janie Mae needs to know that what she did had a bad result even if she did it for the right reason. She's old enough to start taking responsibility for herself." Mother held a dress at arm's length and shook her head. "You're going to have to start letting your sister develop a tougher hide." But Mattie couldn't do it. She was the one who slept with Janie Mae, who knew how everything that was said to Janie Mae during the day came out in her dreams at night, how she thrashed her legs and moaned. And how, if Mattie wasn't there to comfort her, her terror grew and grew until finally she wet the bed, waking herself. Mother knew about the dreams and the bed-wetting, and she attempted to reassure Janie Mae whenever she heard her at night. But usually it was Mattie who calmed her sister. And she intended to protect her from whatever frightened her.

However, Janie Mae's night terrors and the war and the other hurts that brought them on seemed far away to Mattie as she stretched her arms in the warm sunlight. Maybe she could even put up with Virgil on such a day. At the edge of the woods, she took off her sweater and hung it on a limb. Virgil and Janie Mae did the same....

Mattie took the lead down a steep slope behind the house. "Too steep to build on," Daddy had explained one day, "so the government left it in woods. They call them 'greenbelts' and they're scattered all over Oak Ridge." Mattie was glad she lived next to a greenbelt. Last fall she and Janie Mae had often walked home from school through the woods, the dry leaves crunching beneath their feet.

Today the leaves under her feet were soggy from all the rain. She kicked over a clump of leathery oak leaves, slow to decay, and a rich, moist smell drifted to her nose.

With Janie Mae and Virgil behind her, she headed for the foot of the ridge, where a creek meandered. In nice weather she went there often, jumping from stone to stone until she reached a large rock in *the middle of the stream. She liked to sit on the rock and watch the water part and flow past.*

But today she heard the water before she saw it.

The three of them gazed upon a muddy torrent roaring down the creek bed and curling around the rock, only the tip of which stuck out of the stream. "Well, I guess I won't sit on my rock today," Mattie said.

"Why not?" Virgil asked.

"Because I can't get to it without getting into that muddy water."

"Sure you can."

"Come on, Virgil. You can't even see the stepping-stones."

"So? Who needs stepping-stones?"

"Since I haven't grown wings yet, I need them."

Virgil looked her up and down. "I guess that's right, seeing as how you're a girl."

Not that again, Mattie thought. "And what does being a girl have to do with it?" she asked wearily.

"Just about everything, I reckon. Boys don't think twice about jumping that far."

"Oh, really?"

"Yeah, really."

"Next I guess you're going to tell me you can jump that far."

"That's about the size of it."

Mattie leaned against a tree trunk and folded her arms across her chest. "So, prove it," she said.

Virgil paced up and down along the bank. "Okay, I'll do it. But if I make it without getting wet, you gotta jump, too. Or else admit girls can't do what boys can."

Putting up all week with somebody who was crazy was bad. Having to tolerate him on the weekend was double bad....

"Mother's gonna be mad if you get muddy," [Janie Mae] said.

"Okay. Just in case...." And Virgil began stripping out of his clothes. When he was down to his undershorts, he backed several feet away from the bank. Then he bent over, eyed the tip of the rock, and slowly raised his back end in a racer's stance. The next second his feet were thudding against the soggy earth, his arms swinging in rhythm. He ran half crouched to the water's edge. Then he flung himself into the air.

Mattie couldn't take her eyes off the flying figure. Any second now he was sure to land in the muddy water. But to her surprise, his feet smacked safely on the protruding tip of the rock. She stared at him in disbelief. He really could jump that far.

As the teacher shared this excerpt from *The War at Home* by Connie Green (1989) with the class, life in Oak Ridge, Tennessee, during World War II became more immediate and real for the children. They could project themselves into the times more easily through the story's engaging characters.

How Can Story Archetypes Aid in the Understanding of Literature

Storytelling can assist in opening the door to quality literature for children. Inherent in storytelling are ancient archetypes that appeal to our most basic feelings and need to organize and store information.

Archetypes are patterns, images, and symbols that serve as models, templates, or prototypes. These patterns, such as those of the nurturing mother, the trickster, and the hero, according to Jung (1989), reflect not only one individual's images and perceptions, but those of the entire human race. They appear in all cultures and time periods and result in the universal appeal and understanding of stories. The character Virgil in *The War at Home* contains elements of the trickster, and the mother in this story fits the archetype of the nurturing mother.

Archetype (Drabble, 1985 p. 38) may be defined as "a pervasive idea, image, or symbol that forms part of the collective unconscious." Jung's (1989) research on mental activity revealed that repeated images from individuals' dreams matched story formats found in ancient mythology and that this organizational system provided tools to help humans understand themselves and the wide assortment of characteristics that they have. The concept of archetypes and their relationship to the collective unconscious provides a basis for understanding how individuals organize and process the images presented in and through literature. A storyteller who understands the archetypal structure found in literature is able to create characters and events that are believable, even when the story is recognized as fantasy or fiction. Often in the most fanciful story, the listener finds a personal connection either with an event, an image, or a character in that story. With an understanding of archetypes, the storyteller is much better equipped to craft a story that is "dramatic, entertaining, and psychologically true" (Vogler, 1992, p. 13).

From interviews with numerous storytellers, Mooney and Holt (1996, p. 46) report, "The tellers all agree that each story needs characters that are strong and ring true." Many *character archetypes* exist in literature. They are often related to specific characters, for example the "big, bad wolf," the "wicked witch," or the "fairy godmother." Numerous combinations of character archetypes are possible with the myriad of human characteristics that exist. As a listener analyzes characters described through oral narration, the characters become more believable if they are portrayed as having personality dimensions. Younger listeners are often entertained by simple characters that fit a more basic identifiable pattern, such as the beautiful princess or the handsome prince; while more mature listeners are often drawn to more complex characters, containing combinations of archetypes, who appear more realistic.

An example of a character archetype that appears in stories from different cultures is represented by Tom Tit Tot. Tom Tit Tot is described in the literature as an imp or little devil (Livo & Rietz, 1991) as is his counterpart Foul Weather. The trickster is another character model well represented in a variety of folklore. Coyote, Br'er Rabbit, Raven, Ananse the Spider, and Loki are a few of the common trickster characters found in stories.

Behavior archetypes may also be related to specific characters and are often easy to anticipate because of the pattern and the predictability. When listening to stories featuring a hero character, students often expect the hero to accomplish goals and to "do" good deeds. According to Jungian theory, the listener recognizes the traits demonstrated by the character and is able to identify with the story because of an existing subconscious memory. Students visualize or imagine their own reactions to the challenges and temptations that the hero faces in a story. Students can be encouraged to monitor a story by asking "What would I do in this situation?" and "How would I react?"

Analysis of the behavior archetype following a storytelling event encourages discussion. Many students become excited and enthusiastic when discussing how they might have reacted to the challenges that faced a character from a selection of literature. Often students will agree with the behavior of the character and feel that it was quite predictable; other times, they are surprised because of the way the character behaved in a particular situation.

Understanding the concept of archetypes and developing an awareness of human behaviors and traits enable the storyteller to effectively share stories that involve the listener. Such understanding can serve as a guide for choosing appropriate stories for a particular audience. For example, stories that appeal to adolescents often portray characters who demonstrate behaviors and interests that parallel their own at the time. The behavior archetype becomes a tool for the storyteller to allow listeners to see themselves through a character or in a story.

Stories reveal various sets of real world circumstances and the behaviors and relationships surrounding those circumstances. Through literature, students can see various models of how relationships exist and are developed. They are introduced to relationships that exist among individuals, not only in literature, but also in daily life, such as parent/children, husband/wife, friend/friend, grandparents/grandchildren, employer/employee, teacher/student, and sibling/sibling. Through story, students can compare the dynamics of the interactions revealed through literature with their own everyday interactions. The selection that begins this chapter is an excellent example of complex interaction among siblings.

In stories, basic human needs are also reflected through various arche-

typal patterns. Literature provides numerous sources for exploring the psychological needs of the human race. Stories may be found that reveal our
needs for acceptance, security, and love and can also guide us through the
recognition of unpleasant emotions or feelings that we may not want to
acknowledge.

Experiences may be depicted with either happy or unhappy archetypal
patterns. Many times cultural differences are evident in the way the experiences are defined. For example, the concept of justice is viewed differently
from culture to culture, and this is reflected in stories that feature the theme
of justice.

In stories, the archetypal nature of events may reveal individual cultural
values and levels of social consciousness. Story events may be depicted as
either pleasant or distressing. Fables, offering words that teach and guide,
may provide a rich source for analysis of this archetype. The following story,
told to a group of sixth grade students as a writing prompt, is an example of
a popular Aesop's fable.

The Fox and the Grapes

*One hot summer's day a fox was strolling through the country-
side, when he saw a bunch of ripe grapes hanging on a vine near the
edge of an orchard. The grapes were beautiful! They were purple and
plump, filled with delicious juice. The fox, staring at the grapes, said
to himself, "Oh, what luscious grapes, just the thing to quench my
thirst. I must have those grapes!"*

*Stepping back a few paces, the fox jumped high into the air, but
missed the delicious looking grapes. He turned around and jumped
again and again with all his strength. He continued to miss the grapes
each time he jumped. Finally, he became so hot and tired that he gave
up. Walking away with his nose in the air, the fox proclaimed aloud
for all to hear, "Humph, I didn't want those grapes anyway, I am sure
they were sour."*

Moral: It is easy to despise what you cannot obtain.

The fable is one story type that falls under the genre of traditional literature. The next section in this chapter explains more about the various genres
of literature.

Expanding on the concept of archetypes, Campbell (1988), in *The Power
of Myth*, addressed the relationship between Jungian archetypes of the uncon-

scious and common ideas found in mythology from different cultures around the world. Campbell's work in mythology has influenced many who strive for successful story analysis. The ability to analyze a selection of literature enables a storyteller to deliver a more sincere and powerful story for the listener. Campbell (1988, p. 4) says, "When the story is in your mind, then you see its relevance to something happening in your own life. It gives you perspective on what's happening to you."

Livo and Rietz (1986) discuss the archetypal nature of story, as well as the secondary archetypes of motifs, characters, behaviors, relationships, needs, experiences, and events. Much like musical compositions are created from combinations of notes to form original works, stories have developed from these secondary archetypes and are as vast and different as are the behaviors, traits, and characteristics associated with the human race. The combinations of the components provide the storyteller with an array of tools that can be used to enhance human knowledge and awareness.

Motifs are the building blocks, or narrative elements, that fit together to make the story. They are the repeating situations that shape the content of stories and are often descriptive of a given culture. The study of motifs often helps in the understanding of folklore and may serve as a guide for the analysis of myths (Brunvand, 1978). MacDonald (1982) offers a variety of both major and minor motifs which include ones that explain the origin, or the "why," of basic realities. "Spider and the Sky God" is an example of a story that describes the origin of storytelling. It features a popular character, Ananse the Spider, who is also a cultural hero of the Ashanti in West Africa.

Patsy Cumby's second graders knew the character Ananse. They had been listening to several stories featuring Ananse the Spider for a number of days and were eager to hear more about the antics of this particular "trickster/hero." They were also very curious about this story because it promised to explain where the stories came from.

"This is a special story," the storyteller began. "It is a story that explains something. In this story, you will hear about how stories came to be. And it won't surprise you to find out that our friend, Ananse the Spider, had something to do with the first stories."

ℰ᪥᪁᪥ℰ

Ananse and the Sky God

A long, long time ago before there were any stories told on earth, there lived a spider named Ananse. Everyone knew Ananse. He was known by so many because of his beautiful spider webs. Even though Ananse was very popular, he had a secret wish. He wanted to be able to spin a story as well as he could spin a web. There was one problem with his wish. At that time all the stories in the world belonged to the Sky God.

One day Ananse decided to make a bargain with the Sky God, so he spun a beautiful web that reached all the way to the place the Sky God lived. Ananse approached the Sky God and asked him the price of his precious stories.

The Sky God laughed and laughed and said, "Little Ananse, greater ones than you have tried to buy my stories. Such a small one as you could never pay the price." Ananse responded, "I will pay whatever price you ask. Name the price, and I will pay it."

The Sky God stopped laughing and looked at Ananse and said, "You cannot buy my stories. However, you can do these things: bring me Onini, the python; Mmoboro, the hornets; Osebo, the leopard; and Mmoatia, the fairy. Bring these to me, and then we'll talk."

Ananse agreed and began climbing down his web back to earth. He returned to his village and began to search for the things that the Sky God had demanded.

Ananse cut a branch from a palm tree and some vine creeper and went into the jungle, near the river, where Onini lived. He walked along the bank of the river, talking to himself, pretending to have a disagreement.

"It is longer than Onini," said Ananse.

"It is not longer than Onini," said his imaginary companion.

Finally Ananse said, "There is Onini, the python. Let us ask him."

Listening, Onini asked, "What is going on here?"

"Oh, I am Ananse the Spider, and I am arguing with myself that the palm tree branch is longer than you. First I say it is true, then I say it is not true."

Onini thought for a moment, then he offered, "Please, come measure me with the branch. We will see who is right."

Ananse told Onini that he would measure him, but instead he laid the stick down beside Onini and quickly wound a vine around the python so that he could not escape. Onini was now ready to meet the Sky God.

Next, Ananse filled a calabash with water and went into the forest. Before long he heard the great buzzing sound of Mmoboro, the hornets. He climbed a tree and sprinkled water on the hornets and then poured some on himself. Then he placed a huge plantain leaf on his head. Finally, Ananse said to Mmoboro, the hornets, "My brothers, the rain has come and you need shelter. You can find all the shelter you want in this calabash bowl. In here, the rains will not drown you."

The hornets buzzed, "Thank you brother spider, we are grateful."

Just as they all flew into the bowl, Ananse quickly placed the large leaf over the bowl and carried it to the place where Onini was. Now Mmoboro was ready to meet the Sky God.

Ananse then set off to track down Osebo, the leopard. Anansi had dug a deep hole in the jungle path and covered the hole with branches. When he returned to the hole, he found Osebo lying at the bottom of the pit.

"Oh, poor Osebo, look! You have fallen into this pit and if I were to try to get you out, you would only return tomorrow to try to eat me and my children," said Ananse.

"Oh, no, Brother Spider, I would never do anything like that. Please help me get out, and I will never catch you or your children, or even your cousins," pleaded Osebo, the leopard.

Ananse cut bamboo sticks from a nearby grove and stuck them into the pit. Osebo climbed out of the pit, but near the top there was a cage and, as Osebo climbed up, Ananse lifted the door and then let it close behind Osebo. Osebo found himself out of the pit but trapped inside the cage and ready to meet the Sky God.

Ananse quickly returned home and began to carve the image of a doll from the odum tree. He then collected sticky fluid from the gum tree and painted the face and body of his doll with it. In the hands of the doll, Ananse placed some mashed yams. He gently placed the doll near the spot in the forest where the fairies came to play; then he waited. Before too long Mmoatia, the fairy, came by and saw the doll. Mmoatia said to the doll, "Hello, little friend, I am hungry. Will you share your mash?"

When the doll did not answer, Mmoatia became angry and she threatened to slap the doll. She asked again and, when the doll still did not answer, Mmoatia raised one hand and slapped the side of the doll. Her hand stuck. She raised her other hand to slap the other cheek and, when she touched the doll's face, that hand stuck. Mmoatia didn't know what to do. Before long her hands and feet were all stuck.

Just then, Ananse jumped out from his hiding place and began to spin a huge web around the fairy, the python, the hornets, and the leopard. He placed them on his back and continued to spin another web, on which he climbed to the sky.

Ananse approached the Sky God and declared, "I have brought the payment for your stories."

The Sky God couldn't believe it. He proclaimed to all who could hear, "Many have come and gone and tried to buy my stories. They have all failed. But today, before us, is Ananse. He has brought to me Onini, the python; Mmoboro, the hornets; Osebo, the leopard; and

*Mmoatia, the fairy. From this day and forever I give my stories to him
and they shall forever be called Spider Stories."*

*From then on Ananse would travel from place to place all over
the world, spinning his stories so that they might live forever in the
memory of all who listen.*

How Can You Use Storytelling to Expose Students to a Variety of Types of Literature?

Storytelling is a natural way to introduce different *genres* (categories or
types) of literature to students. Many students have limited ideas of the kinds
of stories found in books, and storytelling can be the key for revealing possibilities to them. When they have heard a story from literature, they often want
to get the book to read it for themselves, or to read another one like it, or to
read one by the same author. Genres that you may wish to expose students to
include picture books; contemporary realistic fiction; historical fiction; fantasy and science fiction; traditional literature; poetry; and nonfiction, including
biographies, autobiographies, and other informational books.

Picture Books

Picture books are books that depend on pictures for completeness. For
very young children, picture books are a wonderful vehicle for storytelling,
but they can be used with older students as well, for some of the books are
very sophisticated in content.

Wordless picture books offer intriguing pictures that provide the impetus
for telling a story, and they are particularly good for enticing children to tell
stories to partners as they both enjoy the pictures. When you tell a story from
a wordless picture book, the children see representations of the ideas that you
present orally, and the visual context allows them to enlarge their vocabularies. When they tell stories from these pictures, they use vocabulary that is
stimulated by the pictures, helping them to incorporate new terminology into
their speaking vocabularies.

Picture books that are accompanied by text are often read to the students,
and this, of course, involves oral interpretation of the words on the part of the
reader. However, *telling* the story while showing the pictures has many advantages. First, you don't have to move the pictures out of the students' view to
see the words. Second, you don't end up turning your head away from the
children or blocking their view of your face with the book. When you tell the
story while showing the pictures, be sure that you remain synchronized with
the pictures that are currently being shown. Memorize any repeated phrases

or sentences, especially rhyming parts, so that you deliver them exactly as written, and do so with appropriate expression. This memorization will allow your telling to be predictable enough that the children can chime in with you on predictable passages, drawing them more completely into the experience of the story.

Some picture books, like *Rosie's Walk* (1968) by Pat Hutchins, have little text, and the text does not really tell the good part of the story. The text merely tells where Rosie, the hen, walked. The pictures show a fox stalking Rosie and being repeatedly frustrated. The children could have a great time telling the whole story after you share the pictures and the sparse text.

You may want to choose picture books that illustrate a familiar rhyme, story, or song to present. Doing this will make the preparation for telling relatively easy for you and will provide a familiar experience for the children, which may allow them to join in with the telling and become more a part of the literature experience.

In choosing picture books, you should look for accurate illustrations that correspond to the story's content, complementing the setting, plot, and mood and enhancing characterization. The illustrations should avoid stereotypes of various types of people, as well. The story should have a good, age-appropriate plot, a worthwhile theme, and appropriate style and language for the children. Humorous stories are good for attracting children to the pleasures of literature (Norton, 1991). Tales like Margot Zemach's *It Could Always be Worse: A Yiddish Folktale* and Verna Aardema's *Why Mosquitoes Buzz in People's Ears* are good choices for primary grade children. The rich language in *Why Mosquitoes Buzz in People's Ears* makes it especially effective. Arthur Ransome's *The Fool of the World and the Flying Ship* is good for older elementary students. Adolescents can be exposed to Toshi Maruki's *Hiroshima No Pika*, a picture book that is not appropriate for young children.

Picture books have content representative of all the other genres, from fantasy to nonfiction, and they present a wide range of themes. Therefore, they are a fertile ground for introducing the elements of the other genres and/or promoting the study of any theme that is the focus of class activities.

Some suggestions for wordless picture books to use with storytelling for elementary students are Peter Collington's *The Angel and the Soldier Boy*, John Goodall's *Story of a Main Street*, Mitsumasa Anno's *Anno's Journey*, and Chris Van Allsburg's *The Mysteries of Harris Burdick*. *Story of a Main Street* can be used with older students to enhance historical understanding of architecture, clothing, and transportation over time. *Anno's Journey* and *The Mysteries of Harris Burdick* are also good for use with older students and provide excellent stimuli for storytelling (Norton, 1991).

Contemporary Realistic Fiction

Today there are many books that offer *contemporary realistic fiction—*

stories that have characters, settings, and plots that could possibly live, exist, or happen today. These stories present possible real-life happenings that can engage students who are experiencing similar situations or who want to find out, through the eyes of a story character, what things that they have not experienced are like. These stories can help children understand and come to terms with themselves and their world (Huck, Hepler, & Hickman, 1993). Many issues of concern to children are presented in contemporary realistic fiction, and discovering that this is true may draw students to these books.

Younger children may enjoy stories such as Beverly Cleary's *Ramona* stories or Judy Blume's *Tales of a Fourth Grade Nothing*, whereas older students may relate to Katherine Paterson's *Bridge to Terabithia* or Cynthia Voigt's *Homecoming* or *Dicey's Song*. Sawyer (1962) recommends James Ramsey Ullman's *Banner in the Sky* for students who are indifferent readers. They are drawn to the display of courage and the action in the story. Obviously you cannot tell an entire young adult novel, or even most elementary grade chapter books, in one sitting. You may want to serialize your telling, telling an episode each day, or you may want to tell excerpts from the books to entice the students to get the books and read the stories for themselves.

Historical Fiction

Historical fiction is set in the past. Often real events and characters are included, but fictional characters and their involvement in the historical events are included, as well. These stories must have authentic settings and characters that are believable for the time period depicted. They can be used to enrich history studies, as well as to lead the children to this literature genre. Many historical fiction works, such as Laura Ingalls Wilder's *Little House* books and Newbery Award-winning books like Lois Lowry's *Number the Stars* provide numerous opportunities for storytelling. Excerpts from the complete works, such as the one from *The War at Home* that opened this chapter, may be told; or the stories may be serialized, although books for younger children could be told in a single presentation.

The excerpt from *The War at Home* depicts an authentic setting and a situation that was true to the period involved, but it is peopled by fictional characters and describes a fictitious event.

Fantasy and Science Fiction

Stories that fit into the genre of *fantasy* include imaginary elements. These stories could not really happen. They may involve shape-changing, magical transformations, and fanciful settings and characters. Animals or inanimate objects may talk. Books like Deborah and James Howe's *Bunnicula*, E.B. White's *Charlotte's Web*, Natalie Babbitt's *Tuck Everlasting*, and Richard Adams' *Watership Down* are fantasies that have appealed to a wide range of age groups, from elementary school to adult.

Science fiction must be based on some scientific phenomenon or a scientific phenomenon that is projected to be possible in the future. Alfred Slote's *My Robot Buddy* is an example of a science fiction story in which robots are a part of daily life. Madeleine L'Engle has produced many intriguing science fiction selections that not only explore such areas as astrophysics and cellular biology, but also reflect knowledge of theology, folklore, classical literature, and history (Huck, Hepler, & Hickman, 1993).

You may want to serialize most of these stories or tell excerpts to entice the children to read the rest on their own. Science fiction stories may fit into a science class, if they are based on current scientific fact, rather than visions of possible future scientific advances.

Traditional Literature

Traditional literature has already been referred to repeatedly in this book. It is based on stories that have been passed down from generation to generation orally. After the printing press came into being, people began to capture these stories in books. Nursery stories, such as "The Little Red Hen," "Little Red Riding Hood," "The Three Little Pigs," and "Goldilocks and the Three Bears," qualify for this category, as well as more complex stories, such as "Molly Whuppie," "Hardy Hardhead," and "Snow White and the Seven Dwarfs." Many folktales feature animals that have human characteristics, tricksters, or simpletons. *Fables*, stories such as "The Fox and the Grapes" that have morals, are included in this genre. The stories often begin with "Once upon a time..." and end with "and they lived happily ever after" or with some other formulaic beginning or ending. Characters are often stereotyped as all good or all bad, and the stories are often very moralistic, with good prevailing over evil. The plots of these stories are often simple and straightforward. Setting is generally not very well-developed. There are often three or four episodes in the story, depending upon the culture from which the story is drawn.

These stories are wonderful to tell because they have been passed down orally over the years, and they seem to be fitted to the tongue. Additionally, since many of them are highly predictable, the children in the audience have the pleasure of guessing outcomes successfully. The story structures are often sequential, circular, or cumulative (Stoodt, Amspaugh, & Hunt, 1996). All of these structures facilitate telling.

Folktales, with their limited characters and straightforward plots, are naturals to use with flannelboards to draw the younger children into the story. "The Old Woman and Her Pig" and "The House That Jack Built" are two stories that Betty often tells with the flannelboard. Both are cumulative tales that children quickly learn to retell with the aid of flannelboard pieces.

Poetry

Poetry is a natural element to include in storytelling, since narrative poems tell stories, and even short lyric poetry and most free verse have some elements of setting, characters, and theme that are the building blocks for stories. Children who purport to hate poetry are often drawn to poems with marked rhythm and rhyme, and the imagery in much free verse attracts many children, as well.

Mother Goose rhymes are good to use with young children, as are rhymes to accompany physical activities such as skipping and jumping rope. Finger plays for young children are often set to verse, and some of them are ministories. "Itsy Bitsy Spider," a popular finger play, is an example of an episode that could be a small part of a story. In addition, many picture books are written in rhyme. Some are even illustrated versions of songs that the children can readily learn to sing. "The Old Woman Who Swallowed a Fly" is a song that has been turned into picture books by various people.

Older students enjoy poems such as "Casey at the Bat" by Ernest Lawrence Thayer. Secondary students enjoy "The Highwayman" by Alfred Noyes and many works by Edgar Allan Poe.

One thing is sure. Select poetry that you enjoy, and you will soon have the children involved in it enthusiastically.

Nonfiction

Nonfiction books present factual material. *Biographies* and *autobiographies* depict the lives of individuals. Obviously these would be good to use in a history class. Other nonfiction books exist that are appropriate for social studies, science, mathematics, and other content areas. These include nature books, books that show how to do things, and accounts of events. They should be chosen for accuracy and adaptability to telling. Biography and autobiography are stories that lend themselves easily to telling. Sawyer (1962) recommends Elizabeth Yates' *Amos Fortune, Free Man* and Hildegard Swift's *Railroad to Freedom* (about Harriet Tubman). Life cycle books and books about discoveries and historical events also are good choices. Stories about how to make things may naturally go along with art. As you tell a story involving a paper-cutting activity, for example, you can have the students work through the steps in paper cutting as the story progresses. In the end, the students have not only heard a good story, but they have a work of art, as well.

Hearing true stories provides students with background for facing the real world and reading in content area materials. It is also a way to draw into books some children who are not oriented toward fiction.

The teacher continued to read from *The War at Home*. The children's changing facial expressions showed involvement with the story and a sharing of Mattie's amazement at Virgil's leap across the swollen creek.

He looked over his shoulder, his mouth turned up in a triumphant smile. But the next minute he paid for it. His arms flailing wildly, the smile frozen on his face, he slowly tipped backward into the water. When he stood up, water swirled around his thighs, and his undershorts were the color of Janie Mae's doll dresses.

He waded out of the creek and grinned at Mattie. "Okay, let's see how far you can jump now."

"Oh, no you don't," Mattie said. "The deal was I had to jump only if you made it dry. And nobody in his right mind would call you dry."

Virgil looked at muddy rivulets streaming down his legs and across his feet. He laughed. "I reckon I did get a little wet."

Dang, Mattie thought, he even loses with good humor.

He disappeared for a few minutes behind a large oak. Then he emerged wearing his blue jeans, shirt, and shoes. He flung his muddy undershorts over a limb. "They'll be dry enough to put back on when we head home. Reckon Aunt Lucy'll never know the difference."

Mattie looked at the muddy undershorts and remembered Janie Mae's doll clothes. She doubted Mother had gone blind since then (Green, 1989, pp. 22-27).

 Suggested Activities for the Teacher

1.   Locate excerpts from chapter books or young adult novels that would be good to tell to your class. Photocopy these excerpts and file them for use in specific units or as motivational tools.

2.   Practice telling the segment from *The War at Home* presented in this chapter. Plan to use it to encourage the reading of historical fiction or to enrich the study of World War II.

Suggested Activities for Use with Students

1.   Have students bring in tellable stories from each genre as that genre is studied in class. Have them place these stories in a "resource corner" of the room. When all genres have been presented, have each student choose one story from the resource corner to learn and share it with the class.

2.   Have young children form pairs and tell stories from wordless picture books to one another. Let older children write stories from these books, practice the stories, and tell them to younger children while showing the pictures.

3.   Let students search favorite chapter books or young adult novels for excerpts that they can learn and share orally with their classmates as a way to entice the classmates to read the chosen books.

References

Adams, R. (1974). *Watership Down*. New York: Macmillan.

Anno, M. (1978). *Anno's journey*. New York: Philomel.

Babbitt, N. (1975). *Tuck everlasting*. New York: Farrar, Straus, & Giroux.

Barton, B., & Booth, D. (1990). *Stories in the classroom*. Portsmouth, NH: Heinemann.

Blume, J. (1972). *Tales of a fourth grade nothing*. New York: Dutton.

Brunvand, J. H. (1978). *Study of American folklore: An introduction*. New York: W. W. Norton.

Campbell, J., with Moyers, B. (1988). *The power of myth*. New York: Doubleday.

Chocolate, D. M. N. (1993). *Spider and the Sky God: An Akan legend*. Mahwah, NJ: Troll Associates.

Collington, P. (1987). *The Angel and the soldier boy*. New York: Alfred A. Knopf.

Drabble, M. (1985). *Oxford companion to English literature* (5th ed.). Oxford: Oxford University Press.

Goodall, J. (1987). *Story of a main street*. New York: Macmillan.

Green, C. J. (1989). *The war at home*. New York: McElderry.

Hague, M. (1985). *Aesop's fables*. New York: Henry Holt and Company.

Haley, G. E. (1970). *A story, a story*. New York: Aladdin Paperbacks.

Howe, D., & Howe, J. (1983). *Bunnicula*. New York: Atheneum.

Huck, C. S., Hepler, S., & Hickman, J. (1993). *Children's literature* (5th ed.). Fort Worth, TX: Harcourt Brace Jovanovich.

Hutchins, P. (1968). *Rosie's walk*. New York: Macmillan.

Jung, C. G. (1989). *Analytical psychology: Notes of the seminar given in 1925*. Princeton, NJ: Princeton University Press.

Livo, N. J., & Rietz, S. A. (1986). *Storytelling: Process and practice*. Littleton, CO: Libraries Unlimited.

Livo, N. J., & Rietz, S. A. (1991). *Storytelling folklore sourcebook*. Englewood, CO: Libraries Unlimited.

Lowry, L. (1989). *Number the stars*. Boston: Houghton Mifflin.

MacDonald, M. R. (1982). *The storyteller's sourcebook: A subject, title and motif index to folklore collections for children*. Detroit, MI: Neal-Schuman in association with Gale.

Maruki, T. (1982). *Hiroshima no pika*. New York: Macmillan.

Mooney, B., & Holt, D. (1996). *The storyteller's guide: Storytellers share advice for the classroom, boardroom, showroom, podium, pulpit and center stage*. Little Rock, AR: August House.

Norton, D. E. (1991). *Through the eyes of a child* (3rd ed.). New York: Merrill/Macmillan.

Paterson, K. (1977). *Bridge to Terabithia*. New York: Crowell.

Ransome, A. (1968). *The fool of the world and the flying ship*. New York: Farrar, Straus, & Giroux.

Sawyer, R. (1962). *The way of the storyteller*. New York: Viking.

Slote, A. (1974). *My robot buddy*. New York: Lippincott.

Stoodt, B. D., Amspaugh, L. B., & Hunt, J. (1996). *Children's literature: Discovery for a lifetime*. Scottsdale, AZ: Gorsuch Scarisbrick.

Ullman, J. R. (1954). *Banner in the sky*. New York: Harper Keypoint.

Van Allsburg, C. (1984). *The mysteries of Harris Burdick*. Boston: Houghton Mifflin.

Vogler, C. (1992). *The writer's journey: The mythic structures for storytellers and screenwriters*. Studio City, CA: Michael Wise Productions.

Voigt, C. (1981). *Homecoming*. New York: Atheneum.

Voigt, C. (1982). *Dicey's song*. New York: Atheneum.

White, E. B. (1952). *Charlotte's web*. New York: Harper & Row.

Zemach, M. (1976). *It could always be worse: A Yiddish folktale*. New York: Farrar, Straus, & Giroux.

Chapter 6
Using Storytelling to Enhance Learning In and Through Literature—Part 2

The Story of Thomas and Henry

Before we begin our unit on The Canterbury Tales, *I want to tell you a story. A long time ago, in England in 1163, hundreds of years before any of us were born, a terrible quarrel began to brew between two very stubborn men. Men have argued since the beginning of time, but this was a very special argument between a powerful king and a stubborn archbishop.*

In those days, the Roman Catholic Church had enormous influence on the lives of people all over Europe, and the Pope had great power; in some cases, even a king could not go beyond a Pope's ruling. The Church was organized like a well-run government. The Pope was the head of the church, and for each country, an archbishop was appointed to take care of the church's business in that country.

In those days, the church had jurisdiction over the behavior of its priests. So, in the unlikely event that a priest committed a crime, he was tried by the church, not by the court of the king of the country where the crime was committed. As you can imagine, the punishment given to a priest who broke the law was not always as severe as kings and courts thought it should be. So, in order to keep kings happy, the Pope allowed kings to appoint the archbishops for their countries. But, although he was appointed by the king, the Archbishop of Canterbury had to answer to the Pope. You can see what a delicate arrangement that could be for a poor archbishop because, if you remember, the scripture says, "Man cannot serve two masters." And, as you will find out if you listen carefully, it proved to be a very bad situation for the men in this story.

That brings us back to the argument of two stubborn men in the twelfth century. One of the men was Henry the Second, King of England, and the other man was Thomas Becket, who was the Archbishop of Canterbury, the head of the Roman Catholic Church in England. Before that, he had been Henry's chancellor; and he and Henry had been very good friends. Thomas had done such a good job as Henry's chancellor that the king appointed him Archbishop of Canterbury. He did so for what he thought was a very good reason. You see, Henry had become very unhappy with the fact that his court could not try a priest who had broken the law of the land. But he could not get the old archbishop to give up the church's right to try priests who broke the law. So when the old archbishop died, here was Henry's chance to make a clever political move. No doubt Henry said to himself, "If I appoint my good friend, Thomas, as Archbishop of Canterbury, he will make it easier for me to gain the right to try priests in my court rather than the church's court." Well, Henry may have thought that, but that is not what happened.

When Thomas became Archbishop of Canterbury, and had the awesome responsibility for the Church in England, he took that responsibility very seriously. He came to believe that the church, not the state, should be responsible for bringing unlawful priests to justice. That's when the argument started. And it grew more heated and less open to solution for eight years. Thomas and Henry wrote letters, had meetings, and sent messengers back and forth to each other. But they could not agree on this very important issue. The longer the argument went on, the more stubborn each man became.

Finally, one day after receiving yet another quarrelsome letter from Thomas, Henry slammed his fist down on the table and shouted, "Will no one rid me of this troublesome priest?" He said later that he did not really mean for anyone to take him literally, that he was just expressing his anger because he was so frustrated. So maybe we should let what happened next be a lesson to us all. We ought to say only what we mean, and mean what we say. Otherwise, unfortunate things can happen, just as they did in this story.

Four "yes" men, who very much wanted to please the king, heard Henry's shouting, realized his frustration, and took him literally. They saw a perfect opportunity to do Henry a favor and get in his good graces. So, on December 29, 1170, they got on their horses, rode into the town of Canterbury, and on to the Cathedral where they saw Thomas at the altar praying. There, in the most revered church in England, these four henchmen cut Thomas down in cold blood. They struck him so hard that his blood ran onto the floor of the church, and part of his skull was cut off. Even some of his brain matter fell onto the floor. It was a brutal, unholy act. When the murderers left, other priests, who had fled for their lives, took up Thomas's body for burial. They saved some of the flesh, bone and blood that lay on the floor and put it in a small urn, which remained in the church. When the people from Canterbury heard of the archbishop's murder, they came to the Cathedral to pray. Some of them later reported that while they were praying in the Cathedral, they had not only been forgiven of their sins, but they had been healed of their afflictions as well.

Now you know how fast that kind of news travels, even without radio and television. A few days after Thomas Becket's death, people began visiting his tomb as a sacred site. They believed that after a visit to Becket's grave their afflictions were healed. And the news spread all over England.

Three years later, the Pope, Alexander III, declared Thomas a saint. And for 300 years after that the people of England made sacred pilgrimages to the tomb of Thomas Becket.

And King Henry? Well, it took him a little longer than it did the common folks. They mourned Becket's death right away. It took Henry four years; but, finally, in 1174, Henry asked for forgiveness for his responsibility in Becket's death and was absolved of his sins.

What does all this have to do with a literature class? Well, I'll tell you; almost 300 years later in England, people were still making their way to Canterbury Cathedral to pray at the tomb of Thomas Becket; and a very observant writer who lived near there decided to use that journey as a frame for a series of stories that we know today as the Canterbury Tales. *That writer's name was Geoffrey Chaucer.*

For many years, Suellen told this story or a version of it to high school seniors to whom she taught the *Canterbury Tales*. She learned early in her career that telling the history of the feud between Thomas Becket and Henry II as a story captured and held students' attention much better than delivering the information as a lecture. It provided an interesting introduction to a piece of literature that is not always easily understood by secondary students. Also, the storytelling approach was very appropriate for the study of the *Canterbury Tales*, since so many of them came out of an oral tradition; and his book could be said to be Chaucer's formal, literary representation of stories he had heard and read during that time in history.

Suellen saw evidence of the impact of her "Story of Henry and Thomas" one night with a group of theater students who were taking a break from a rehearsal. One of them said, "Ms. Alfred, tell that story about Thomas Becket." He turned to his buddies lounging on the stage and said, "Listen to this, y'all; you gotta hear this story." Then in a hollow theater, on an empty stage, Suellen told the story to a group of high school actors who, even though they were not enrolled in her senior English class, listened quietly to the narrative of Thomas and Henry.

The power of a good story has been used for centuries by teachers who have known that narrative is almost always more interesting than exposition. Shaw (1996) has discovered the power of narrative with her juniors and seniors at Asheville High School in North Carolina. She asks the students to research and write a news article about an important event in history that relates to some work of literature. Shaw calls her students' work "creative nonfiction." She requires her students to research the historical events as a newspaper writer would research a news story. They must create a mock interview of the people involved in the event and weave quotations from that interview into the news story. And they must tell the story from a particular participant's point of view, even if that participant is a fictional character. Finally, they must read their stories to the class. As a result, instead of writing a routine report that can be easily copied from the encyclopedia, students frame the information in the context of a story which seems almost always to be much more interesting. When Suellen asked Shaw how she answers critics who say that she is asking her students to stray from the truth in their creative nonfiction narratives, Shaw replied that all of the established facts must be in the students' reports; even the fictitious characters must be the kind of people who would most likely be involved in the events, and the fictitious conversations must refer to the events as they are happening or have happened.

How Can You Use Storytelling to Teach the "Classics"?

Storytelling is a natural introduction to literature. Ross (1996, p. 31) could easily be speaking of storytelling when she writes, "Quality books are those whose rich illustrations inspire us, whose language lingers on our tongues, whose characters become part of our lives, and whose themes remain with us long after we've finished reading." Let us look at some ways that teachers can use storytelling to teach literature.

The Canterbury Tales

As the story that introduces this chapter shows, *The Canterbury Tales* lends itself to a number of storytelling applications. For example, when Judy Champney teaches Chaucer, she asks students to complete a project that relates in a creative and unique way to one of the stories in the *Tales*. She gives the students the opportunity to retell tales in their own words and to use some kind of visual medium to enrich their performances. For her project, one of Judy's students retold "The Pardoner's Tale" using a large sheet cake that she had covered with green icing to represent grass. The cake served as a kind of storyboard. At the beginning of the story, the cake had only the green icing on it. As the student began the story, she introduced certain items and characters that she had made from cardboard cutouts glued to bamboo skewers so that they would stand up easily. As she proceeded through the story, she placed the cutouts of the characters strategically on the cake to illustrate the setting and the interaction of the characters in the tale.

Of course, we hope the student's hands were clean, because after she finished her presentation, every student had a piece of "Pardoner's Tale" cake.

The Greek Myths

Actually many selections from the traditional literary canon lend themselves nicely to a storytelling approach. After all, great literature has lasted over time in large part because it tells intriguing stories. Certainly a body of stories as time-tested as the Greek myths is perfect for storytelling, especially with high school students who may not have the kind of reading ability required to read such complex works independently.

Rosen (1988) writes about working in a north London suburb with a group of multiethnic, bilingual students aged 12 years and older who had a reputation for being difficult in the classroom. Many of the students who had been expelled from other schools came to class with a variety of emotional and academic problems.

In order to help her students appreciate classical literature, Rosen (1988, p. 79) introduced students to Greek mythology by telling the story of Tantalus. She writes, "My experience tells me that a told story gives rise to a wider scope of responses than any other language stimuli in the repertoire of an English teacher" (p. 91).

In a later assignment Rosen introduced the story of Orpheus and Eurydice. As a prelude to the story, she read lines from works by Shakespeare and Milton to show the students how the ancient Greek myth is referred to in literature written long after the period during which the myth originated. Also, she shared the music from various operas that use the Orpheus and Eurydice theme. After emphasizing to the students the endurance of such a beautiful story, she told it as a storyteller would. Afterward, students wrote their own versions.

Frankenstein

Finally, another example of the relationship of storytelling to the "classics" is the story surrounding the inspiration for Mary Wollstonecraft Shelley's *Frankenstein: Or, The Modern Prometheus*. Although the novel was first published in 1818, in recent years it has steadily gained critical acclaim, and it is now being taught in secondary schools with increasing frequency. Students are especially intrigued by the prospect of reading *Frankenstein* when they are told that Shelley wrote it when she was 19 years old and that she was the first person to write science fiction (Sunstein, 1989, p. 4). Before assigning *Frankenstein* to her students, Suellen introduced the novel by telling the curious story about the dream that inspired Shelley to write the book. This version of the story is based on the accounts given by Bigland (1959, pp. 93-96) and Sunstein (1989, pp. 117-131).

❧❧❧

Now listen to this story closely, because if you have ever had a hard time thinking up something to write about, this story will make you feel better. Let me tell you, if you have trouble thinking of a good story to write, you are in very good company. Around two hundred years ago, nineteen-year-old Mary Wollstonecraft had the same problem. She had run off from her home in London, England, with a famous poet, Percy Bysshe Shelley, a married man whom Mary's father strongly disliked. For a number of complicated reasons—religion, money, and politics among them—Mary and Percy left England and traveled throughout Europe. During the summer of 1816, they wound up in Geneva, Switzerland, where they rented a villa. Soon, George Gordon, Lord Byron, the English poet, rented a villa next door to theirs. Mary and Percy often visited Byron and other friends and spent hours conversing about poetry, politics, and love. One night, they decided that "before the evening was out, they would each write and share a ghost story" (Bigland, 1959, p. 92). Mary drew a blank, and was upset with herself that she could not think of a thing.

For several days afterward she worried about her inability to invent a ghost story. Then, one night, as a group of friends gathered for their usual discussions, the topic of conversation turned to the "nature and principal of life" (p. 93) and whether life could be restored to a corpse by some yet undeveloped scientific method. No one knows for certain what inspired these musings. Maybe Byron, Shelley, and others in the group had read about Luigi Galvani, an Italian scientist, who made a dead frog move by touching it with an electrically charged wire. Galvani wrote about his experiments in 1790; and it wouldn't surprise me if Shelley and Byron had read Galvani's work some 20 years later. Like most well-informed people today, they enjoyed speculating about future developments in science. They even suggested that it might be possible to "assemble component parts of some creature" (Bigland, 1959, p. 93) and cause it to come to life. No doubt all this talk about bringing corpses back to life had a great effect on Mary Shelley's imagination. In fact, she said so herself. When she went to bed that night, she had a very vivid dream about a young scientist being terrorized by a creature that he had made. The dream scared Mary so badly that when she woke up, she couldn't stop thinking about it. And then she realized that if her dream had scared her so badly, it would scare others as well. And so, the next morning, she proudly announced to her friends that she had thought of a story.

Well, her story was a hit with all her friends, so much so that she decided to publish it. At first, she wanted to write it in the form of a short story; but her sweetheart, Percy Shelley, suggested that she turn it into a novel. And much to our delight, she did. Out of a scary storytelling session, a young woman, not yet 20 years old, wrote one of the most highly regarded novels in the world and became known as the inventor of science fiction! And that's how the novel Frankenstein *was born.*

After that introduction, the students tackled *Frankenstein*, a pretty tough "read," enthusiastically.

How Can a Retelling Help Students?

Students who have trouble with writing or discussing stories sometimes respond well to assignments that involve simply retelling a story they have heard. Retelling can be an especially effective introduction to teaching students how to discuss the elements of a short story as they relate to the whole of the work. Eighth and ninth graders frequently find it difficult to differentiate between summary and analysis.

Given the fact that many students have not yet developed analytical or critical skills in literature, it makes sense to ask them initially to retell a story that has been assigned to them. A retelling is quite different from a summary. Unlike a summary, in which a student is asked to condense a story into its basic main ideas, a retelling requires a student to reproduce the story with detail, characterization, and style. Retelling integrates one's own style with another's story. Students can even use key phrases from the original and thus "import alien language—syntax, diction—for their own uses" (Andrasick, 1990, p. 107).

Students can be asked to present their retellings in written or oral form and respond to others doing the same. Inevitably, one "reteller" will put greater emphasis on some elements of the story and lesser emphasis on others. As students listen to or read the retellings of others, they can compare their versions with those of their classmates and discuss why they believe the events they used were important to the story. In doing so, they show the teacher not only the extent to which they comprehended the original story, but also the extent to which they are able to discuss important elements of the story and the way in which the author uses them to weave the story together into a whole tapestry. In this way, students have taken an intermediate step between summary and analysis and are not likely to forget the story, even after the test is over, because they have made it their own. At the end of this chapter, you will find a retelling of *Romeo and Juliet* by a secondary student, Dusty Smith.

Rosen (1988, p. 72) explains her rationale for asking students to retell stories. "The fact is that there are very few pupils who can immediately absorb a written text and feel eager to compose their own as a result....As English teachers we know that if all our pupils are going to respond to what has been selected for them to read, there must be a period of sharing, of communal mulling over before everyone feels able to write, in pairs, in groups, as a whole class, or even, at times, all three in sequence."

While some teachers may see the above activity as a bit too controlling of their students' creative process in speaking and writing, we must remember that some students need more guidance than others. The activity can provide that guidance.

You may say you do not want to spend on one story the time required to complete the process outlined above. Certainly such an approach is not appropriate for every class every time. However, using this approach with younger secondary school students gives them an interesting, effective, and interactive introduction to the elements of the short story. Students can use this process independently as they read, respond to, and analyze other works in a short story unit.

How Can the Elements of Fiction
Be Taught Through Storytelling?

Storytelling is very helpful when it is taught in conjunction with the short story genre. If students are given an opportunity to tell personal and family stories, or to learn and tell an established story that appeals to them, they are practicing the elements of fiction before they ever learn what those elements are. Some students, however, may have trouble framing an original story, particularly if they come from a family that is not very verbal. In such cases, you may want to ask students to begin working with a single element of a story.

Setting

Tell or read the students a story or begin with a taped story of a literary selection. Choose one in which the place and or the weather is an important factor. Jack London's widely anthologized story, "To Build a Fire," is a good example of the importance of setting to the outcome of the story. "The Day the Cow Ate My Britches" by Ray Hicks is also a good one. It can be found in *Best-Loved Stories Told at the National Storytelling Festival*, and it is available on tape in Hicks' own words. Before telling the story or playing the tape, give the students the chart in Figure 6.1 and ask them to listen for parts of the story in which the place and/or the weather are very important for the plot of the story. For example, Hicks' "The Day the Cow Ate My Britches" is based on a childhood experience of a cold day and a warm heart. As a boy, Hicks was stranded at his girlfriend's house by a great snowstorm. In the story, he tells us that with the snow comes the cold wind blowing through a hole in the drafty bedroom where he spends the night. In a desperate attempt to keep warm, he stuffs the hole in the bedroom wall with the only chinking material he has, his pants. And, of course, since the snow outdoors has covered up any grazing that was available to the family cow, she is willing to eat anything that appears to be organic and chewable, *i.e.*, his pants. The cow's natural desire to satisfy her hunger leads to an embarrassing conflict that the poor trouser-less boy must solve. All these are simple events that inexperienced students can grasp easily.

It doesn't take a great analytical mind to understand the influence of setting on the plot of "The Day the Cow Ate My Britches." As the students listen to the story, have them fill in the chart in Figure 6.1. We have included in that chart an example of how the chart might be completed.

When students have finished filling in the chart, have them work in small groups to discuss and compare their observations. Then, play the tape or tell the story again, and ask the students to review their charts and make any additions or deletions they think are necessary. At the end of the activity, tell them that they have been working with the *setting* of a short story, the time and place and environment in which the story takes place.

To underscore the importance of setting, you may want to read them the following comments by Donald Davis (Mooney & Holt, 1996, pp. 47-48):

> To me, a wimpy story is a story that is thoughtful but doesn't land concretely enough in any particular place for me to be able to really see it. So, the more specifically and visually concrete a story is, the more it really works well.

Character

You can use a similar chart for listening or reading for other elements of a story such as characterization or conflict. For example, to emphasize character development, complete the chart shown in Figure 6.2.

If you decide to use charts, it is vital that you avoid turning the activity into isolated seat work where students simply fill in the chart without interacting with the text, their classmates, or the teacher. The chart should lead to substantive interaction among the members of the class.

Figure 6.1 How the Weather Influences Decisions in "The Day the Cow Ate My Britches"
by Ray Hicks

> As you listen to the story, concentrate on points where the place and the weather have a great influence on what happens next. For example, listen closely to Ray Hicks' discussion of the cold, the snow, and the hole in the bedroom wall. How do those elements influence what the main character decides to do or what happens in the story? In the blanks below, on the left side of the page write the weather or the place, and on the right side write the decision the main character makes or the thing(s) that happen because of the place and/or the weather.

Weather or place (To be filled in by the student. Answers will vary.)	What the main character decides to do or what happens (To be filled in by the student. Answers will vary.)
Example:	Example:
Snow piles up deeply on the road.	Ray has to spend the night in a drafty room.
The room becomes cold because of the hole in the outside wall.	Ray patches the hole with his pants.
Because of the snow, the cow cannot graze.	The cow becomes hungry and eats Ray's pants.
The cow eats Ray's britches.	When he wakes up, he has no pants to put on.
The kitchen is the place where the family goes to eat breakfast.	Ray decides that going into the kitchen without his pants is too embarrassing. He acts sick so he won't have to get out of bed without his pants on.

Plot

If students seem to have trouble grasping the structure of plot, you may want to use the Freytag Pyramid, which was developed by Gustav Freytag in 1863. "Although Freytag meant [his] diagram to describe a typical five-act tragedy, it may be adapted to apply to most works of fiction" (Griffith, 1990, p. 46). Figure 6.3 is an illustration of Freytag's Pyramid, showing how a typical story progresses from the initial unstable situation that begins the conflict with the exposition that gives the reader or listener the background information necessary to understand the context of the story. Then comes a series of events during which time the characters seek to resolve the conflict. These events move in the rising action toward the climax. Some say that in the nar-

Figure 6.2 Character Development in "The Day the Cow Ate My Britches" by Ray Hicks

Concrete words describing the kind of person the main character is at the	Does this show change? Yes No	Elements in the story that caused the change
Beginning of the story		
Middle of the story		
End of the story		

Figure 6.3 Freytag's Pyramid

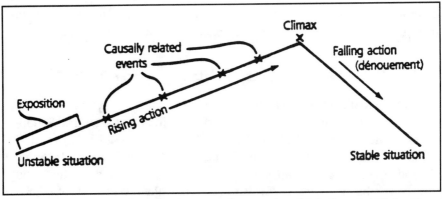

Source: Griffith, Kelly. *Writing Essays About Literature: A Guide and Style Sheet.* 3rd Ed. San Diego, CA: Harcourt Brace Jovanovich, 1990, p. 47.

rative, the climax is the most intense event. However, this event could be defined as the emotional climax. That point can be different for each reader. A more concrete definition of climax is found in Holman (1980, p. 84): "... in dramatic structure 'climax' is the term used to designate the turning point in the action, the place at which the rising action reverses and becomes the falling action." In other words, the *climax* is the point in the story at which events begin to move in a different direction. After the climax comes the falling action, and the plot resolves into a situation that is more stable than it was in the beginning.

Conflict

As Freytag's Pyramid shows, a sequence of events carries the plot. However, the interactions among characters are at the heart of those events, and with interaction comes conflict. In *external conflict* a character struggles against other characters, or institutions, or deities, or natural forces. In *internal conflict*, a character struggles with his or her own values and principles. In working with "The Day the Cow Ate My Britches," students should have no trouble identifying the conflicts, both external and internal, that the main character faces. He faces a number of external conflicts with the deep snow, with the cold air in his bedroom, with the drafty house, and with the hungry cow. He also faces internal conflict in his problem-solving process, in his romantic attraction to a girl, and in his deep embarrassment about the prospect of facing her without any pants on. As students work with the charts in Figures 6.1 and 6.2 and move through the events in "The Day the Cow Ate My Britches," encourage them to identify the conflicts that Hicks faces, and show them how those conflicts influence the plot.

While a familiarity with the structure of the story is important, it is equally important that teachers integrate a discussion of these elements in the reading, listening, and telling of stories. Rather than giving students a cold, disembodied lecture about the elements of the short story, it is better to integrate a discussion of those elements into a discussion of actual stories that may illustrate a particularly strong emphasis on one or more of them.

How Does Storytelling Relate to Narrative Poetry?

The activities discussed above will relate well not only to a unit on the short story but to a unit on narrative poetry as well. Poems like "The Shooting of Dan McGrew" by Robert Service, "Paul Revere's Ride" by Henry Wadsworth Longfellow, and "The Rhyme of the Ancient Mariner" by Samuel Coleridge (Ernst, 1983), all tell stories and can be related to storytelling. Elizabethan ballads, such as "Sir Patrick Spens" (Pooley, et al., 1968) or John Niles' delightful version from East Tennessee (Niles, 1961) and John Niles' humorous ballad "The Old Man and the Door" (Niles, 1961), also relate nicely to storytelling.

You may start by reading a narrative poem to the students. One full of action and suspense like "Paul Revere's Ride" works nicely. As you read, be careful to avoid falling into a sing-song sound. Read from one punctuation mark to another, not from line to line. Let the rhyme and rhythm reveal themselves naturally. Before you read, ask the students to listen to the rhythm and the rhyme of the piece and to take notes on the events of the story.

After reading the poem, tell the students they may retell the story of the poem in prose. After doing their own retelling, ask them to discuss the way in which regular rhythm and rhyme affected their understanding, response, and enjoyment of the poem in contrast to hearing someone retell it in prose. Also, lead the students in a discussion of the benefits of listening to or reading rhymed and rhythmic narrative poetry. Ask them to try their hand at writing a rhymed, rhythmic narrative poem based on an experience they have had.

Conclusion

These two chapters on using storytelling with literature contain only a few ideas about using storytelling to teach literature. We hope that you will let your own imagination soar and develop your own effective ways of using storytelling with your literature students.

Dusty Smith had read *Romeo and Juliet* in English class. He had also watched several video and movie versions and had listened to taped recordings of this ever-popular love story. Dusty's story begins with a summary of his favorite scene.

Romeo and Juliet are one of the most famous couples of all time. There isn't anyone who doesn't know who they are, even if they don't know every detail of the play. They represent true love. They also show how mixed up things can be when lots of people try to interfere with a situation. My favorite, from Romeo and Juliet, *is the death scene. It shows how everything can end in tragedy if you fall in love too quickly.*

Juliet was being forced by her parents to marry someone else. They didn't know that she and Romeo had already fallen in love and secretly been married by Friar Lawrence. Friar Lawrence had tried to help them throughout the story, even though at times he didn't want to. It was his idea to plan the pretend death of Juliet. She begged him to help her come up with some plan to keep from having to go through with the marriage her parents had arranged. Knowing that she loved Romeo and was already married to him, Friar Lawrence felt that he should do something to help. His idea was for her to take a drug that would make her sleep and appear dead. She would look dead, but in a few days, after the funeral, she would wake up and then she and Romeo could be together.

Juliet came to the Friar and got the potion. She took it just like they planned. Her parents thought she had died and held a funeral for her. Friar Lawrence was supposed to get word to Romeo about the plan, but things didn't work that way. Romeo found Juliet and believed that she was dead. He thought that she had killed herself. He tried to drink the same potion. There wasn't enough of the drug left, so he stabbed himself with his dagger and died there beside Juliet.

Juliet woke up just after Romeo killed himself and saw what he had done. She grabbed his dagger and stabbed herself. Nothing turned out like it should have. Their parents and other townspeople found them in the tomb together and realized how wrong they had been to try to keep them apart.

Even though Romeo and Juliet were really young, they probably could have been happy if everyone had left them alone. If their parents had been different, they wouldn't have had to marry so early and maybe they could have had more time to just date and get to know each other, like kids today. Who knows? They might have decided they didn't even like each other. But they weren't given that chance.

 ### Suggested Activity for the Teacher

Check with your Media Center for tapes, recordings, or CDs of accomplished speakers reading narrative poems. Listen for the rhythm and cadence of their reading. Choose one of those poems as a model and practice reading it yourself so that you can read it with expression to your students.

Suggested Activities for Use With the Students

1. Using Dreams

Ask your students to become dream-inspired storytellers just as Mary Shelley was. Knowing that Mary Shelley's masterpiece started with writer's block and ultimately grew out of a dream, students may want to use their own dreams as kernels for their own stories. The assignment below will be a useful one for your own dreamy students:

Mary Shelley's inspiration from a dream can be a good example for you if you have trouble thinking up something to write about. Instead of trying to "think" up something, why not "dream" up something? The assignment below will take you approximately a week to complete, but if you are diligent, you may find some great ideas for a story right in your own head.

For the next seven nights, try to go to bed as early as you can without reading or watching television before going to sleep. Keep a pad of paper and a pencil by your bed. Tell yourself that when you wake up the next morning, you will remember your dreams.

If you should awaken in the night immediately after a dream, quickly write down as much of the dream as you can remember. Then go back to sleep.

When you wake up the next day, before you even get out of bed, write down as much of any other dreams as you can remember. It is important to write down the dream before you get out of bed and stir around, because moving our bodies around when we first get up can cause us to forget our dreams.

After you have written down a number of your dreams over the week, take a look at your notes and use the details to put together a fantasy story or a science fiction story using the characters, events, and places you dreamed about. You need not share any part of your dream that is too embarrassing or too personal; share only those parts that you would be willing to share with a general audience.

2. Use the following procedure to encourage students to make a story their own.

Before teaching the genre of the short story, choose a short story from your literature anthology that contains a great deal of irony or suspense. "The Monkey's Paw," "The Pit and the Pendulum," and "The Most Dangerous Game" are good choices. Tell the students that you are going to tell them a story. Ask them to listen as closely and as actively as they can because soon they will be asked to retell the story themselves. Then, tell—do not read—the story to your students in your own words as dramatically as you can. After telling it, ask your students to do the following:

a. After you have heard the story, rewrite it in your own words with description, dialogue, and suspense. Write it as if you were going to tell it to a group of younger students who will listen to someone only if the speaker is very dynamic in his or her presentation.

b. After writing the story, practice telling the story to a partner. You may use your own ideas and interpretation, but be sure to include the main characters and the main events that you heard when the teacher told the story.

c. Retell the story to the class with expression, gesture, and dramatic flair.

d. As your fellow students present their retellings, listen actively, take notes comparing one person's retelling with another's, and be prepared to share your comparisons in class discussion.

After students have finished all their retellings, give these instructions:

a. Silently read the story as it was written by the author. As you read, write your informal responses to the sections of the story that are significantly different from the way the teacher retold it and to the sections that are markedly similar. Comment on how these differences affect your response to the story.

b. After you have read the story, review responses in preparation for group discussion.

c. After you have reviewed your reading responses, use them as a part of a group discussion about the story.

d. Use the ideas that arose in the group discussion to write a paper about the process of hearing, retelling, reading, and responding to a story. Also, use notes from your response journal to write several paragraphs in which you compare your reaction to hearing the story with your reaction to reading the story.

e. Read your paper to a small group and be prepared to read it to the rest of the class.

References

Andrasick, K. D. (1990). *Opening texts: Using writing to teach literature.* Portsmouth, NH: Heinemann.

Barrows, M. (Ed.). (1957). *One thousand beautiful things.* New York: Spenser Press.

Bigland, E. (1959). *Mary Shelley.* New York: Appleton-Century-Crofts.

Ernest, P. E. (1983). *The family album of favorite poems.* New York: Putnam.

Griffith, K. (1990). *Writing essays about literature: A guide and style sheet* (3rd ed.). San Diego, CA: Harcourt Brace Jovanovich.

Hicks, R. (1991). The day the cow ate my britches. *Best-loved stories told at the National Storytelling Festival* (pp. 1320-134). 20th Anniversary Edition. Jonesborough, TN: National Storytelling Press.

Holman, C. H. (1980). *A handbook to literature* (4th ed.) Indianapolis, IN: Bobbs-Merrill.

London, J. (1960). To build a fire. In Frank Walker (Ed.), *Jack London: The call of the wild and selected stories.* (pp.142-157). New York: The New American Library.

Mooney, B., & Holt, D. (Eds.). (1996). *The storyteller's guide: Storytellers share advice for the classroom, boardroom, showroom, podium, pulpit and center stage.* Little Rock, AR: August House.

Niles, J. J. (1961). *The ballad book of John Jacob Niles.* New York: Bramhill House.

Pooley, R. C., Anderson, G. K., Farmer, P., & Thorton, H. (1968). *England in literature.* (p. 54). Glenview, IL: Scott, Foresman.

Rosen, B. (1988). *And none of it was nonsense: The power of storytelling in school.* Portsmouth, NH: Heinemann.

Ross, E. (1996). *The workshop approach: A framework for literacy.* Norwood, MA: Christopher-Gordon.

Shaw, E. N. (1996). Their voices tell the story: Using creative nonfiction to examine literary periods in historical contexts. A Paper Delivered at the National Council of Teachers of English Convention, Chicago.

Shelley, M. W. (1848). *Frankenstein: Or, the modern Prometheus.* London: Richard Bently.

Sunstein, E. (1989). *Mary Shelley: Romance and reality.* Baltimore, MD: Johns Hopkins University Press.

Chapter 7
Using Storytelling to Teach Drama

❧❧❧

The Head Start children had assembled eagerly in the largest classroom in the building. The school had no auditorium, and the room wasn't big enough to provide chairs for everyone, so all the three- and four-year-olds were gathered on the floor in eager antici- pation for the show that was to begin. The big kids from the high school were going to do a show for the little kids at Head Start.

The theater group from the local high school had scripted "Rumpelstiltskin" into a theatrical piece for this presentation. The story revolves around an evil dwarf who demands a woman's first- born baby in return for his help in spinning straw into gold. He will return the child only if she can guess his name. Fortunately, a mes- senger whom she sent to the countryside chances to overhear Rumpelstiltskin proclaim his name, and reveals the name to the hero- ine. She is able to tell the dwarf his name and keep her child.

As the show began, the children settled down with wide-eyed attention. The Head Start teachers were a little surprised by how quiet and well-behaved they were. As the production proceeded, the tension mounted as the desperate young woman tried to guess Rumpelstiltskin's name. The high school student who portrayed Rumpelstiltskin was doing an outstanding job of building suspense every time he asked her if she could tell him his name. Especially gratifying to the Head Start teachers was the fact that this adolescent was from the low socio-economic area in which the Head Start pro- gram was located. He had shown remarkable talent for music and acting during his high school days; and he had "come back home" to share his talent with the children of his community, a number of whom knew him and his family. In fact, in that community, though his

fellow actors did not know it, James went by the distinctly untheatri-
cal nickname of "Bubba."

Among the children in the audience, the excitement continued to
build as James portrayed Rumpelstiltskin as a very objectionable
character, taunting the heroine with the question of his identity.
Apparently the tension was too great for one four-year-old. The third
time that James demonically delivered the line, "Do you know who I
am?" one heroic four-year-old jumped to his feet and shouted, "I
know who you is. Your name is Bubba." The children cheered. The
teachers laughed. And James just kept going with the performance.
Only a slight smile spread across his face as he struggled to stay in
character. And he succeeded. Soon after that, the young woman who
heard not only the actor's name from the four-year-old, but the char-
acter's name from the messenger, told him that his name was
Rumpelstiltskin. And everyone, except Old Rumpel, lived happily ever
after.

This story is an example of one way in which students at all levels can
use storytelling through drama. It also illustrates how skillfully an older student can affect the response of his audience.

How Do Drama and Storytelling Relate to Each Other?

When asked "What do you think theater can bring to storytelling?" Jay
O'Callahan replied, "Theater can teach us that it is important to allow each
character an entrance. Storytellers in their enthusiasm can often rush by characters...someone who has studied theater can simply tell us to pay attention to
the moment—to allow the character to be savored before we move on"
(Neimi, 1988, p. 11). O'Callahan also states that "Storytelling can bring an
immediacy back to theater....It invites the listener to surrender to the
story....[Storytelling] awakens imagination and our sense of drama. It can
refresh us in the deepest sense. And the theater can use that" (p. 11).

Barbara Freeman says that one of the biggest differences between storytelling and theater is movement. When she puts her stories in a theatrical
setting she feels she has "the chance to act out those stories, not only in our
minds' eye, but literally on the stage" (Neimi, 1988, p. 12). Connie Reagan-
Blake says that theater can help her "develop a deeper feeling of stage pres-
ence" (p. 12). She also sees acting as "becoming at one with whatever it is that
you're putting across to the audience. I think that good actors and good storytellers are the ones who can do this" (p. 12).

Differences Between Storytelling and Drama

While storytelling and drama have much in common, their differences are important when we teach students how to incorporate one into the other. An obvious example is the way each is written. In a story, all the details, conversations, action, and interaction among characters can be narrated by one person standing in one place: a teller who has no need for props, lighting (except perhaps a spotlight), set, or actors. Such simplicity is a great part of its appeal. One person with his or her voice alone can mesmerize an audience and take them mentally to places they have never been.

Drama, on the other hand, relies on a script that is a kind of guide for actors; it tells them what the set looks like, where they are to stand, where they are to move, what they are to say, and often how they are to say it. The playwright does not generally have the luxury of narrating. He or she must rely on actors to carry words and the story. That may explain the spelling of the word "playwright." One definition of the word "wright" is "a person who makes or repairs" (Neufeldt & Guralink, 1991, p. 1542). A playwright is more of a craftsperson who puts an entire production together than a writer or a teller who merely puts words on paper or speaks them.

The students who scripted and enacted Rumpelstiltskin in the story that began this chapter had turned from storytellers into playwrights and actors. A project like theirs can take a number of different forms. Remember, however, that the group performing Rumpelstiltskin was composed of confident theater students. Not all students in a regular classroom will be as skillful and as poised as they were. You may have to start on a smaller scale.

How Can You Encourage Reluctant Actors?

If the above assignment is too overwhelming for inexperienced students, you will want to start with dramatizing ideas through hand movements or facial expressions. For a variety of reasons, some students will initially be reluctant to participate in physical activities. With such students you will want to start small with some activities similar to the ones below.

Using Hand Movements to Communicate

Ask students to think about how hand movements communicate certain ideas or feelings. Give them these instructions:

Show what kind of hand movements you would use to show that you are feeling confused; you want a person walking or driving toward you to stop; you want someone to come toward you; you disagree with what someone is saying. These simple hand movement activities can show students how a small part of their body, such as a hand, can be a powerful medium of communication. And, of course, hand gestures are very important for effective storytelling.

Using Facial Expressions

Facial expressions are also an effective way to use the body to communicate feelings or ideas. For example, ask students to stand silent and still. Then give them these instructions:

I am going to read to you a short scene. At the end of the scene I will ask you to show only with your facial expressions how one of the characters in the scene would appear as he delivers certain lines.

1. John and Mark are driving from Nashville, Tennessee, to Birmingham, Alabama. They have taken a route with which they are completely unfamiliar. Mark suspects that they are really lost.

   His suggestion to John that they pull into the next gas station to ask for directions falls on deaf ears. John assures Mark that they are on the right road. Mark disagrees. Finally, Mark's frustration overcomes him as he shouts to John, "We are lost! I know it, and you know it; but you are too stubborn to admit it. Pull over to the side of the road and let me drive!"

   Show me what Mark's face looks like as he utters that last sentence: "Pull over to the side of the road and let me drive!"

   Show me John's face as Mark utters that last command.

2. It is award night for the top athletic scholar in the school. No one knows who has been elected by the faculty. Mary Johnson has been a strong runner on the cross-country team for four years, played varsity basketball for the last three, and kept an A average all through school. However, a few of her best friends also have outstanding records athletically and academically. She feels herself go into a numb daze when the principal says, "The winner is Mary Johnson."

   Show me Mary's face when she hears her name called. Show me Mary's face if she had heard the name of a good friend.

Whole Body Movements

Hand movements and facial expressions are a beginning. When students feel comfortable with them, perhaps they will lose their reluctance to move to a more physically demanding activity. For example, to help students become comfortable with their own bodies in a given space, work with them on whole body movements. You can use the same scenarios above, only this time, instead of asking students to show you hand gestures or facial expressions, ask for body postures or attitudes. Suellen saw a very interesting whole-body warm-up activity performed by a high school student who later became a theater director. He imitated for his classmates a melting block of ice. As he began, he stood stiff and straight. When he finished with the imitation, he lay limp and spread out on the floor.

Try these walking exercises:

Walk across the room several times as if you are

> a person going to meet his or her sweetheart at a dance;
>
> a basketball player who has just sprained her ankle on the court but doesn't want the coach to know so that she can stay in the game;
>
> a student who is trying to leave school early without getting caught;
>
> a scholar who is trying to read and walk at the same time.

Make up your own kind of walk and tell us about it.

Make up your own kind of walk and let others guess the situation it illustrates.

These exercises in hand movements, facial expressions, and various walking styles can help you feel more comfortable when you practice dramatizing your own scenes from stories. Practice them daily for the next week by doing the following:

> As you encounter characters or events in your academic reading, think about how the characters would use their hands, facial expressions, and walking styles to express their inner thoughts as they react to situations in which they find themselves. Pantomime those movements, walks, and expressions just to see how they feel. You may want to do this privately, so that an unknowing observer will not conclude that you have developed some sort of chronic muscle spasm that requires emergency medical attention.

For an interesting pantomime activity, see Cottrell's Sequential Pantomime Game (Cottrell, 1987, p. 60).

From Body Movements to Enacting Scenes

As they progress from body movements to enacting scenes, students can use the activity developed by Cooper and Collins (1992) in which the teacher reads or tells a story to the class and then asks students to enact just one simple action or small scene from the story. Read a story like "Cinderella" and divide the students into small groups. Ask students in each group to pantomime different parts of the story. For example, ask how Cinderella would mop the floor after learning that she can't go to the ball (Cooper & Collins, 1992). Ask the students to show through their movements the disappointment Cinderella must feel. With "Little Red Riding Hood" the students could enact the section in which the wolf smells the goodies in the basket and stalks the girl (Cooper & Collins, 1992). High school students can pantomime amusing scenes from literature, such as Tom Sawyer whitewashing a fence, Huckleberry Finn watching his own funeral, or Scout's reaction to her first snow in *To Kill a Mockingbird*.

Sometimes students tend to overdramatize the scenes. To discourage overacting, Gillard (1996, p. 53) "assigned people-watching for homework."

When students watch people expressing themselves verbally and physically in actual situations, students see firsthand authentic expressions of thoughts and feelings.

Enunciation

For help with enunciation and pronunciation, ask students to recite the tongue twisters that Cooper and Collins (1992) have gleaned from John Moschitta's *Hilarious Tongue Twister Games*. Here are the first lines from three of those tongue twisters. Each line should be repeated quickly three times so that the audience can clearly hear each syllable.

"Free Tree Twigs" (Cooper & Collins, 1992, p. 96).

"No need to light a night light on a light night like tonight" (p. 96).

"The sixth sick sheik's sixth sheep is sick" (p. 97).

These and other tongue twisters will help students to concentrate on using tongue, palate, lips, and teeth effectively, so that when they speak, they can be distinctly understood.

Moving from Story to Drama

All of the preparation work discussed above is really a precursor to enacting scenes from stories. Students can move from pantomiming a short scene to pantomiming an entire story. However, it is important to choose a story that lends itself well to dramatic enactment. In some cases, students may find it necessary to add movement and action not specified in the original story.

Also, students should consider the realities of the time constraints, the location of their performance, and the need for the dialogue and the action to convey the plot to the audience. As "playwrights" they do not have the luxury of a traditional storyteller who can narrate and explain. Drama is a very specialized way of storytelling. Students must *show* the audience the story.

Creative Drama and Reader's Theater

"Not all performances need to be formal plays where parts are memorized, sets built, and costumes made" (Moore, et al., 1994, p. 259). Betty used creative dramatics with great success in her work with primary grade students, using storytelling to teach language arts. These activities are described in detail in Chapter 3.

One way to help students feel comfortable on stage is the use of *reader's theater*, "the oral presentation of drama, prose, or poetry by two or more readers, with characterization when necessary, narration if desired, coordination of material to constitute a whole, and the development of a special reader-audience relationship" (McCaslin, 1984, p. 262). Prior to asking students to script a story, ask them to develop a reader's theater production wherein they have the story right in front of them and can read an assigned part from it. Each character from the story can be read by a different student, and one or two students can read the narration. This approach can help students to read with expression, to understand the importance of delineating different characters through different voices, and to experience the enjoyment of reading for others.

Sandy had good success using reader's theater. One particularly useful resource she used is *Cowboy* (Adams, 1988), a collection of reader's theater scripts based on songs, poems, and legends. One of the scripts is based on Robert Service's narrative poem, "The Shooting of Dan McGrew." To help students see the subtle differences between poetry, dialogue, and storytelling, you can divide the students into three groups. Ask one group to read the narrative poem as Service wrote it. Ask the second group to devise and tell the story as an eyewitness might have told it. Ask the third group to perform the script as it is found in *Cowboy* (Adams, 1988). Other narrative poems could be presented in a similar way.

How Can You Encourage the Scripting of Stories?

McCaslin (1987) has written a script based on "The Three Wishes," a story that, according to her, "contains the basic elements of a play:

1. A plot that holds interest

2. Plenty of action

3. A worthwhile theme

4. Characters who motivate the plot

5. Conflict

6. Humor

7. Climax and a quick and satisfactory end" (McCaslin, 1987, p. 102).

These elements are helpful guides in the search for stories that are appropriate for scripting. McCaslin's script can be used as a model.

How Can You Show Students The Difference
Between Storytelling and Dialogue?

To help students understand how scripting works, show them a copy of a play script. For older students, you could use the Dan McGrew script mentioned above. For younger children the script based on the Yiddish folktale "Things Could Always Be Worse" is included in *How To Do Plays with Children* (Moore, et al., 1994). For students of any level, the layout of the script gives a good example of how dialogue and stage instructions work. Note that at the beginning of many scripts you will find a kind of exposition explaining the time, the place, the opening set, and the characters who will be involved. Also, note that, instead of narration, the script will describe in parentheses or italics what the actor is supposed to do as he/she delivers a line.

As students work on scripting stories, they may want to share their skits with younger children at a different school. However, you must caution them to be realistic about the logistics of transporting the material for their props and set. All the props, costumes, and parts of the set must be constructed so that transporting them does not take more creativity and energy than the performance does.

The caution about easy mobility of props and sets is vital. Sandy Smith did not heed that warning when she and her secondary students decided to transport an entire cabin from one school to another. Here is the story in her own words.

❧

It was pouring rain. The roads were icy, and here I was driving a straight-shift truck. I hadn't driven a straight-shift in a while. But I got the hang of this gear shifting pretty well. I didn't make any big bobbles. We were making great progress, driving carefully down a busy highway. After a while, one of the boys in the cab of the truck quietly mumbled, "Well, there it goes."

I was not sure what he said. Just as I was turning my head to ask him to repeat what he said, my eyes panned across the rear view mirror. In the rear view mirror I saw our cabin blow off the back of our truck. It was circling up in the air. It looked just exactly like the clip of the house in the tornado from the movie The Wizard of Oz. It took me several minutes to stop the truck because I just went blank. I didn't know how to stop it. I didn't know where the clutch was. I didn't know where the brakes were. But finally I got it stopped. Our cabin hit the highway and spun around, and then it flew from one side of the two lane highway back over to the other side and finally ended up in the ditch. Suddenly, I put the truck in reverse and backed up to claim our stuff. As I got out of the truck it dawned on me that I had not even looked to see if anyone was behind us. What if there had been a car behind us?

When the students and I got to the cabin, it had come to rest off the highway. The cabin was huge. Usually five or six kids would be involved in helping to load the cabin, but they weren't with us. Well, the three of us got out of that truck, rushed over to the ditch, and had that thing picked up and on the back of that truck in 30 seconds flat. While we were standing there, bent over to pick up that cabin, I felt like Wonder Woman or Superman picking up the corner of a house. But just as I bent over with my rear end facing the road, a truck whooshed by, hit water, and sprayed it over every one of us. My hair was drenched, and my clothes were soaked. I didn't care. We were desperate to get that cabin on the truck.

When we finally got to where we were going, we just fell in the door of the school laughing. The story has a happy ending. We got the cabin safely to the elementary school, used it as part of the set, and went on to deliver our performance. But the memory of that wet and desperate day has not faded. It took me two or three years before I was willing to take that cabin anywhere else. Every time I see Grant and Andrew, the boys who were with me that day, we get hysterical.

 ## Suggested Activities for The Teacher

1. Refer to Appendix B for sources of stories appropriate for scripting. From your school or local library obtain a number of these books to use with your students. They will be especially helpful for the student activities listed below.

2. Before using the first activity for students listed below, choose a brief story from one of the books listed in Appendix B and try your hand at scripting the story.

Suggested Activities for Use with Students

1. Give students the directions below:

   Listen to a story chosen by your teacher with the idea that you will enact the story yourself. After listening to the story, discuss with your class the following questions as they relate to an enactment of the story:

   > "Who are the people? What are these people really like? What are they doing when we first meet them? Where does the first scene take place? What kind of house do they live in?" (McCaslin. 1987, p. 18. Also, see McCaslin, pp. 122-145).

   After the discussion, the teacher will divide you into groups of three or four and assign each group a portion of the story to act out as you listen. Your group should pretend you are going to be in a silent movie and discuss how you will silently enact the portion of the story assigned to you. The teacher will play the story a second time and cue your group when it is time to go into action. Present your planned silent enactment as your part of the story is told. Listen and observe quietly as other groups enact their portions of the story.

2.   Give the students the directions below:

Work in groups of three or four. Choose a very short story from a children's book. Read the story carefully. Then, working together, rewrite the story in dialogue form. Do not use a narrator. Show any action that the story describes, and use simple props to illustrate key parts of the setting. Your ultimate product will be a short skit lasting no more than 20 minutes; thus, you may have to condense the story somewhat, but be sure to include all the key events that are vital to an understanding of the story. Be sure that you keep scene changes to a minimum. In fact, it is best to have no more than two settings for the story so that you will not become overly involved in changing the set from one scene to another.

At the appointed time, participate with your group in reading the dialogue of your story.

3.   Give to the students these directions:

After each member of the class has told a personal story, break into groups of three or four. Choose one personal story told by a member of your group and script it for a twenty-minute presentation.

References

Adams, W. (1988). *Cowboy*. San Diego, CA: Reader's Theatre Script Service.

Cooper, P., & Collins, R. (1992). *Look what happened to Frog: Storytelling in education*. Scottsdale, AZ: Gorsuch Scarisbrick.

Cottrell, J. (1987). *Creative drama in the classroom, grades 4-6*. Lincolnwood, IL: National Textbook Company.

Fitzgerald, B. S. (1962). *World tales for creative dramatics and storytelling*. Englewood Cliffs, NJ: Prentice Hall.

Gillard, M. (1996). *Storyteller, storyteacher*. York, ME: Stenhouse.

McCaslin, N. (1984). *Creative drama in the classroom* (4th ed.). New York: Longman.

McCaslin, N. (1987). *Creative drama in the intermediate grades: A handbook for teachers*. New York: Longman.

Moore, J. E., Hall, G., Tryon, L., & Franco, B. (1994). *How to do plays with children*. Monterey, CA: Evans-Moore.

Neimi, L. (1988). Storytelling in a theater setting. *The National Storytelling Journal*, (Winter), 1988, 11-12.

Neufeldt, V., & Guralink, D. B. (Eds.). (1991). *Webster's new world dictionary* (3rd college ed.). New York: Prentice Hall.

Chapter 8
Using Storytelling to Teach Art and Music

While Georgia O'Keeffe is associated with her paintings of large flowers and cow skulls, one of her most stunning paintings is neither a flower nor a skull. It is a huge painting of clouds. At 8 feet high and 24 feet long, it covers one wall at the Art Institute of Chicago. The story of "Sky Above Clouds IV" is found in Georgia O'Keeffe: A Studio Book *(1976).*

On a flight from New York to New Mexico, Georgia looked through the window to find that "the sky below was a most beautiful solid white. It looked so secure," she said, "that I thought I could walk right out on it to the horizon if the door opened. The sky beyond was a light clear blue....I couldn't wait to be home to paint it" (O'Keeffe, 1976, no page numbers).

When Georgia returned to her studio in New Mexico, she first sketched the clouds on a large sheet of paper, 9 feet by 24 feet. Realizing that an oil painting of that size would be a monumental challenge, she sought help in the design and construction of a stretcher for the canvas. She decided to paint it in her garage. As she progressed through the project, she found it very difficult to stretch, hang, and paint on such a large canvas; but her determination and perseverance drove her to complete the work. As Georgia worked on "Sky Above Clouds IV," she faced not only enormous tasks of constructing the stretcher, preparing the canvas, and finally painting the picture, she also "was afraid that the rattlesnakes would come in [the open door] behind me as I worked" (O'Keeffe, 1976, no page numbers).

At its completion in 1965, "Sky Above Clouds IV" was so large that transporting it to its first home in the Amon Carter Museum in Fort Worth, Texas, required a 30-foot truck. The painting was so long, it had to "hang in the hall with part of it reaching into the next room" (O'Keeffe, 1976, no page numbers). *Later it was taken to the Art Institute in Chicago. The size of the painting meant that some galleries or museums could not display it because they simply did not have enough room, "so it still hangs in Chicago"* (O'Keeffe, 1976, no page numbers).

How Can You Use Storytelling to Teach Art?

Although it may be true that a picture is worth a thousand words, it is also true that words are often good companions to pictures. They can help us articulate our responses to and interpretations of pictures; they can help us share our ideas with others. Storytelling can be a useful tool in the teaching of art.

The Story Quilt Project

Katherine McGhee of Tennessee Technological University worked with students at Prescott Central Middle School in Cookeville, Tennessee, to make a story quilt. The project was inspired by Faith Ringgold's *Tar Beach*, a Caldecott Honor Book, based on Ringgold's story quilt or "quilt painting [also entitled *Tar Beach*] that incorporates a written story" into its design (*Ringgold*, 1991, Book Jacket Notes). The quilt painting combines autobiography, fictional narrative, painting, and quilt making in one art form. It is a quilt with a story written on fabric strips sewn around the border as an integral part of the work (*Ringgold*, 1991, pages not numbered).

Ringgold's art is inspired directly by personal family stories told by her mother, Willi Posey Jones, who watched her grandmother, Betsy Bingham, "boil and bleach flower sacks to line the quilts she sewed. Susie Shannon, Betsy's mother, was a slave in antebellum Florida who made quilts as part of her duties. Ringgold's quilt designs echo the African-influenced, repetitive geometric design characteristic of many Early American Quilts" (*Ringgold*, 1991, last page).

The story for *Tar Beach* is fictional. But, like the quilts that were inspired by family stories, *Tar Beach* was inspired by Ringgold's "memories of childhood" in Harlem when her family would go up on the roof on summer nights to cards and visit. After creating the story quilt, Ringgold modified and published the text and the quilt pattern in a children's book by the same name. Thus, we see in Faith Ringgold an artist whose work is the direct result of stories told to her by her mother and stories she herself told about her own childhood.

McGhee (1996) invited Ringgold to speak to her art education students at Tennessee Tech. After Ringgold's visit, the college students worked with upper elementary school students at Prescott Central Middle School to combine quilt making and storytelling. The two art forms together give students a rich opportunity to express their creativity with craft, color, and writing. While the Prescott students were not asked to display their quilts and share stories orally, McGhee said that the project could easily be modified for oral storytelling.

Dinner at Aunt Connie's House (1993) is another Ringgold children's book. This picture book evolved from one of Ringgold's story quilts entitled *The Dinner Quilt*. The story is about two children who learn through painted portraits hung on Aunt Connie's wall about the contribution that strong African-American women have made to American history and culture. Ringgold says, "Art can be more than a picture on a wall—it can envision our history and illustrate proud events in people's lives" (Ringgold, 1993, no page numbers).

Using Memory to Create Image

A similar use of art was demonstrated in a reader-response workshop in which Probst and Sipe (1992) led participants through a number of reader-response activities to prompt personal involvement with a poem or short story. One assignment required participants to draw a picture or a design that was closely associated with a significant family event. Each participant then shared his or her picture with members of the small group. Suellen drew a pattern of a quilt that had been given to her mother by a very special family friend. Then she told this story:

❧

When I was growing up, my mother had a close friend who was quite a bit older than she was. We children even called her Granny. Because our mother's own mother died when Mom was only six years old, I think Granny fulfilled a kind of mother role that Mom needed in her life. Granny and Mom both enjoyed homemade quilts. One day, Granny gave Mom a quilt top that she had made and left the rest of the quilting up to Mom. With the rigors of a full-time job and caring for three children, Mom put the quilt top away and never finished quilting it.

Years later, when we children were grown and married and were starting households of our own, my sister asked Mom if she would give her that quilt top that Granny had made. Our mother found it hard to say "no" to her children; so with great reluctance, she gave the quilt top to my sister. Later she felt a bit resentful that Sis would dare ask her for something so precious.

On Christmas day, we all gathered at Mom's house to exchange gifts. My sister had given her a rather big box, with no hint whatsoever about its contents. When Mother opened the box, she was tearfully surprised to see the very quilt top that Granny had made; my sister had taken it to someone who had finished it into a completed quilt, with batten, back, and stitches. So Sis turned out to be far more sensitive than Mom had realized.

Suellen had not thought of that story in years until she was asked to draw a design or picture that represented a significant family event. The design that she drew in that workshop was her attempt to duplicate the design of Granny's quilt.

While some may say that such an assignment is using art to teach storytelling, the idea of attaching a design or a picture to a significant family event is certainly an effective way to motivate a student to draw, sculpt, or paint.

The Story Behind the Scene

Very often in the teaching of writing, teachers will ask students not only to write an essay, but also to write an account of the process involved in writing the paper. Emanuel (1997) asks her students to write about not only "the placing of the words on the page, but also the mental process which preceded the act of writing"—how that piece of writing began and developed into its final form. Writing about writing gives students an idea of the process involved in bringing a final work to fruition.

Similarly, telling a story about how a piece of art began and developed into its final form can help painters, sculptors, and other artists gain an understanding of the challenges inherent in creating their art. Such an account can also be a valuable review of the whole process and lend insight into the kinds of changes the artist will make in his or her next artistic venture. It can also enhance a viewer's appreciation of a work of art. For example, while Suellen was very impressed with O'Keeffe's painting "Sky Above Clouds IV," she gained an even deeper appreciation of the work after reading O'Keeffe's account of how she created it.

Rather than asking students to verbalize their review of their work in an analytic vein, ask them to simply narrate sequentially the way the idea came to them; what challenges or conflicts they found in the choice of materials, space, color, design, composition, and balance; and the way they met the challenges or resolved those conflicts as they completed the final work. If students view the challenges inherent in the project as kinds of conflict in a story line, they can construct a story with themselves as the protagonist, the work of art as a challenge to be faced or a conflict to be solved, and the process of creating the piece as the plot that shows how the challenge was met or the conflict was resolved.

A variation of this approach involves looking at the finished product as if it were created by someone the artist does not know and then writing a story about the kind of person who is represented by the work on display. What does the completed work say about the artist? Ask them what assumptions they would make about the artist, if they had not created the piece themselves (Emanuel, 1997).

Other Stories Behind the Art

A valuable resource to help young students appreciate the works of the masters is Ernest Raboff's *Art for Children* (1988), a series of books on the works and lives of sixteen painters. Each book contains handsome prints of important paintings and interesting stories behind them.

ceǝɔ

How Can You Use Storytelling to Teach Music?

Over 200 years ago, a man named George Handel lived comfortably in London, England. Even though he was born in Germany, George had made quite a name for himself as a brilliant musical composer in England. In 1741 George received a letter from his friend Charles Jennen who wrote that he had put together a large collection of Biblical passages about the coming of a Messiah and he wanted George to write a musical composition to go with that collection.

After he read Charles' letter, George decided he would write the music to these beautiful Biblical passages. So, on Saturday, August 22, 1741, George Frederic Handel went into the front room of his house in London and began to work. What happened after that is a mystery. Some people say that he simply pulled out melodies that he had already written and set them to the new words, and that he worked like he usually worked, quickly and skillfully. Others say that when he entered his studio on that fateful day, he began to work on a project that resulted in the most miraculous musical composition of his life.

For 24 days the composer remained in the little room. Some say that he ate very little and slept even less. His servant brought regular meals and left them on the floor outside his door. Often the servant would return with another meal, only to find that George had not touched the platter that had been left there earlier. Sometimes the servant would look in the room to find George in tears as he composed certain parts of the oratorio. At one point, he is supposed to have said, "I did think I did see all Heaven before me and the great God Himself."

George worked almost non-stop for 24 days. When he came out of his room on September 14, he had produced "Messiah," a lengthy work of music for choir and orchestra that is still sung in churches around the world today. The most famous part of "Messiah" is the "Hallelujah Chorus," which moved King George II so much when he heard it that he stood out of respect while it was being performed. In those days, when the king stood, so did everyone around him. The whole audience stood with the king during the "Hallelujah Chorus." That tradition is still observed when the work is played today. So when you hear the "Hallelujah Chorus," stand up to honor a musical genius who produced a masterpiece in only 24 days. (This story is based on accounts taken from Burrows, 1991; Flowers, 1948; Myers, 1948; Tobin, 1964.)

Music is the closest thing to a universal language. We are often moved by its beauty even though we may speak a language that is very different from that of the composer. However, sometimes words of a story like the one above about Handel's "Messiah" can heighten our appreciation of music and of the musician who created it. Thus, telling the story behind the music is an effective way of motivating students to listen to and/or perform a piece of music that may not interest them otherwise.

Speaking and Singing Are Sisters

A number of music educators believe that in their early years, the speech of children has a kind of melodic form to it. "Children's early speech is 'musical' in its form and expression...with often rhythmical, sustained pitch and pointed repetition....As speech becomes more mature it becomes less 'tuned' and rhythmical as the purpose becomes more semantic" (Glover & Ward, 1993, p. 177). The observations of Glover & Ward (1993) point to the importance of building upon the inherent musicality of children's speech. Musical speech is a valuable tool for storytellers.

Glover and Ward recommend teaching children to appreciate the unique sounds found in dialects different from their own to help them become aware of the musical elements of language. Suellen saw powerful evidence of students' ability to appreciate this musical nature of language when she invited some guest speakers from Scotland to read poems to her untraveled East Tennessee high school seniors. Suspecting that her students would have trouble understanding the guests' thick Scottish accents, Suellen encouraged them to listen simply for the rhythm and expression of the sounds. "Now when our visitors come to read for us," she said, "you may find that unless you listen very carefully, you will not understand their Scottish dialect very well. Don't let that stop you from appreciating the rhythm and lilt of the language. In fact, your inability to understand what the readers are saying will give you a special opportunity to hear the very musical sound of English as it is spoken in a dialect you have not heard before."

After the Scots had read the poems and left the classroom, one student told Suellen that she really did listen just for the rhythm and pitch of the voices and found it very pleasant, very musical. As Mark (1978, p. 90) observes, "Children learn musical concepts from the texture, dynamics, pitch patterns, and rhythms of speech....Their musical knowledge grows from their experiences." Mark's observation reflects Carl Orff's approach, which is still used today, wherein he began music education with "speech as a springboard for musical experiences" using "the rhythmic pattern of language" (Wheeler & Raebeck, 1972, p. xix) and "the natural chant of childhood (the falling minor third)" (p. xx). In fact, if we think back on our own childhoods, we may well remember the melodic sound of our parents calling us to come in for supper. More than likely, that melody was made up of a falling, or descending, minor third as shown in Figure 8.1.

Figure 8.1 Descending Minor Third

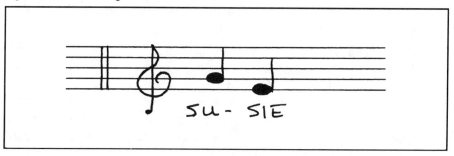

To help students hear the musical quality of speech, play recordings of experienced storytellers like Jackie Torrence, Donald Davis, Heather Forest, Doug Lipman, or David Holt. Before playing a recording, give the students the text of the story and a listening guide such as the one that follows.

Storytelling Listening Guide for Students

As you listen to a tape recording of a professional storyteller, please do the following:

1.   Follow along with the written text of the story. Listen for the aspects of the performance below and, in the space provided, write your comments about how that particular aspect affected important parts of the story,

such as mood, characterization, and suspense. You may also comment about other aspects not mentioned here. You will need to use a separate sheet of paper.

Aspect: The rise and fall of the storyteller's voice

Comment:

Aspect: The changes in volume of the storyteller's voice from very soft to very loud

Comment:

Aspect: The changes in the storyteller's pace from fast to slow

Comment:

Aspect: Other dynamics and expressions in the voice of the story-teller

Comment:

Aspect: The storyteller's phrasing and use of breaths and "rests"

Comment:

Other Aspects and comments:

2.   As you listen, take notes on the similarities you see between the telling of a story and the performance of a musical work such as a choral piece or a piano sonata. Also, think of melodic lines, original or published, that would fit a certain part of the story.

3.   After listening to the story, work in small groups of no more than four, and brainstorm melodic lines that you think would fit a particularly interesting part of the story. You may create an original melodic line, use melodic lines that already exist from established works, or use a combination of both. The choice of the instrument(s) for expressing the melodic line is up to the group. Your group should be prepared to perform its melody for the rest of the class.

The activity above can also be used with ballads. For example, you may want to let students use a listening guide as they listen to an expressive reader or speaker as he or she reads or recites the words to the ballad, "John Henry." Then have the students listen to someone play the melody of the ballad. Finally, have them listen to someone sing the ballad, or have them sing it themselves. Discuss with them how the words and the music work together to create quite a different response from the response to the melody or the words alone. Books such as *Gonna Sing My Head Off* (Krull, 1992) and *The Funny Story Book* (Nelson, 1984) have very appropriate songs for these activities.

Using Ballads

Music and storytelling are close partners in teaching students to appreciate and learn both disciplines. Certainly the ballad forms of poetry and music are unique versions of a story. A ballad like "Barbara Allen," for example, contains a central character, a conflict, and a resolution. An awareness of the tension and suspense inherent in the ballad can have a positive effect on the musical interpretation of the song. Thus, teaching the important parts of the story as well as the important parts of the musical composition can encourage greater musical facility among singers and players. For example, you can read the words to "Barbara Allen" aloud to the class and discuss the major tone and mood of the story. Then, play a recording of someone singing the ballad "Barbara Allen." Provide a written score of the ballad for students to follow. Then discuss how the music affected the students' responses to the story. Also, discuss how the melodic line reflects the sense of the words set to it.

Livo and Rietz (1991) list a number of ballads that would work well with the activities discussed above. Some of the suggested ballads are "Clementine," "The Fox," "As I Stepped Out One Evening," and "The Grey Goose."

A great number of children come to school having already developed a sense of narrative form. Although they probably could not clearly articulate that sense, they know that a story has a beginning, a middle, and an end. "There are links between musical form and narrative form. Both have openings, themes, repetitions, endings. But these are expressed in different ways in language and music: 'Once upon a time . . .' as a beginning, or a crash on the cymbals as an ending" (Glover & Ward, 1993, p. 178). Because of children's sense of story, storytelling can be an effective part of music instruction.

Music That Tells Its Own Story

Kevin Fletcher (1997), an elementary music teacher, uses the frame of a story to teach his kindergarten students a sense of rhythm and melody. Instead of teaching the discreet skills of rhythm, Kevin makes up a story in which the children must use rhythm to participate in the story. He also uses stories to teach a major scale without using the terminology. By the time the children sing a given song that centers around a very funny man, they have essentially sung a major scale without knowing it. Kevin theorizes that, if he can let kindergarten students pleasantly experience certain musical essentials such as rhythm and a major scale without teaching them as discreet skills, he will give them a memorable experience on which they can build when their music teacher in a higher grade teaches these concepts in a more formal way.

Using Story To Teach Perspective in Music

Schafer (1965) describes how he used story and setting to teach the idea of perspective in music. He discussed the unusual music of Charles Ives' composition entitled "Putnam's Camp." The piece sounds rather cacophonous with the melodies of several marches being played simultaneously. To help students see that this kind of confusion was purposeful, Schafer told the following story.

Once when "Putnam's Camp" was being performed, Charles Ives was in the audience, listening intently. After the concert, someone implied that the scrambled music must have been the result of poor playing by the orchestra, and apologized to Ives, the composer, for such a confusing sound. But Ives said "Wonderful how it came out! Every man for himself—just like a town meeting" (Schafer, 1965, p. 75).

The story of Ives' comment about the performance helped students to see that the music in "Putnam's Camp" is supposed to sound confused. As they discussed the piece further, students began to see that the composition sounded a little like several bands converging at the same street corner in a parade and then marching away from each other. This "picture" is created by having some music more prominent in the "foreground" and other music less prominent in the distance. With this observation, Schafer goes on to discuss the idea that perspective in music is very similar to perspective in painting, film, or theater. (We could easily add "storytelling" to his list.)

Musical Storytelling with Artistic Objects

Just as objects can be used to motivate storytelling with words, they can also be used to motivate storytelling with music. For example, Schafer showed a group of sixth graders a very ugly mask and asked the students to make noises with their vocal chords to indicate the sounds a person might make if she or he came upon the mask unexpectedly. He then asked the students to make up a brief story about the mask, perform it as dramatically as they could, and then express those same emotions with percussion instruments. As they experimented with sounds, the students elaborated on their extemporaneous story, which they entitled "The Mask of the Evil Demon," and "told" each part of the story with instruments and sounds that were appropriate for that part. Schafer (1965, p. 47) says that when the children left the classroom, he saw them continuing to talk about the story, "and the fierce dance of the mask carried right out into the schoolyard, down the streets, and into life."

The activity described above isn't appropriate for very young children. However, they could be asked to look at masks with different facial characteristics and expressions. The children could make up stories about the masks and act out the stories with musical accompaniments on simple rhythm instruments. They could then discuss why certain musical sounds matched certain parts of the stories. To extend the activity into visual arts, the children could go on to create their own masks about which they would create stories and music. Such a multidisciplinary activity would help children see the close relationship that can be forged among music, language, and art.

Sandy and her colleague Barbara Winningham created a multidisciplinary project wherein music became the primary storytelling medium. They wrote for their students a production entitled *Between the Lines: A Musical Revue*. The script uses American songs from the Colonial Period through the 1980's to tell the story of American history. *Between the Lines* is a good example of a multidisciplinary combination of storytelling, drama, and history, all carried by its primary medium, music.

Music in Context

Music can be related to the familiar frame of a story. As a result, students learn a number of musical concepts within the context of a familiar pattern, relating new learning to acquired knowledge. For example, many traditional Native American stories could be accompanied by rain sticks, drum beats, or other rhythm makers. Students could create from a variety of instruments the sound effects related to specific stories. While some students tell the stories, other students could use instruments to create the sounds of hoof beats, thunder, wind, rain, and desert or forest animals. Teachers can build students' confidence in using instruments by helping them become familiar with the sounds of orchestral instruments.

Peter and the Wolf

Probably the most famous musical work that relates musical instruments to a story is *Peter and the Wolf* by Serge Prokofiev, the Russian composer of the mid-twentieth century. Prokofiev wrote both the music and the words for the narrator. The story centers around the dangers faced by a boy who encounters a wolf and feels the responsibility of protecting his animal friends from this dangerous predator. As the narrator spins the story, the orchestra plays Prokofiev's music. In that music, he matches the following creatures with the following instruments: bird and flute, duck and oboe, cat and clarinet, grandfather and bassoon, wolf and three French horns, hunters and drums, and Peter and all the strings of the orchestra. In preparation for playing a recording of *Peter and the Wolf*, you may want to show students the instruments mentioned above, with a label on each. As you play the recording, point to the instruments when you hear them on the recording.

Play a recording of *Peter and the Wolf* and ask students to discuss why they think Prokofiev chose those particular instruments to represent those particular creatures. For example, as they discuss what the sound of a flute and the sound and movement of a bird have in common, they begin to discuss "timbre" or the unique properties of sound produced by each instrument. In conjunction with the music, you may want to use Loriot and Muller's retelling of Prokofiev's story (Loriot & Muller, 1986).

After playing *Peter and the Wolf*, read to the students a familiar story. Since they have been thinking about a wolf, "Little Red Riding Hood" would be a good choice. Before reading the story, ask the students to think about the instruments they just heard when they listened to *Peter and the Wolf*. As they listen to "Little Red Riding Hood," have them write down the instrument that they think would best represent each character in that story. Of course, choices would vary depending on the students' familiarity with orchestral instruments. If they know about instruments other than the ones used in *Peter and the Wolf*, they may choose instruments for "Little Red Riding Hood" that are not heard in *Peter and the Wolf*. For example, one student may choose the string bass to represent the wolf, while another may choose the tuba. Both choices could certainly do the job of making listeners think of a wolf. Thus, it is important to give children flexibility in their choices. At the end of the story, the teacher could discuss with the class the various instruments chosen and why those instruments can represent a given character.

Other Applications of Story to Music

You could tell *The Story of the Nutcracker Ballet* (Hauzig, 1986) as an introduction to the popular ballet. Students can discuss how the story relates to the music that they hear and to the dancers that they see. *Swan Lake* (Helprin, 1989) can be used in the same way.

You may want to use the following story as a motivational device for budding composers.

⚜

Listen. It's the "Ode to Joy," the choral section for the last movement of Beethoven's Ninth Symphony. *How high those sopranos sound! They say that singing this work is a real challenge for sopranos. Why would Beethoven write the music so terribly high? Some people say he did so because he forgot the sound and the range of the human voice. But I get ahead of myself.*

Ludwig Von Beethoven was born in Germany in 1770. His musical talent flourished at an early age, and when he became a young composer at the beginning of the nineteenth century, Beethoven's music became extremely popular. He was in demand all over Europe. Then, at the height of his career, he began to become aware of an increasing difficulty with his hearing. By the time he had finished the Ninth Symphony, *he had become quite deaf. In fact, when it was first performed in 1824, three years before his death, Beethoven was so deaf he was unaware of the applause that followed until one of the soloists motioned that he should turn and face the audience.*

While Beethoven's disability prevented him from hearing the sounds around him, it never kept him from composing the music of his soul. (This story is based on accounts found in Hickock, 1975, and Buddon, 1982).

 ## Suggested Activities for the Teacher

1. As you begin your next work of art—drawing, clay pot, weaving, painting, or sculpture—think about the creative process as you move through it. After you have finished, speak into a tape recorder a narrative related to how the idea came to you and how you decided on the materials, dimensions, design, composition, medium, space, color, and so forth. After you have finished dictating, transcribe your notes into a kind of "story behind the scenes" and share the story when you display the work. You may even want to post the story along with the piece when it is in a show.

2. Before teaching performers to sing or play a piece of music, research the life of the composer, especially the circumstances surrounding the creation of the work. Develop the information into an oral story. Tell the story to the music students, and ask them to think about the story as they rehearse and perform the piece.

Activities for Use With the Students

1. Give these directions to the students:

    For this assignment, you will do not only art, but storytelling as well. As you proceed with the work at hand (drawing, sculpture, pottery, weaving, painting, etc.), think about the process in which you are involved. After you have finished your piece, speak into the tape recorder provided, and narrate the process you followed as you progressed through the work. Use the questions below as a guide for your narration. When you are finished with your dictation, transcribe your notes on paper. Share them with a partner and ask for suggestions on how they can be strength-

ened. Write them in final form, and attach them to or near your work
when we put it on display.

Questions to Guide your Narration

The questions below are to serve as guides to your thinking. Please
avoid simply answering them independently of each other. Rather, use
them to weave together a story about the process you went through to
finish the work.

a. What did you see, hear, taste, smell, feel, do, dream, and/or remember that led you to begin this work?

b. What factors were involved in your decisions about color, medium,
   design, shape, composition, balance, dimension, space, and/or other
   elements of your work?

c. What frustrations, problems, conflicts, or challenges did you face as
   you began to put the work together?

d. How did you solve those problems? Be specific.

e. What personal artistic limitations did you face as you worked on your
   piece?

f. What did you do in the process that worked well?

g. How different is the final product from the vision you first had of the
   work?

2. Give the students these instructions: In the library find a print or photograph of one of your favorite paintings or sculptures. Then find information about the artist and about how that work came into being. Find the
   story in the artist's own words, if possible. Bring the print or photograph
   to class. Show the print and tell the story that lies behind it.

3. Tell the students: Choose a brief story from your literature class that
   lends itself well to illustration. Draw one scene from the story as accurately as you can, based solely on the details provided by the author.
   Display your illustration to the class, give a brief summary of the story,
   and read aloud or tell the section of the story that is illustrated by your
   drawing.

4. Have each student choose a partner and trade drawings (paintings, sculptures, etc.). Then give the students the following instructions:
   Look at your partner's work carefully. Write an outline of a story that
   seems appropriate to the work. Include at least two main characters that
   face a simple conflict or problem, show how they solve the conflict or
   problem, and show how the work of art relates directly to the story.
   Display your partner's work and share your outline with the class.

5. Ask students to follow the instructions for the activity below:

In your literature anthology, find a very short story that you think would lend itself to a musical interpretation. Find specific places in the story that you wish to interpret either with a musical composition of your own or with a recording of existing music. If you use a recording of someone else's music, be sure to note the name of the composer, the title of the work, and the names of the performers.

Practice reading the story aloud and playing the music at the appropriate point in the story. When you feel confident that you have effectively coordinated the music with the story, read the story aloud to your classmates with the accompanying music.

6. This multidisciplinary activity will involve students who are interested in storytelling and/or theater, drawing, and musical composition and/or improvisation. It may also require the cooperation of teachers in those disciplines. Form groups of students who show some aptitude in each discipline mentioned above. Each group must have one student who is accomplished in each area; they may want to use a multimedia computer program to complete their project. After forming groups, give the students this assignment:

You will work in your group to produce a story that you will tell and/or perform, illustrate, and accompany with music. Regardless of your individual talent, you will make some contribution to each of the components of the production.

Create an original story appropriate for telling to the group. It can be a trickster tale, a hero tale, a fable, or any other form that works. Write the story, and as you do so, create a storyboard with panels that illustrate the major scenes in the story. Along with the writing and drawing, develop a musical theme or a series of melodies that illustrate the story well. You may improvise your own music, use music that has already been written or use a combination of both. You may play a musical instrument, sing, or play a recording.

The sequence you follow to complete the project is up to you. You are not required to start with the story. You may want to start with musical improvisation or with drawing and build the story from what the music or the drawing tells you. Regardless of the process, your group will present the story to the rest of the class; and everyone in the group must participate in the presentation.

References

Buddon, J. M. (1982). Beethoven. *Encyclopaedia Britannica* (Vol. 2, p. 797) Chicago: Encyclopaedia Britannica, Inc.

Burrows, D. (1991). *Handel: Messiah*. New York: Cambridge University Press.

Emanuel, C. (1997). Personal conversation. Tennessee Technological University, Cookeville, TN, March 17.

Fletcher, K. (1997). Personal conversation. Cookeville, TN.

Flowers, N. (1948). *George Frederic Handel: His personality and his times*. New York: Charles Scribner's Sons.

Glover, J., & Ward, S. (Eds.). (1993). *Teaching music in the primary school*. New York: Cassell.

Helprin, M. (1989). *Swan Lake*. Illustrated by Chris Van Allsburg. Boston: Houghton Mifflin.

Hickock, R. (1975). *Music appreciation* (2nd ed.). Reading, MA: Addison-Wesley.

Hautzig, D. (1986). *The story of the Nutcracker Ballet*. New York: Random House.

Krull, K. (1992). *Gonna sing my head off: American folk songs for children*. Illustrated by Allen Garns. New York: Alfred A. Knopf.

Livo, N. J., & Rietz, S. A. (1991). *Storytelling: Folklore source book*. Englewood, CO: Libraries Unlimited.

Loriot, & Muller, J. (1986). *Peter and the wolf: A musical fairy tale by Serge Prokofiev*. New York: Alfred A. Knopf.

Mark, M. L. (1978). *Contemporary music education*. New York: Schirmer.

McGhee, K. (1996). Personal conversation. Tennessee Technological University, Cookeville, TN, December 15.

Myers, R. M. (1948). *Handel's Messiah: A touchstone of taste*. New York: Macmillan.

Nelson, E. L. (1984). *The funny songbook*. Illustrated by Joyce Behr. New York: Sterling.

O'Keeffe, G. (1976). *Georgia O'Keeffe: A studio book*. New York: Viking.

Probst, R., & Sipe, R. (1992). Principals and practices in teaching literature. A Workshop. National Council of Teachers of English Convention, Louisville, KY.

Raboff, E. (1988). *Art for children*. New York: Harper & Row.

Ringgold, F. (1991). *Tar Beach*. New York: Crown.

Ringgold, F. (1993). *Dinner at Aunt Connie's house*. New York: Hyperion.

Schafer, R. M. (1965). *Creative music education: A handbook for the modern music teacher*. New York: Schirmer.

Smith, S., & Winningham, B. (1992). *Between the lines: A musical revue*. Livingston, TN: Overton County Schools.

Tobin, J. (1964). *Handel at work*. New York: St. Martin's Press.

Wheeler, L., & Raebech, L. (1972). *Orff and Kodaly adapted for elementary school*. Dubuque, IA: Wm. C. Brown.

Chapter 9
Using Storytelling to Enhance Learning in Social Studies

Sequoyah as a young boy lived in the Cherokee village of Tuskegee in the Smoky Mountains of Tennessee near the Cherokee capital, Echota. His mother was a Cherokee woman named Wur-teh. His father was thought to be a white man named Nathaniel Gist, who lived among the Cherokees for years as a hunter, explorer, and soldier, but went back to live with his own people about the time Sequoyah was born. Sequoyah grew up speaking only Cherokee. He helped his mother with farming and home chores that were generally considered by Cherokees to be women's work.

Sequoyah traveled to other villages to trade, and there he saw silversmiths working. He secured tools of his own and became a skilled worker in silver. After his mother died, he moved to the Village of Coosa in Alabama, got married to a woman named Utiya, and worked as a blacksmith and silversmith.

Many of the Cherokees admired the white men and were convinced that the white men had great power because their books, which the Cherokee referred to as talking leaves, were magic. Sequoyah hated to see so many Cherokees taking up the white men's ways. He argued that the books were not magic. He told his Cherokee associates that he would make marks for Cherokee words and have the same magic. Council leaders and others laughed at him, but he was convinced that he could do this.

The War of 1812 delayed Sequoyah's plans for the development of Cherokee writing. He enlisted to fight on the side of the Americans against the Creeks. When white soldiers got letters from home, he thought of his plan, and his resolve became stronger than ever.

When Sequoyah returned home he busily worked on his idea for

*writing the Cherokee language. First, he tried to make a picture for
every word in the Cherokee language. He put them on pieces of bark.
He soon saw that this approach wouldn't work.*

*One day, listening to bird sounds, Sequoyah decided that sounds
were the key to writing. He started by pronouncing his name in sylla-
bles and making a different mark for each syllable. When he found the
same syllable in other words, he could use the same mark for it. Piles
of bark grew in the house. He worked day and night.*

*Sequoyah's wife got angry. "All you do is play with pieces of
bark," she said. Then she threw the stacks of bark into the fire.*

The class was thunderstruck. How could anyone be so cruel and insensitive as to destroy all of that work? They leaned forward to hear more about an
important historical personage who had seemingly taken on an impossible
task. Hadn't writing evolved over centuries? Could one man possibly think he
could develop a writing system all alone?

Why Is Storytelling Especially Well-Suited to Social Studies Instruction?

The social studies curriculum includes such areas as history, geography,
and current events. Storytelling is a natural technique for social studies
instruction, because it can bring people, places, events, and situations to life
for students who might never see them as anything but a collection of facts to
be read and memorized.

History

History is obviously a rich area for storytellers, for history is the story of
the past. Of course, that story is composed of many interrelated smaller stories that together form a coherent picture of previous events, complete with
their casts of characters and unique settings.

Textbooks in history sometimes cover an entire war, political movement,
social movement, or technological revolution in a single chapter. Needless to
say, there is little room for elaboration: names, places, and dates abound;
causes, connections, emotional implications, and human reactions often are
missing. These, of course, can be supplemented by having students read a
variety of other references and trade books on the topic. Unfortunately, many
students are unwilling or unable to manage this supplementary reading to the
extent that is desirable to develop clear understandings of the issues. In this
case, you, as teacher, have to step in. Your judgment can be used to direct the

students to the supplementary materials that they can reasonably be expected to handle independently, leaving a vast collection of materials that most of the class will not have the time or the ability to access. From that collection, you must decide what ideas are most important for you to transmit to the students. From these sources you choose people and events that you want the students to know more about than they can get from their personal reading. You take these events and form them into stories that will bring them alive for the children, connecting them with real individuals doing things for authentic reasons, and showing the consequences of these individuals' actions for themselves and others. Ellis (1997) and Blair (1991) point out that the topic you choose to tell about has to interest you, or you won't do a good job of communicating with your students through a story about it. You need to be deeply involved in the story.

Betty chose the topic of Sequoyah when she wanted to tell about a Native American who had had a major impact upon the development of his people. She read every account of Sequoyah's life that she could locate. They covered many aspects of his life, and some were contradictory. Using the ones that had closest agreement and backing by scholars of which she was aware, she began to piece together a story of his life that would not be too cluttered with detail to make a comfortable telling, but would contain the essential facts that were pertinent to his development of a writing system. She discovered other accomplishments that could have been highlighted, but she saved them for possible other stories, in order to keep the focus upon the one that was most appropriate for her immediate purpose. The result was the opening/closing story in this chapter.

When researching and writing a story from history, it is valuable to collect both primary source material, such as letters, journals, old photos, newspapers and so forth, and secondary source material, such as books that give an overview of the times, helping you to set the story in its actual context. Details of daily life add authenticity. Include historical events, foods the people ate, expressions that they used in speech, prices and wages, means of transportation, types of housing, games they played, household items, and types of clothing (Ellis, 1997; Black, 1992; Ellis, 1994; Golden, 1994).

Ellis (1997) suggests that sometimes you may tell a story about real events in history through the eyes of a fictional character, but that even then you must be true to the facts. You should develop a character with whom your intended audience can identify, if you are creating a fictional character. A character with the same age as the intended audience and with some of the same dreams and problems will enhance the story (Black, 1992).

You also need to have some conflict in your story, because it will be the heart of the story (Ellis, 1997). In the story that Betty developed about Sequoyah, there were several sources of conflict—the antagonism of his wife toward his work and, as you will see later, the suspicions that he was performing witchcraft and the disbelief of the council leaders after the syllabary was finished provide needed tension in the story.

Understanding the time period in which your story takes place is important to the development of an effective narrative. Sequoyah's story shows how his invention of the syllabary had a major influence on the Cherokee nation, which was transformed from a nation with no writing system to a widely literate nation. This, among other things, puts the Trail of Tears experience of many Cherokees into sad perspective. These people, some of whom were more literate than the ones who took their land, were trapped by circumstances into a tragic event.

Point of view has to be considered when doing a historical story. The story of Sequoyah that Betty told is in third person, told by a narrator outside the action. Blair (1991) points out that this is the safest point of view if you are not completely at home in the time period. There is less chance of including anachronistic comments. The story could have been told from Sequoyah's point of view, or through the point of view of a fictional contemporary of Sequoyah or that of his daughter, to name only a few possibilities. Ellis (1997) suggests telling the story from several different points of view to help listeners see a more complete picture of history. For example, a Cherokee's evaluation of Andrew Jackson's presidency would most likely emphasize very different issues than one written by a white person. "For the native peoples who lived here, the experience of being 'discovered' was very different from that of the explorers" (National Storytelling Association, 1994, p. 116), so telling that story from the different perspectives could definitely be beneficial for the students. Ellis (1997) also points out that if the students say that you can't teach them about their history because you are a different race or from a different ethnic group, challenge them to teach you about their history.

For a unit on Christopher Columbus, you may want to tell some stories that were being told in 1492. *Stories From the Days of Columbus* (Young & Young, 1992) is a book of tellable stories from that time. The stories are not about Columbus, but they are the stories that were being told by the mainly illiterate Portuguese, Italians, Spanish, Caribbean Islanders, and Aztecs when Columbus was making his voyages. These stories may help students relate better to the people of that time when they hear the folktales, fables, and legends that these people told. They may thus be better able to take the point of view of these people who were impacted by Columbus's actions.

Karen Wanamaker (1996) dresses up in period costume to tell tales from Laura Ingalls Wilder's history. She is able to set a mood that draws the listeners into the time period very effectively with her authentic dress. Children love to examine the unusual attire, and it adds to their appreciation of the daily lives of women from that time in history.

Barbara Blair (1991) tells stories in the role of Sarah Godbertson, an English housewife from the 17th century, who was married three times and widowed twice. Her stories include how each of Sarah's husbands was chosen and the reasons that she married them, illuminating family life and mortality in the 1600s, a topic appropriate for history or sociology class.

Other historical characters are routinely portrayed by storytellers who have studied their lives in depth. Ralph Archbold as Benjamin Franklin, Alice McGill as Sojourner Truth, Dan Bassuk as Abraham Lincoln, and Karen Golden as either Amelia Earhart or Pancho Barnes (one of the first female stunt pilots) are a few examples (Brown, 1991). As a teacher you may want to choose a character to portray, but be aware that you must do a great deal of research and put much energy into such a project. If the prospect of taking on a character to that extent is daunting to you, but you recognize the value of it in the curriculum, you may prefer to arrange a class visit from a professional storyteller in your area who has done this extensive preparation.

You may want to portray the daily lives of ordinary people during a particular time period, perhaps Americans who stayed at home during World War I and suffered the effects of the war in a way different from that of the combatants. You may want to especially focus on local history, to help the students see the connections that people they know may have with the past.

Other cautions are to avoid anachronistic dialogue and to avoid letting costuming overpower the story. Modern language in a story set in the past destroys the authenticity, and too much attention to costumes may shift the focus away from the story itself (Ellis, 1997).

Elizabeth Ellis tells stories about heroic women, such as Mary McLeod Bethune (African-American teacher), Delia Ackley (explorer), and Margaret Sanger (founder of Planned Parenthood), partly because they are a way to fight sexist and racist attitudes. She likes to show students history through the eyes of women and minorities, an unusual perspective for many students, who have primarily been exposed to a white, male perspective. However, she also does it because she thinks that you can't hate a person once you know his or her story (Shaw, 1993).

There are many stories that can be used when teaching about the Civil War, or, as it is known in many sources, the War of the Rebellion. Storyteller Craig Roney (1994) has adapted a Civil War story originally written by Ambrose Bierce that gives a chilling picture of the conflict. He calls the story "A Cold Night." It can be found in *Tales as Tools* from the National Storytelling Press (1994) and *Once Upon a Folktale* by Gloria Blatt (1993). Craig suggests using the story to teach facts about the Battle of Stones River, to introduce new vocabulary words, to show use of troop-movement maps of the battle, and to initiate discussion about many aspects of the war. He also suggests storytelling about the war, creation of art projects, and writing activities to follow the experience (National Storytelling Association, 1994).

A family story from the War of the Rebellion is shared by Charles A. Sherrill, Director of Public Services, Tennessee State Library and Archives:

When I was a boy, my grandfather told me the story of what happened to HIS grandfather during the Civil War. His grandfather was a wealthy plantation owner named Bird Henson. (I always remembered this because the name seemed so strange to me.)

Bird lived near the town of Pikeville in the Sequatchie Valley of Tennessee. He was too old to fight in the Civil War, so he stayed at home. During the war a troop of Union Army men marched into the Sequatchie Valley and set up their camp on Bird's land. They tore down his fences and burned them for firewood; they trampled his fields and ruined his crops; and they stole all the livestock and everything else they could find from the plantation. But they were under orders not to molest the citizens, so they left Bird and his family alone.

Then one night three men snuck into the house and pushed Bird into a chair in the parlor. They demanded to know where he had buried his money. He wouldn't tell, so they took a hot poker from the fire and held it to his bare feet.

His little daughter, Addie, heard what was happening and snuck out of the house. She ran across the footbridge, going to a neighbor's house for help. When she ran across the bridge, the planks rattled loudly. The men in the house, hearing that commotion, thought someone was coming to the house, so they ran off. That little girl's noise was the only thing that saved Bird Henson and his family from losing all their money to the Yankees.

This story was met by gasps of horror by the audience. Then Mr. Sherrill authenticated his family story with this word on historical research.

Years later, in doing research on my family, I found a letter in the National Archives that makes me think this family story has some truth in it. It was written September 29, 1863, by Capt. George S. Clark of the 15th Pennsylvania Cavalry. Capt. Clark reported, in part, "I have the honor to report that an abundance of forage exists in the Sequatchie (Hog Trough) Valley, there not having been any forage trains in that section previous to the 26th day of September, when I reached there....The road is...steep...but smooth...it being 1 1/2 miles from the top of the ridge to its foot, where lives Mr. Henson, a wealthy man and a rebel. Out of his abundant cornfields we loaded our wagons." Of course, Clark wouldn't report officially about all the other damage done to Bird Henson's farm, but to me this one clue buried in the Archives was enough to confirm an old story passed down through the generations (Sherrill, 1997).

This story shows how each family's history makes up a part of the history of our nation and how family stories that have been passed down orally can help us to understand more about events in times past. This story would make the horrors of war distressingly obvious to students.

Sparky Rucker is an African-American storyteller who portrays black cowboys and black soldiers, dressing the parts. He tells true stories about slavery, including one about an ancestor of his who was sold on the auction block and separated from her mother without being allowed to say goodbye. He also adds appropriate music to his presentations. He believes that he helps young audiences feel a link to their ancestors (Shaw, 1993). You may know of other African-American storytellers who could share similar stories and music with your students, or you may be able to do much of it yourself.

Historical tales are everywhere. In trying to locate tales related to Pennsylvania State Parks, Hamilton (1986) found stories about a Russian prince who became a priest in the wilds of Central Pennsylvania, wildcat loggers, railroad ghosts, hunters, trappers, and Indians from the past.

In Chicago's Field Museum of Natural History there is an Africa Exhibit that offers visitors a chance to learn about Africa, partly through storytelling. In the hull of a slave ship, a videotape of a woman, a teenager, and two men telling stories in African languages (Ibo, Wallof, Hausa, and Yoruba) gradually changes to English and Spanish. These individuals tell about their capture and enslavement. A visit here would make a wonderful field trip for students in the area, because the telling of the stories in the African languages as well as English makes them have more impact and gives more feeling of "being there." Teachers in other areas may be able to locate resource people who speak other languages and are able to provide a similar experience for students.

When studying about Abraham Lincoln, you may wish to tell stories about how a young girl influenced him to grow a beard, some of his own anecdotes about his Illinois childhood, and how he used his sense of humor. You may also want to include a story or two from African-American folklore about how he visited plantations in disguise to find out how slaves were treated. In these stories, he treats slaves kindly, reflecting the sentiments of the black population of that era (Garcia-Barrio, 1986).

Storyteller Ray Gray tells stories about the Battle of Gettysburg through the voices of two fictional 13-year-olds. He remembers not liking school very much, and he liked to intake ideas in the context of stories, so now he goes into schools to hook students on learning (Shaw, 1993).

Source books for both you and your students to use in order to prepare good stories about the Civil War are *Bull Run* by Paul Fleischman (1993) and *Now Is Your Time!* by Walter Dean Myers (1991). Myers provides a nonfiction presentation, whereas Fleischman has created sixteen fictional characters from different walks of life and presented their thoughts and experiences during the war. Fleischman's book would be good for students to use to develop a reader's theater script or short skits for presentation to the rest of the class.

Freedman's *Children of the West* (1983) would be good source material for stories about the experiences of pioneer families as they traveled west in Conestoga wagons and settled down on the frontier. This book also contains information about Native American children.

For a gripping account of the famous Chicago fire of 1871, Murphy's *The Great Fire* (1995) can be consulted. Students can compare his carefully researched account with the many stories that have circulated about this historic event.

Teaching the horrors of the Holocaust is difficult, at best, because it is hard for students to take in the atrocities that occurred. First-person accounts of events, not just of the brutality but, also of the heroic deeds of many who sought to save the endangered people and/or fight back against the menace, may be the most effective way to introduce this painful period of history. Friedman (1986) tells of the reaction of students who said that they had not understood the Holocaust until they heard her tell the stories of its effect on people their age. They also showed ignorance of the persecution of Christians as well as Jews. Some of the stories that she tells are in the book *Escape or Die: True Stories of Young People Who Survived the Holocaust* (Friedman, 1982).

In a study of the Holocaust, a tellable story that is accessible for younger students, but still powerful for secondary students (and adults), is *Terrible Things* (Bunting, 1980). This story is an allegory that makes its point quite thoroughly.

Bill Coates is a sixth-grade teacher who leads his classes to become storytellers through a social studies project that starts at a cemetery. The students find the grave of a 19th-century pioneer that has an epitaph. The children follow a paper trail through county courthouses and various other locations, searching for letters, diaries, census data, deeds, death certificates, and obituaries to help them reconstruct the person's life history. They even collaborate with students in the town where their subject was born in order to get more information. They also look at the significant local and national events that occurred during the subject's life. Finally, they assume the person's identity and write a diary, including only facts. The book is published with the help of the local historical society and parent volunteers. The project is concluded with a tribute to the subject at the gravesite, where the students tell the story they have uncovered (Shaw, 1993).

Studies of Native Americans should contain factual stories like the one about Sequoyah at the beginning of this chapter; factual ones about more contemporary Native Americans, such as Wilma Mankiller; and examples of the folk literature. Folk literature of Native Americans should not be treated as if it were the same for all tribes. Indeed, the stories vary widely among groups. Both Sequoyah and Wilma Mankiller might be involved in a study of the

Cherokee. In that study, *Cherokee* folklore would be included. The following folktale from the Cherokee could be used:

[This story was told by Martha Sauceman from Texas. She now lives in Silver Point, Tennessee. Her mother was a full-blooded Cherokee.]

Back when the earth was young, the Great Spirit left his paints where his children could get them. The raven was jealous that the Great Spirit had made his brother the eagle so beautiful. The raven persuaded the beautiful eagle to try to paint him to be beautiful. When the eagle had finished, Raven looked into the river. The raven hated what he saw and became very angry. He fought with the beautiful eagle. During this battle, the Great Spirit's paints were spilled. The colors mixed and fell onto the raven making him all black—black head, black eyes, and black breast. The raven dove into the river to try to wash off the ugly blackness that had engulfed him. The color would not wash off, because it was indelible. The Great Spirit told the raven that he would forever be blackened because of his hatred of the eagle's beauty.

Geography

Geography, like history, can be illuminated by appropriate stories. Tales of the hardships of westward travel in the days of Conestoga wagons and oxen, rather than interstate highways, can make the natural features of the land, such as mountains, lakes, and rivers, take on significance in the minds of the listeners that they may not have had before. Or you may make use of fictional characters to focus on natural features: one teacher told stories about how Paul Bunyan made the Great Lakes. She had the children look at the lakes on the map when she told the stories, making the entertaining and outrageous stories a link to the real lakes. She then let the students choose another location and make up a tall tale about how Paul Bunyan affected it (Pearmain, 1991). This lesson may have culminated with the students sharing their stories orally, or they may have committed them to written form.

Bryce Steven's story in Chapter 1 would be a good one to use when studying the area around Mount St. Helens or when studying volcanic eruptions and their effects on the surrounding countryside. Stories such as the ones in the book *Pele: Goddess of Hawaii's Volcanoes* (Kane, 1987) could be used for the same purpose when studying the volcanic Hawaiian Islands. The picture book *The Village of Round and Square Houses* by Ann Grifalconi (1986) could be used for a similar purpose when studying African geography in primary grades.

The Story of the Chinaman's Hat by Dean Howell (1990) is a picture book with an interesting fanciful story about the origin of an island in Hawaii. It could also be used as a vehicle to lead the children to trace a route from China to Hawaii on a globe.

The picture book *Grandfather's Journey* (Say, 1993) could be told while showing the pictures of the various bodies of water and landforms. The journeys could also be traced on a map or globe.

A discussion of bodies of water and the building of canals could lead to singing the song "Erie Canal" and locating the Erie Canal on a map. More information on use of music is found in Chapter 8.

The story *Sweet Clara and the Freedom Quilt* by Deborah Hopkinson (1993) can be told, and the use of the quilt as a map to freedom discussed. Other stories that involve journeys, such as the Laura Ingalls Wilder *Little House* books, can be used to construct maps of the travels of the characters.

Current Events

Storytelling is also a valid component of current events. Politicians, for example, tell story after story to sway people to their points of view. But storytelling may play a less flamboyant part in community affairs. Communities that treasure the stories of their pasts may move more readily to cooperate to control their futures. Niemi (1986) says, "In community organizing, storytelling functions as a mirror and a hammer. As a mirror, it reflects the lives and values of the community. As a hammer, it shapes the dreams and strategies for getting to 'happily ever after.'" Happily ever after may be related to such issues as nuclear safety procedures or environmental concerns, for example. Students can be helped to see how proponents of causes use story to further their causes, and they can be taught to recognize and resist propaganda in story form. One way to make them familiar with such propaganda is to have them develop a story designed to further a cause they choose. Using the technique themselves sensitizes them to its characteristics. Storytelling is as old as civilization, but it is as current as today in its ability to inform and persuade.

Storytelling may also be used to heal wounds caused by current events. When Hurricane Hugo hit South Carolina in 1989, children in two elementary schools were helped to make videos of their stories and those of others who lived through the hurricane. The children taped each other's stories and the stories of other people in the community. They further used their creativity by writing and performing raps about the storm. They used vivid images of the wind, the noise, and the devastation left behind by the storm. The children generally chose the more upbeat stories to put on the tape, but there was undoubtedly value in the darker stories that were told only for their classmates (Nash, 1991).

Since crime is frequently in the news, you may want to use a story like the personal story Gail Hyder told in Chapter 3 to link the concerns about crime in the abstract to a particular crime that affected children's lives. Unfortunately, if you begin with a story like this one, you may be able to collect an appalling number of personal stories about brushes that your students or their families have had with crime, opening the door to a more personal discussion of the problem.

For What Instructional Purposes Can You Use Storytelling?

Storytelling can be used profitably for a number of different purposes. It can be used in introductory, basic instructional, and extension roles.

First, storytelling can be used to introduce a unit or lesson in order to promote interest in the topic to be studied and to build background information about the topic that will help the students understand the material in the textbook.

Storytelling can also provide much basic content for the body of a unit, as the teacher passes along material that is not covered or is inadequately covered by the book and the supplementary readings available to the students. It can also be used by the students to present information during the progress of a unit, when they have interviewed primary sources or collected information from printed sources that the other students have not read.

Finally, storytelling is a good extension activity, for students can go beyond the original scope of the unit and read additional sources that they share with their classmates through storytelling. Groups of students can also construct and tell stories based on the material that they have just studied in an effort to internalize it more fully. They may then present these stories to their own classmates or students in other classes who are studying the material.

Another extension activity related to storytelling that students might take part in is listening to storytelling tapes by professional storytellers and primary sources and scripting one or more of the stories for a reader's theater presentation.

The possibilities are only limited by class time and the imaginations of you and your students. Remember stories as a high interest entry into your content.

Eager to find out how Sequoyah dealt with his crushing setback, the students leaned forward, listening intently.

Sequoyah moved to a cabin in the woods to start over. His daughter, Ahyoka, joined him and helped him with his work. Using white men's writing—that he could not speak or read—he borrowed many

marks from their alphabet and gave them Cherokee sounds, but he needed more marks, so he had to devise some new symbols.

Some people in Coosa thought Sequoyah's writing was a way of casting bad spells, and they were afraid. They burned his cabin and all of his work on the syllabary, but Sequoyah remembered his symbols this time. He wrote them on a large piece of buckskin.

Sequoyah decided that he needed to leave Alabama, so he and his daughter moved west to Arkansas, where Sequoyah married Sally, a Cherokee woman who believed in his dream. With her encouragement, he finished his syllabary.

Sequoyah wanted to take his syllabary as a gift to the tribal council, so he and his daughter, who had learned to read all eighty-six symbols, returned to Tennessee. The leaders were hostile when he spoke of his writing system. Sequoyah wrote words and his daughter read them, but the leaders thought it was a trick or a spell he had put on Ahyoka.

Finally, in desperation, Sequoyah sent his daughter to the far end of the village, away from him and the leaders. The leaders dictated words for Sequoyah to write. Then his daughter came back and read the words. Then the procedure was reversed, and the daughter wrote messages that Sequoyah read. The leaders were almost convinced. They allowed Sequoyah to teach several young men to read and held a similar test for them. At last the doubts were gone!

Sequoyah and Ahyoka taught others to read. Many people learned rapidly, some in a month or less. When they returned to Arkansas, they took letters written by Cherokees to family and friends. Literacy spread quickly among the Cherokee.

Eventually, the Cherokee started a newspaper, printed in both Cherokee and English, the Cherokee Phoenix. *The Tribal Council in 1824 presented Sequoyah with a silver medal carved with two crossed pipes, symbols of the Eastern and Western Cherokees he had joined through his alphabet. He finally was given the honor he deserved for his outstanding achievement.*

 Suggested Activities for the Teacher

1.   Make a list of the units that you teach during the year for one or more history or geography classes. Picture the events, places, and people that you would like to have the students remember from these units. Choose

several that you think would be appropriate as the subject of a story telling presentation, such as the one on Sequoyah in this chapter.

2. Gather material from which to craft stories about each subject that you identified in Activity 1. Start with the topic that you plan to present first in class, and read all of the background information that you have on that topic. Choose a focus for the story that you want to tell, such as a major accomplishment of an individual, the account of an event and its aftermath, the effect of a geographical feature on a particular event or on the lives of a group of people, or something similar. Also choose a point of view from which the story will be told.

Develop a beginning that draws the audience into the story by setting up an unusual situation, introducing an interesting character, or beginning in the middle of exciting action. Tell your story in sequence, using information from the many sources that you have consulted, weaving them into a coherent whole. Close with a satisfying, if not necessarily happy, ending.

Practice this story until you have made it your own and can tell it naturally and comfortably. Then share it with your students at an appropriate time in the unit.

Repeat this process with as many stories as you have the interest in and time for developing. They will enliven your classroom.

3. Locate resource information about the origins of several place names, local and otherwise. Share the stories of these names and your process with your students.

Suggested Activities for Use with Students

1. Ask your students to read the material in the book and passages in supplementary materials that you have located (possibly reference books, trade books, and printouts from Internet searches, for example) about a person, event, or place. Let the students work in small groups to construct stories based on this person, event, or place. Let each student learn the story that his or her group developed, practice it within the group until he or she can tell it well, and then join a new group—reconstituted so that it is composed of one student from each of the original groups—and tell the story to them, listening in turn to the stories that they have developed.

Even if all of the groups have the same assignment and the same resource materials, the stories are likely to be different. Class discussion can center around the differences in the stories and why certain groups emphasized certain aspects of the person, event, or place, whereas other groups did not.

2. Have individual students craft stories on people, places, or events of their choice, based upon extensive self-selected reading about some aspect of unit content. Give them a chance to practice in pairs or small groups in order to fine-tune their stories based on feedback from classmates. Then let them present their stories to the whole class as a part of a special program that highlights students' creative work.

3. Have students interview local people who have lived through historical events, taping the interviews with permission. Then have the students craft the results of the interview into a story or a series of stories to add to a class eyewitness history archive or book to be read by current classmates and students who take the class in the future.

4. Have students research the origins of local place names or the place names that are found in a current unit of study. They may use print sources or Internet searches in their research. Let them share the stories behind the place names with the class. The class may want to produce a class book of place name origin stories for use by others in the school.

References

Black, J. (1992). Creating the history story. *Storytelling World, 1* (Summer/Fall), 3-4.

Blair, B. (1991). Tips for telling from history. *Yarnspinner, 15* (December), 1-2.

Blatt, G. T. (1993). *Once upon a folktale: Capturing the folklore process with children*. New York: Teachers College Press.

Brown, F. (1991). Character building. *Storytelling, 3* (Fall), 8-11.

Bunting, E. (1980). *Terrible things*. Philadelphia, PA: The Jewish Publication Society.

Colson, T. (1990). How to conduct an oral-history interview. *Yarnspinner, 14* (August), 5.

Ellis, E. (1997). Researching and crafting the history story. *Storytelling World* (Winter/Spring), 7-8.

Ellis, R. (1994). Helping students connect with history. In The National Storytelling Press, *Tales as tools* (pp. 124-128). Jonesborough, TN: The National Storytelling Press.

Feldman, D. (1993). An introduction to Africa. *Storytelling Magazine, 5* (Fall), 4-5.

Fleischman, P. (1993). *Bull Run*. New York: Scholastic.

Foreman, G. (1938). *Sequoyah*. Norman, OK: University of Oklahoma Press.

Freedman, R. (1983). *Children of the wild west*. New York: Scholastic.

Friedman, I. R. (1982). *Escape or die: True stories of young people who survived the Holocaust*. Reading, MA: Addison-Wesley.

Friedman, I. R. (1986). The preservation of history through the oral tradition. *The National Storytelling Journal, 3* (Spring), 15-17.

Garcia-Barrio, C. (1986). Gifts from home: African folklore in the Americas. *The National Storytelling Journal, 3* (Spring), 10-14.

Golden, K. (1994). History happened a day at a time. In The National Storytelling Press, *Tales as tools* (pp. 129-130). Jonesborough, TN: The National Storytelling Press.

Grifalconi, A. (1986). *The village of round and square houses.* Boston: Little, Brown.

Hamilton, J. (1986). State parks and storytelling. *The National Storytelling Journal, 3* (Spring), 7-9.

Hopkinson, D. (1993). *Sweet Clara and the freedom quilt.* New York: Alfred A. Knopf.

Howell, D. (1990). *The story of the Chinaman's hat.* Aiea, HI: Island Heritage Publishing.

Kane, H. K. (1987). *Pele: Goddess of Hawaii's volcanoes.* Captain Cook, HI: The Kawainui Press.

King, D. H., & Chapman, J. (1988). *The Sequoyah legacy.* Vonore, TN: Sequoyah Birthplace Museum.

Mooney, J. (1992). *History, myths, and sacred formulas of the Cherokees.* Asheville, NC: Historical Images.

Murphy, J. (1995). *The great fire.* New York: Scholastic.

Myers, W. D. (1990). *Now is your time!* New York: Scholastic.

Nash, J. (1991). Gleanings: Stories from a whirlwind. *Storytelling Magazine, 3* (Fall), 4-5.

National Storytelling Association, The. (1994). *Tales as tools.* Jonesborough, TN: The National Storytelling Press.

Niemi, L. (1986). Some considerations of political storytelling. *The National Storytelling Journal, 3* (Spring), 24-25.

Oppenheim, J. (1979). *Sequoyah: Cherokee hero.* Mexico: Troll Associates.

Pearmain, E. (1991). Searching for ways to bring stories into your home or classroom? *Yarnspinner, 15* (December), 5.

Petersen, D. (1991). *Sequoyah: Father of the Cherokee alphabet.* Chicago, IL: Children's Press.

Roop, P., & Roop, C. (1992). *Ahyoka and the talking leaves.* New York: Beech Tree.

Roney, R. C. (1994). The civil war as seen through story. In The National Storytelling Press, *Tales as tools* (pp. 120-123). Jonesborough, TN: The National Storytelling Press.

Sauceman, M. (1996). Raven story. Personal communication.

Say, A. (1993). *Grandfather's journey.* New York: Scholastic.

Shaw, K. (1993). Recalling forgotten lives. *Storytelling Magazine, 5* (Fall), 14-18.

Sherrill, C. A. (1997). Family story from the Civil War. Personal communication.

Starkey, M. L. (1973). *The Native Americans of the Cherokee nation.* North Dighton, MA: JG Press.

Wanamaker, K. (1996). Learning from Laura. A presentation at the

Tennessee Reading Association Conference, Gatlinburg, TN, December.

Young, R. A., & Young, J. D. (1992). *Stories from the days of Christopher Columbus*. Little Rock, AR: August House.

Chapter 10
Using Storytelling to Enhance Learning in Math and Science

"Another trickster tale, p-l-e-a-s-e!" begged Tyler as he got ready for bed. Sandy had previously chosen Coyote and Rabbit stories to share with him; but tonight she decided to introduce him to a new character, Raven. In this Pacific Northwest Native American *pourquoi* tale, the origin of daylight, the origin of fire, and the formation of inland lakes are explained through the adventures of Raven (Feldmann, 1965). Sandy began her story:

⚜

A long, long time ago when the world was brand new, it was dark. The people had to exist in this darkness without benefit of fire or fresh water. It was a difficult time for all. Gray Eagle had been appointed the keeper of the sun, fire, and water. He did not like people at all and was determined to keep these precious things from them.

It was during this time that Raven saw Gray Eagle's beautiful daughter and immediately fell in love with her. Gray Eagle's daughter was quite interested in Raven, also for, you see, at this time when the world was new, Raven was a beautiful white bird. Everyone admired his snowy-white feathers and would stop and look at him when he flew by.

Gray Eagle's daughter issued an invitation to Raven. He was supposed to visit her at her father's lodge. When Raven approached the lodge, he saw a strange light coming from within the lodge. He had never seen this light before, so he approached it cautiously and very quietly peered inside. Inside the lodge, Raven saw the beautiful daughter of Gray Eagle, but what he saw in the center of the lodge and what was hanging on the side of the lodge captured his attention most. Immediately, Raven realized the value of what he saw and knew what he must do to help his people.

"Hmmm," responded Tyler, as a furrow formed between his brows, "I wonder if...?" Sandy smiled in response to his reaction. Just as she had hoped, Tyler's imagination was engaged. He was actively involved in the story, listening intently and making his own predictions.

How Can You Use Storytelling to Teach Critical Thinking?

The areas of science and mathematics involve problem solving, which depends on critical thinking. In classrooms that emphasize critical thinking skills, students are provided opportunities to solve problems, make inferences, draw conclusions, analyze and evaluate information, and form decisions. While motivational and entertaining, storytelling also provides numerous resources for the application of critical thinking skills.

Storytelling can be used as a strategy to teach and model desired thinking skills in any curriculum area, at any grade level. MacDonald suggests "you can use stories to teach concepts and ideas and morals" (Mooney & Holt, 1996, p. 146).

A group of middle school gifted education students, listening to the following Aesop's Fable, were not only entertained; but, through the telling of the story, they were provided a model for successful experimentation, problem solving, and the demonstration of the scientific principle of displacement.

A very, very thirsty crow came upon a pitcher sitting in the grass. The pitcher was half full of cool, crystal-clear water. The crow tried desperately to take a drink but found it was impossible because his beak was just not long enough to reach the water. Over and over again, he repeated his attempts to reach the water with his beak and was just about to give up in despair when he hit upon a plan. He looked all around and spied exactly what he thought he needed. He went over to the edge of the grass and began picking up pebbles and carrying them back to the pitcher. He carefully placed each pebble on the grass. When he thought he had collected enough, he began dropping the pebbles into the pitcher, one by one. With each pebble the water rose a little higher, a little higher, and a little higher, until at

last it reached the brim of the pitcher. Finally satisfied, the clever
crow was able to drink his fill and quench his thirst.
The moral of this fable: Necessity is the mother of invention.

Following the lesson introduction for the gifted education class, the students brainstormed and categorized strategies used by the crow in order to solve the problem. The students identified the crow's abilities to investigate, inquire, and evaluate. The group's discussion continued, with the students demonstrating a great deal of interest.

The lesson's closure included a review of the brainstormed list of strategies and an explanation of how important problem-solving strategies are in learning concepts. The students stated that, in their opinion, it was very important that individuals understand and develop critical thinking skills in order to be more effective in the areas of math and science.

In this gifted education class, storytelling provided the introduction to an instructional unit for math and science. In an evaluative summary of the unit, the students responded that stories made the material much more "fun, challenging, and stimulating." Several students commented on how the stories helped them to understand the information better. One student wrote, "when I listened to the stories, I felt as if I was an eyewitness to what was happening."

Storytelling is a versatile tool to teach critical thinking skills. It can be used to share new information and present the problem that is to be solved. Storytelling activates background knowledge and helps to establish an individual connection with the new information for each student. Teachers can effectively model the efforts of others in problem-solving attempts by simply sharing selected stories as part of their instructional plan.

How Can Storytelling Be Incorporated into Mathematics Instruction?

As young children interact with their environments, concepts are developed, associations are made, and learning occurs. Many young children appear to integrate the learning of concepts from different disciplines with ease, even in early developmental stages. Evidence of this integration exists in a number of games and activities engaged in by young students. Jump rope jingles, counting rhymes, and counting songs are examples of the integration of oral narration and mathematics, as well as tactile and/or kinesthetic involvement.

The language reflected in these activities is often repetitive and rhythmic. Some of the activities may have originated centuries ago, while others are spontaneously created by the participants to meet their immediate needs. As with other folklore, variants of the games and activities exist throughout a number of cultures.

Counting

Counting games, such as "Eeny, meeny, miney, mo...," and elimination games such as, "one potato, two potato, three potato, four...," are popular examples of integrating the disciplines of math and storytelling (Livo & Rietz, 1991). "Seven Little Rabbits" (Becker, 1995) is an interactive story poem involving counting. As the events of the story unfold, the student counts backwards from seven. Then the story shifts, and the student counts forward to seven. The repetition in the poem encourages the younger students to join in as the teacher shares the poem.

The following jump rope rhymes were the most requested by students in Sandy's youngest special education class. The jump rope activity was selected as a technique to reinforce counting and develop gross motor skills. The story format of the jingle also encouraged language development. All members of the class would circle around the student/jumper and would chant the rhyme and count the number of jumps in unison:

Cinderella, dressed in yellow
Went upstairs to kiss her fella.
She made a mistake
And kissed a snake.
How many doctors, did it take? 1, 2, 3, 4, 5, 6....
(Counting continues until the student misses the jump.)

Johnny over the ocean
Johnny over the sea
Johnny broke a milk bottle
and blamed it on me.
I told Ma
And Ma told Pa.
Johnny got a lickin',
Ha, Ha, Ha.
1, 2, 3, 4, 5, 6,....
(Counting continues until the student misses the jump.)

Problem Solving

In the discipline of mathematics, students often use known information to arrive at a solution that is unknown. Storytelling can provide the necessary introductory information in an interesting way. The problem-solving adventure can begin with a story that encourages inquiry.

Storytelling creates the need for the student to apply critical thinking skills and discover that problems are often opportunities to use familiar strategies to arrive at solutions. Repeated integration of stories with math and science provides models of effective problem solving and impacts the student's attempts to identify solutions. When the teacher shares a story to introduce a science or math concept and solve a stated problem, the student has the option of selecting an unfamiliar strategy demonstrated by a character in a story, using a strategy with which he/she has had experience, or possibly combining efforts, both new and familiar. Stories with related science and math activities encourage the application, analysis, and evaluation of different problem-solving approaches.

"The Mathematician" (Sherman, 1992) and "Dividing the Horses" (Shannon, 1985) are variants of the following story puzzle that requires students to apply knowledge of common denominators, equivalent fractions, and division of fractions:

❧

Down the road, just outside of town, there lived a man. He had a wife and three sons, whom he loved greatly. The man had worked very hard, all his life, and what money he had saved, he had spent on his farm. A few years ago, he became very ill, and he called his family to his bedside. This is what he said, "Sally, you are my wife; I want you to keep the house and land. John, you are my eldest; I want you to have one-half of what I own. Tom, you are my second son; I want you to have one-third of what I own. Daniel, you are my youngest son; I want you to have one-ninth of what I own." Soon, thereafter, the man died.

After the funeral, the family returned to the farm and began dividing what the man owned. To their surprise, the sons discovered that the only thing the man owned, other than the house and land, was seventeen mules. Even though they tried and tried, they just couldn't figure out how to divide the seventeen mules by the fractions their father had determined.

Calmly, the mother said to her sons, "Oh, please let us not worry. I think I know how to solve this problem."

She left the farm and walked next door where she borrowed another mule. She put it in the field with the seventeen mules and proceeded to divide the eighteen mules among the sons. The eldest son received one-half, which was 9 mules. The second son received one-third, which was 6 mules; and the youngest son received one-ninth, which was two mules.

She smiled at her sons and counted to make sure she had cor-

rectly solved the problem. Then she said, "Now, didn't I tell you we could solve this problem? Nine plus six plus two equals seventeen. That is what your father wanted."

After that, the woman took the extra mule and returned it to the neighbor from whom she had borrowed it.

What did the woman do to solve the problem?

Students are encouraged to use their math skills to solve the question presented in the story. Through the character's efforts, as well as group discussion, you discover that the fractions used by the father to divide his possessions, when added together, do not equal one whole. In order to complete the steps to arrive at the solution, the mother recognized that she needed to identify a common denominator in order to divide the whole into the prescribed fractions. The common denominator of 2, 3, and 9 is 18. Her next step was to convert the fractions into the equivalent fractions, 9/18, 6/18, and 2/18. Next, she added the fractions together and calculated the answer to equal 17/18. Then she successfully divided the mules among the three sons, just as the father requested. Once she had divided the mules, she took the extra one and returned it to the neighbor. (Don't try this with an estate lawyer!)

Times Tables the Fun Way (Rodriguez, 1995) is a commercially published program that combines the learning of the multiplication tables with the use of pictures and stories. Additional program materials provide the graphic displays that help to establish the important visual images that accompany the stories and serve as mnemonic devices to help remember the multiplication problems. One of the most popular stories in Vickie Moore's third grade is the one featuring the multiplication problem "4 times 4 equals 16." This particular story features a four-wheel drive (4 x 4) truck that you must be 16 years old to drive.

Math Journals

Currently, many teachers are integrating portfolios and authentic assessment into their instructional programs. The documents contained in a portfolio reflect student learning in a variety of instructional areas. In the curriculum area of mathematics, math journals are often maintained and used as a source for potential portfolio documents. The implementation of math journals provides opportunities for the students to use both teacher- and student-created stories as prompts and/or explanations for mathematical calculations. A sample of an original teacher-created story prompt follows:

Once upon a time the third grade classes at Rickman Elementary School planned a field trip to Opryland in Nashville, Tennessee. Every student in both classes brought in a permission slip to attend. The two classroom teachers and four parents would also attend. One third grade section had 24 students, while the other section had 25. The special admission price for a school group was $10.00 for each student. Adult tickets were $14.00 each. The group also had to pay the bus driver $30.00 for driving them to Nashville. How much money do the third grade classes need to collect in order to make their trip and live happily ever after?

Students solved the problem and demonstrated the calculations in their journals. Teacher-created story prompts integrated storytelling and modeled the connection between abstract math concepts and language. Students were also encouraged to create their own original story explanations from basic calculation problems. These stories were written in the students' journals and shared in class or in cooperative learning groups to explain the thinking process with the support of words, pictures, or objects documented in the journals.

Lisa Morrison (1997) relates a technique that integrates geometry and storytelling. Geometric shapes are introduced by giving them character names, such as Miss Poly Gon and Mr. Quadri Lateral. Each character is described in detail, with the shape and form indicating specific personality characteristics. Miss Poly Gon and Mr. Quadri Lateral marry and produce numerous "children" or other quadrilaterals. Each "child" is named and described in detail. The story can be highly motivational and effective in teaching the recognition and properties of different quadrilaterals. The strategy could help meet the learning needs of a variety of students and could be used to either introduce or close a unit of study on quadrilaterals.

Storytelling aids the teacher in providing an authentic purpose for the use of math skills. A problem-solving exercise that uses an original story prompt or a retelling of a related story can suggest the need for such skills in the students' everyday lives. Storytelling demonstrates the parallels of ideas or concepts while maintaining interest and encouraging the retention of the material learned.

How Can Storytelling Be Incorporated into Science Instruction?

Both the effective scientist and the effective storyteller observe and collect data. Folktales originated as a result of people's observations and perceptions of their environment. In many folktales, animals are featured characters faced with humanlike dilemmas or problems. In order for the storyteller to have composed the story originally, he or she must have observed animals and their characteristics. In addition, he or she must also have collected knowledge and identified perceptions about human nature and the challenges for day-to-day existence.

The Aesop's fable of the "The Crow and the Pitcher," featured earlier in this chapter, illustrates the need for critical thinking but has also been used effectively to introduce a ministudy on inventions and discoveries. (See Appendix B for stories behind the origination of numerous inventions.) Many stories not only provide background or establish a historical account, they also provide a model for innovation. Knowing how a familiar object was created can be entertaining; but, more than that, it can demonstrate the importance of perseverance, problem solving, and creativity. Students can learn a great deal from stories about "the many ways inventors and scientists have succeeded despite discouraging setbacks" (Caney, 1985, p. 21).

Using Knowledge of Science to Create Stories

Using stories to demonstrate their knowledge in science can motivate creative students to master scientific concepts in order to make sure their stories are plausible. As part of an assignment in one of Suellen's classes, Martha Albright (1996) wrote a mystery story in which the reader was asked to use his or her knowledge of genetics to decide whether a number of characters were the biological children of a deceased millionaire. Martha's presentation to the class caused quite an animated discussion as students tried to determine which claimants could have been descendants based on their genetic characteristics, such as hair and eye color.

Teachers can use students' original stories to encourage the problem-solving efforts of the class. Pairing or grouping the students into teams and having them cooperatively brainstorm and think aloud throughout the learning process is an effective instructional technique. Once the solution has been identified, students might also develop a visual aid to demonstrate acceptable combinations of traits. Integrating a story with the study of scientific or mathematical principles strengthens the visual images and enhances the comprehension of the theory to be learned.

The discipline of science presents numerous opportunities to integrate storytelling. The developments in science and the growth of scientific knowledge form an all-inclusive story with a myriad of smaller stories contained within. Problem solving, creativity, and questioning are basic to scientific research. "Stories can give meaning to scientific concepts, by literally opening a child's mind, arousing curiosity, and encouraging a willingness to explore all the possibilities" (Sima, 1995, p. 20).

Early stories were often accounts of important events and accomplishments of an individual person or culture. The literature abounds with folklore that attempts to explain "why" through the use of story (Leotta, 1994). *Pourquoi* tales, also discussed in Chapter 11, are simple forms of myths that attempt to explain the world's natural elements (Sutherland, 1997).

The African folktale, *Why the Sun and the Moon Live in the Sky* (Dayrell, 1968), is an example of a *pourquoi* tale. It is an explanation in story form about the location of the sun, the moon, and water. Sima (1995) suggests using creative dramatics with this story, whereby students recreate the plot and develop visual images through the creative dramatics activity. The story allows for a number of students to participate with limited dialogue, while the teacher or another student serves as the narrator. This folktale and activity is an appropriate choice for introducing the water cycle or a unit in astronomy.

In *Emma's Dragon Hunt* (Stock, 1984), explanations for earthquakes, heat waves, solar eclipses, thunderstorms, and rainbows are explored by the central characters, Emma and her Grandfather Wong, who is visiting from China. This children's literature selection uses elements of the ancient Chinese dragon legends, crediting the mythical creatures with causing certain natural phenomena. It can be used as an introduction to the study of these phenomena.

The relationship between the Native American culture and the natural world, along with a rich storytelling tradition, results in many stories for enhancing science instruction. Many Native American folktales attempt to explain nature, as well as demonstrating respect for it. "The ecological lessons of science and North American Indian stories show us how to care for the Earth...we can help children to discover their own roles in maintaining this fragile balance for themselves" (Caduto & Bruchac, 1988, p. 5).

Sima (1995) suggests two ways you can implement storytelling into the science curriculum. You may begin with a selected story, examining it for relationships to science concepts that you plan to introduce in an instructional unit. Or you may begin with a specific science concept and search for a story to illustrate the concept. The important consideration is the selection of the story. You should select an appropriate story in which the students can identify the basic elements, such as characters, setting, sequence of events or plot, and resolution. It also needs to be simple enough so that the students can successfully retell the story to others.

The ability to identify story elements parallels the ability to follow the scientific process of forming a hypothesis. Much of the information used in science is gathered through observation and experimentation. Effective storytellers observe their surroundings and identify qualities that aid in the development of their stories. The plot of a narrative story follows a sequence much like the logical steps that lead to the formation of a scientist's hypothesis (Leotta, 1994).

Both storytelling and the study of science emphasize creative thinking.

Thinking creatively involves activating existing knowledge, gaining new information, taking risks, and exploring numerous possibilities. The process of creative thinking begins with observation. The ability to observe surroundings effectively is a basic skill in both storytelling and science. Nobel Prize winner Albert Szent-Gyorgyi says, "Discovery consists of looking at the same thing as everyone else and thinking something different" (von Oech, 1983, p. 7).

"Albert Einstein called imagination the greatest power of the human mind" (National Storytelling Association, 1994, p. 132). Storytelling gives a teacher an extremely powerful teaching tool for developing a student's imagination. When listening to a story, the student's imagination is activated and not confined by the need to decode the print. Background knowledge is stimulated and visual images are formed. Sima (1995, p. 20) states, "Storytelling leads students to experience and look at the world in a deeper way."

How Can You Use Biographical Stories to Generate Interest in Math and Science?

Biographical stories are usually the result of information collected through research. There is a great deal of effort maintained to present the story as accurately as possible. Biographers collect authentic research data in a variety of forms and preserve the information in written form. Many biographical selections are available for both adults and children. (See Appendix B for examples of biographical stories.)

The storyteller conducts research for original biographical stories and shares the information through oral language or narration. Sometimes storytellers research their chosen individuals throughout the literature, including published biographies, interviews, and other pertinent documents or related information that might enhance the details of the story.

Using biographical stories in the study of science and math is very effective. It is extremely important for students to understand that great scientists or mathematicians were or are real people, not fictitious characters. Many teachers are successful in emphasizing the importance of risk-taking in problem-solving efforts through the sharing of biographical stories.

Effective biographies present much detail about the featured character. When telling biographical stories, the storyteller is challenged to create the image of a person with whom the listeners can identify and associate. The use of biographies often provides models to enlighten and inspire the listener. Hearing a story about an individual with whom you identify can influence your own behavior patterns. This is extremely important for students who may not receive the encouragement to pursue their goals in reality.

Many biographies vividly describe the challenges and triumphs in the early lives of world-renowned scientists and mathematicians while they were working toward success in their fields. Sharing stories that depict successful individuals facing and dealing with day-to-day obstacles provides models for and reinforces the importance of effective problem-solving strategies. Through the use of stories, students can understand that few successes are immediate or instantaneous. Most inventions and scientific and mathematical discoveries are the result of years of persistent hard work, dedication, and divergent thinking. Many discoveries were made because the individual scientist or mathematician combined his or her knowledge with creativity to search for new possibilities. This desire to question and explore is exemplified in numerous biographies of scientists and mathematicians.

The story of Marie Curie, or Marya Sklodowska, was a favorite story shared during a science unit in Sandy's gifted education class. Curie's life was filled with many obstacles; yet her determination and fascination with science never wavered. Coping with children, continuing her education, and suffering the loss of her spouse made Marie Curie an individual with whom many students could empathize. The students observed that the same issues faced by Curie are contemporary issues with which individuals continue to struggle.

Balsamo (1987) shares several biographical sketches and ideas for activities in the teaching resource *Exploring the Lives of Gifted People in the Sciences*. A guided imagery activity, using a storytelling technique, is integrated into the introduction of an instructional unit on space science. The guided imagery activities are used to establish the mood through the use of a story format with background music. Biographical information about Sally Ride, the first American female astronaut, is included along with follow-up activities.

If you are planning a study of rocketry, *Many Voices: True Tales from America's Past* (Haven, 1995) offers a historical science story featuring Robert Goddard. Goddard is credited with inventing the first liquid-fueled rocket in 1926. The story emphasizes young Goddard's enthusiasm and excitement for science. It demonstrates his attempts at experimentation and describes his failures. Along with the story, there are several suggestions for activities, experiments, and questions. Following the use of Goddard's biography and the suggested activities, students should comprehend the importance of experimentation. Students should also realize that scientific experimentation involves learning from failed attempts.

The life of inventor and scientist Thomas Alva Edison was another popular biographical subject with the gifted education students. The students were extremely interested in the period of Edison's life when his friends and family all considered him a failure. Even though Edison worked at many different jobs, he never abandoned his interest in creating or inventing. The events in his life reveal a tenacity and creativity that ultimately led to significant contributions to society.

The story of Alexander Graham Bell and the invention of the telephone illustrates how experimentation may result in a different outcome than the inventor planned. Bell's scientific experiment was an effort to provide assistance to the deaf. While researching the plan for his communication aid, he happened upon the basic idea that led him to the design of the telephone. What he discovered was that the vibration of sound can be converted to electrical currents, which can then be transmitted through wires from one location to another. Even though some documented research by other inventors existed before Bell's efforts, he is credited with the actual implementation of the theory and the resulting product.

Even Bell's moment of discovery provides an interesting story for students. Bell and his assistant, Mr. Watson, were in different locations of the house prepared to test the invention. Only moments before the experiment was to take place, Bell spilled some acid on his coat. He immediately called for his assistant to help him, "Mr. Watson, come here! I want you!" Alexander Graham Bell's plea for help became the first transmitted message using the new invention, the telephone (Reader's Digest Association, 1976).

How Can You Use Stories of the Unexpected as a Motivational Technique?

For centuries, stories of unexpected scientific discoveries have been told. Many students find these extraordinary stories interesting and unique. The following story about an unknown prospector (Burke, 1978) might be used to introduce a science unit on metallurgy.

❧❀❧

Many centuries ago in western Turkey, while searching for gold, a prospector stumbled upon an unexpected discovery that impacted the world. On a mission for the king, the prospector was panning for gold in the Pactolus River.

The gold was panned, then smelted into small nuggets. The process of smelting was difficult and burdensome. Often, sheepskins were used to filter the gold and separate it from other substances collected from panning. Gold dust would become trapped in the greasy sheepskin. When filled, the fleece was hung and allowed to dry. At this point in the process, the fleece was extremely valuable. With the constant threat of theft, the fleece had to be carefully guarded and protected. There are stories still told today of a man called Jason and his followers, the Argonauts, whose quest to capture such a valuable fleece took them on many adventures.

When the fleece was dry it was placed in the fire and burned, leaving the gold, which was then melted into ingots. The weight of the ingots determined the value. After the value was assigned, the ingots were stamped and could be used as currency.

While panning for gold, the prospector noticed other stone fragments in the water. He observed what occurred when the larger gold pieces rubbed the surface of one of the flinty, black stones. When the stones were rubbed by pure gold, the scratch marks appeared yellow. Different colors resulted when they were rubbed with gold mixtures including silver or copper. The purity and value of the gold were now determined much more easily than before. Forgeries were easily identified by comparing scratch marks made by a suspect ingot with those made by pure gold. Evidence of the use of the flinty, black stone was recorded by Herodotus, a Greek historian. The stone was later identified by geologists as schist.

The unknown prospector changed the world forever with his accidental discovery. Not only did this discovery impact the science of metallurgy; it also influenced language. Its common name, reflecting the stone's original function, has been retained throughout the centuries and is still used today as a metaphor. The flinty, black stone, now identified as schist, was referred to as a touchstone. The term touchstone *is used today to express the idea of a set of criteria for evaluation. Even though his discovery was so important, the name of the prospector was never recorded and is still not known today.*

Combining stories and involvement of students in hands-on experiments can be an interesting and effective way to illustrate scientific principles and enrich the science curriculum. The following story illustrates the scientific principle of specific gravity and provides numerous enrichment opportunities for experimentation:

The quest for scientific knowledge has been valued for centuries. In many ancient civilizations, scientists were respected and often served as counselors to those in power.

King Hiero II of Sicily had a scientist whom he respected and depended on to help him solve problems that others could not solve. Archimedes was the scientist that King Hiero II called when he needed help with a particular problem.

One day, Hiero called Archimedes to him and told him of his dilemma. The king had recently commissioned the royal jeweler to create a new gold crown. Before the crown was officially presented to the king, gossip spread concerning the ornament. Eventually the stories reached the king. His crown was not 100 percent gold! He was furious! But before he could accuse his royal jeweler he knew he needed proof. So he called upon Archimedes to help him discover the truth about his crown. Archimedes listened to the king's request and then he pondered the dilemma. Archimedes thought and thought but could not come up with a solution. He knew the king depended on him to solve the problem and identify a way to prove that the crown was or was not 100 percent gold.

Archimedes was so preoccupied with finding his solution that there seemed to be nowhere he could escape it. He thought of nothing else, day after day. On one particular day, Archimedes was entering a tub filled with bath water and observed that when he lowered himself into the water a certain amount of water spilled over the sides. Suddenly he had his solution! He stood and shouted, "Eureka!" and ran naked from the bathhouse, through the streets, all the way home.

What Archimedes realized was that he had discovered a way to measure the volume of the crown to determine if it was indeed 100 percent gold. First, he weighed a quantity of gold and a quantity of silver. Some gossips had told that the royal jeweler had mixed both gold and silver to create the crown; therefore, Archimedes had to compare the weights of the metals. He determined that the same weight of gold and silver had different volumes. When he placed the two quantities into separate containers of water, the silver caused more water to spill over.

Archimedes concluded that when a solid object sinks, it displaces water equal to its volume. He then continued his experiment and placed a piece of pure gold that had the same weight as the crown in one container filled with water. He placed the crown into a second container identical to the first and containing the same amount of water. Sure enough, the crown made a greater amount of water spill over than the pure gold did. This experiment proved that the royal jeweler was guilty; he had not created a crown of pure gold (Jones & Wilson, 1987).

The story of Hanson Gregory's cooking innovation provides an opportunity for exploring accidental or unexpected discoveries. Follow-up cooking activities allow students to discover how scientific principles can be observed in many ways. Even the everyday routine of preparing food may involve a scientific principle or theory in creating the resulting dish.

Cooking activities are extremely popular with younger students. Observing the physical changes that occur when ingredients are combined and following the sequence of a recipe encourage students to inquire and predict. Students can also experiment with different ingredients or varying amounts to discover the different outcomes possible. Cooking also provides numerous opportunities to apply math skills as well. The following discovery story is one that could be reenacted through a follow-up cooking activity in the classroom:

Hanson Gregory loved the fried cakes his mother prepared in the kitchen of their home in Maine. The one part of the treat he didn't enjoy eating was the center; it always remained doughy and soggy, never quite done. One day, while in the kitchen with his mother, he had an idea. He wondered what would happen if he poked a hole into the center of the cakes with a fork. He suggested to his mother that the cakes just might fry more evenly and not be so soggy in the middle. So he tried it!

Both he and his mother were pleasantly surprised by the outcome of Hanson's spontaneous experiment. Years later, he grew up and became a sailor. Gregory traveled all around the world but never lost his taste for those special fried cakes. During his travels, Gregory prepared the treats for his shipmates and shared his secret with others. Soon stories of Gregory's fried cakes with holes spread. Even though fried cakes had been eaten and enjoyed for centuries, Gregory was credited for inventing a part of the cake not eaten. As a result of a simple kitchen experiment, Hanson Gregory discovered a new food, doughnuts with holes. Today, we eat them by the dozens and give very little thought to how the hole came to be (Aurandt, 1980; Leo, 1964).

How Can You Use Urban Legends in Teaching Scientific Discovery?

Some technological or scientific advances have received unusual responses from the culture for which they have been developed. In many cases, these advances have spawned imaginative stories developed as a result of the lack of understanding and possibly fear. The stories are often told as true stories; however, in most cases there is little or no evidence to document their authenticity. Urban legends often reflect a culture's initial reaction to a new discovery or invention.

Integrating urban legends with science encourages students to investigate and discuss possible anxiety created by scientific advancements. The impact and importance of advertisement and public awareness can be introduced, as well as the importance of being an informed consumer. Students are also led into the research process by proving or disproving the plausibility of such stories.

The introduction of microwave ovens and tanning beds has spawned several versions of urban legends. High school students are continually reporting the sad news of some unknowing female who, in a desperate rush to get a tan, remains in the tanning bed too long. She returns home to prepare for her upcoming date and hours later dies while attending her senior prom. The autopsy supposedly reveals that she was literally baked to death. The possibility of this could be the subject of study.

Cohen (1983) reports that some earlier urban legends involving stories of pets or animals that end up in washing machines or dryers have parallel story variants. Some of the more recent tales involve an individual placing an animal into the microwave to dry after giving it a bath. The individual leaves the animal inside the oven and returns moments later only to find that the animal or pet has been baked to death. These particular stories generate a great deal of student discussion about the plausibility and/or foolishness of such events. Cautions to avoid such behavior should be given.

By integrating urban legends into instructional units of science, the teacher provides opportunities for students to apply critical thinking skills. The events of the stories can be analyzed and investigated. Questions concerning the validity of the story arise. The story components are synthesized and evaluated. In many cases, urban legends are quite familiar to the students and can easily be used as a technique to bridge the distance between the students and the science concepts being taught.

Interrupting the Raven bedtime story, Tyler sat up in bed and responded, "I'll bet I know what the light is, but, what else did he see? Does Gray Eagle's daughter know he's there, and is he going to steal something?" he inquired excitedly. Sandy continued the story:

Just then, Gray Eagle called to his daughter to come to him outside the lodge. Raven hid himself as she walked out of the lodge and joined her father. In the next moment, Raven quickly entered the lodge and snatched the gourd of fresh water from the wall. He seized the sun and moon and scooped up a brand of fire in his beak as he soared from the lodge through the smoke hole.

Raven continued to fly, higher and higher into the dark sky. As Raven flew, carrying the sun, the sky became so bright that Raven found the perfect location and hung the sun in the sky. Later when the sun grew weary and set, Raven found the perfect location to hang the moon.

Continuing to fly inland, carrying the fresh water, Raven found the perfect locations to drop the water from the gourd. Each time the water touched the land, a new freshwater lake or stream would spring up providing much water for the people all over the world.

Raven continued to fly with the brand of fire in his beak. As he flew, the dark smoke covered his beautiful white feathers and changed them to black. Before long, the fire began to burn his beak and he was forced to drop the brand of fire onto the jagged rocks below. The fire was swallowed up by the rocks. That is why, when you strike two rocks or stones together, sparks of fire will appear.

Raven helped to bring light, fresh water, and fire to the people; but, in doing so, he was changed forever. His beautiful white feathers, for which he had been so admired, had been permanently charred by the black smoke from the fire brand; and that is why today Raven is a black bird.

Tyler looked at Sandy for a moment, smiled, and then stated emphatically, "I guess I'll just have to try that with two rocks tomorrow." Immediately, the story of Raven had provided the impetus for an investigation into the science of geology.

 Suggested Activities for the Teacher

1. Identify math and science concepts as instructional goals. Collect stories and selections of children's literature that can relate to the concepts. Design the instructional unit, integrating the selected story. Provide for "hands-on" activities or experimentation in the instructional plan. Look for stories that demonstrate problem-solving efforts and model critical thinking.

2. Identify and collect biographical stories that can be related to math and science concepts in your instructional plan. Integrate the stories into the plan. Create a classroom display featuring a specific mathematician or scientist during your instructional unit. Have the students enhance the display by completing related art work or writing activities.

3. Script a selected story into a reader's theater or play. Collect props and costumes, then integrate the presentation into the instructional plan.

4. Create your own original stories to use in your instructional plan for teaching math or science concepts.

5. Organize a team-teaching approach with a colleague. One teacher might assume the role of the storyteller, while the other assumes the role of the scientist, inventor, or mathematician. Plan a presentation whereby the storyteller shares the story while the scientist or mathematician demonstrates a principle or experiment while the students watch and listen. After the presentation, the students could replicate the same experiment or conduct a related one.

6. Dress in costume and use appropriate props to tell a selected story. If the story is biographical, deliver it in first person, if appropriate. Following the story, allow students the opportunity to interview your character.

7. Before telling a story involving nature or natural elements, plan to tell your story outside or take the students on a nature walk as a follow-up activity.

8. Encourage research skills among your students by discussing current scientific or mathematical discoveries. Scan journals or newspapers and listen to media reports of ongoing experiments or current discoveries. Create a file of these for quick discussion topics. Initiate the activity with the following or a similar phrase: "Did you know...?" The topics could be used as prompts for the development of student-created original stories.

Suggested Activities for Use with Students

1. To emphasize the importance of observation, divide the class into pairs. Involving one pair of students at a time, instruct the students to look carefully at each other for a timed 15 seconds. At the end of the 15 seconds, ask one of the students in the pair to leave the room. The remaining student, or eyewitness, describes the other student, offering and recording on paper as many details as possible. Continue through the class until each pair of students has participated. A standard set of questions can be used as a guide. For example, the questions might include information about color of eyes, distinguishing marks, color of hair, description of dress, left-handed or right-handed, height, and evidence of jewelry. Success with this activity could be beneficial to them as storytellers as well as scientific observers.

2. Regularly engage students with activities such as optical illusions, brainteasers, mental puzzles, mazes, riddles, and imagination exercises.

3. Have each student research a different scientist or mathematician. Host a "VIP Science Fair" where each student displays models, pictures, or any information gathered from his or her research. The models should demonstrate the significant discovery with additional biographical information provided in visual form. As viewers visit the fair, the student/scientist should be prepared to tell the story, in first person, behind the invention or experiment. Information concerning how the scientist formed the idea, how the research was conducted, and what process led to the development of the invention should be included.

4. Have students regularly maintain math journals that document original stories or explanations of math concepts.

5. Have students regularly maintain science journals that document individually conducted science experiments. The students should record the sequence of the experiment using the scientific inquiry method. Students should formulate a question or hypothesis, make predictions, collect data, interpret and report results, and evaluate and communicate outcomes. In addition, students should be encouraged to identify stories related to each experiment to share with the class. The stories might involve both folklore and other literature selections.

6. Have students create original *pourqoui* tales to explain the "why" of a selected natural element or phenomenon. The tales might represent different cultures and be shared orally.

7. While listening to commercially recorded nature audiotapes, have the students compose poems or stories that use the environment depicted in the tape. For example, play a recorded tape with sounds and music related to the rain forest. Instruct the students to close their eyes and listen to the sounds. Through the use of guided imagery, the students can engage their imaginations to create a composition set in the surroundings reflected in the audiotape.

8. Have the students read or listen to a variety of myths. Have them compare and contrast various cultural myths regarding star constellations. As a culminating activity, the students might draw or construct models of the constellations for a display.

References

Albright, M. (1996). Scientific ponders: Millionaire. Unpublished manuscript, Cookeville, TN.

Aurandt, P. (1980). *More of Paul Harvey's the rest of the story*. New York: Bantam Books.

Balsamo, K. (1987). *Exploring the lives of gifted people in the sciences*. Carthage, IL: Good Apple.

Becker, J. (1995). Seven little rabbits. In *Juba this and Juba that* (pp. 10-17). Selected by Virginia Tashjian. Boston, MA: Little, Brown.

Bennett, W. J. (Ed.). (1993). The crow and the pitcher. In *The book of virtues* (pp. 532-533). New York: Simon & Schuster.

Burke, J. (1978). *Connections*. Boston, MA: Little, Brown.

Caduto, M. J., & Bruchac, J. (1988). *Keepers of the earth*. Golden, CO: Fulcrum.

Caney, S. (1895). *Steven Caney's Invention Book*. New York: Workman Publishing.

Cohen, D. (1983). *Southern fried rat & other gruesome tales*. New York: Avon Books.

Dayrell, E. (1968). *Why the sun and the moon live in the sky*. Boston, MA: Houghton Mifflin.

Feldmann, S. (Ed.) (1965). How Raven helped the ancient people. In *The storytelling stone*. New York: Dell.

Haven, K. (1995). Launching a scientist: Robert Goddard's first attempt at rocketry. In *Many voices: True tales from America's past* (pp. 98-102). Jonesborough, TN: The National Storytelling Press.

Jones, J., & Wilson, W. (1987). *An incomplete education*. New York: Ballantine Books.

Leo, A. R. (1964). Hungry Hanson. In *Childcraft: Scientists and inventors*, Vol. 11 (pp. 98-99). Chicago, IL: Field Enterprises Educational Corporation.

Leotta, J. (1994). Stories plus science equals discovery. In *Tales As tools* (pp. 139-140). Jonesborough, TN: The National Storytelling Press.

Livo, N. J., & Rietz, S. A. (1991). *Storytelling folklore sourcebook*. Englewood, CO: Libraries Unlimited.

Mooney, B., & Holt, D. (1996). *The storyteller's guide*. Little Rock, AR: August House.

Morrison, L. (1997). Personal conversation. Cookeville, TN.

National Storytelling Association, The. (1994). *Tales as tools*. Jonesborough, TN: The National Storytelling Press.

Reader's Digest Association, The. (1976). *Strange stories, amazing facts*. Pleasantville, NY: The Reader's Digest Association.

Rodriguez, J. (1995). *Times tables the fun way*. Sandy, UT: Key Publishers.

Shannon, G. (1985). Dividing the horses. In *Folktales from around the world* (pp. 47-49). New York: Scholastic.

Sherman, J. (1992). The mathematician. In *A sampler of Jewish-American folklore* (p. 104). Little Rock, AR: August House Publishers.

Sima, J. (1995). Story-enhancing your science classes. *Storytelling Magazine, 7* (May), 20-23.

Stock, C. (1984). *Emma's dragon hunt*. New York: Lothrop, Lee & Shepard.

Sutherland, Z. (1997). *Children & books* (9th ed.). New York: Addison-Wesley.

von Oech, R. (1983). *A whack on the side of the head*. New York: Warner Books.

Chapter 11
Using Storytelling to Promote Understanding of Cultural Diversity

"Every really good story in the world has a trickster in it," commented Tyler as he settled comfortably into his blankets. As he readied for bed, he eagerly discussed the possibilities for the upcoming bedtime story and finally decided on a Native American tale about one of his favorite characters, Coyote.

⚜

Everyone knows Coyote. And everyone knows that Coyote always seems to find trouble no matter where he goes. One reason for this might be that Coyote is never satisfied. He always wants to be like the other animals and do things like the other animals rather than just being himself.

On this particular day, Coyote was just wandering along in the desert and heard a noise that sounded like laughing and singing, so he went up to take a look. Coyote saw a large group of blackbirds chanting and dancing. He watched the birds for a while, and he knew that he had never seen anything like this before. First they would sing and chant, and then they would stop and spread their wings and fly all throughout the canyon. They would fly in a circle and then land back where they had begun.

"Oh, if only I could fly," thought Coyote. "I would be the greatest coyote in all the world!" So Coyote called to the blackbirds and asked the chief if he could join them.

"This foolish coyote wants to be like us," the Blackbird Chief said to his flock. "No," he called to Coyote, "you may not join us, because this is not a coyote dance. It is a blackbird dance."

Coyote would not take "no" for an answer. He asked a second, and a third, and a fourth time. He continued to ask until finally the chief agreed to let Coyote join.

"Oh, thank you!" said Coyote. "May I fly, too?"

"Maybe, you can," said Chief Blackbird, while plucking a feather from his left wing. He then told his flock to do the same. The chief and all the other blackbirds plucked feathers from their left wings and stuck them in Coyote. Coyote yelped and squirmed until the blackbirds declared that he was ready to fly.

Tyler interrupted and said, "Oh, no! Something will happen, because Coyotes can't fly! I know the birds are going to trick him!" Tyler had listened to stories about Coyote before and he knew what to expect. His knowledge of the folklore of a culture different from his own had been growing for some time through hearing these bedtime stories. As Tyler's mom continued the story about Coyote, Tyler lay still, listening intently.

Soon the birds began their chanting and singing. They hopped from one foot to the other, and Coyote joined them. Even though Coyote sang a bit off-key and did not always step in rhythm with the others, he was quite proud of himself.

Before long the blackbirds spread their wings, and Coyote did the same. The blackbirds began to fly, and so did Coyote. His flight was awkward. He was not nearly as graceful as the blackbirds. He tilted from side to side. Since Coyote only had feathers from the left wings of each bird, he was off balance. Before long Coyote fell to the ground crying "Wait! Don't leave me!"

The blackbirds returned and gathered around Coyote. The chief declared that Coyote needed balance, so he plucked a feather from his right wing. The other birds did the same. Once the birds finished, Coyote said, "Now I am perfect. I can fly just as well as the rest of you!"

Tyler and the storyteller smiled secret smiles and Tyler interjected, "Look out, Coyote, they are going to trick you again! He just won't ever learn!" Tyler was using his past experiences with trickster stories to predict the outcome of this one.

Why Can Studying Stories From Different Cultures Be Valuable in Building Understanding of These Cultures?

"We tell stories for two reasons—so others can understand us and so we can understand ourselves" (Griffin, 1989, p. 41). Using storytelling to promote the understanding of cultural diversity encourages students to develop divergent thinking skills through sharing, participation, and cooperation. "Storytelling is older than history and is not bounded by one civilization, one continent, or one race" (Baker & Greene, 1977, p. 1). Its universal nature allows it to function as a key to cultural understanding.

The power of storytelling enables students to be introduced to the general knowledge about a culture, its history, and its location. Students can be taught the importance of communication, understanding, and cooperation with others. But most importantly, storytelling can provide students with an opportunity to see beyond the stereotypes and develop a respect and concern for the future of all.

How Can Similarities Among Cultures Be Discovered Through Stories?

"It seems patently clear that the more diverse we become racially and ethnically, the more important it is that we not only learn to tolerate differences, but also to celebrate what we all hold in common" (Chavez, 1993, p. 3). In an attempt to recognize and develop an appreciation of cultural similarities and differences, the role of the storyteller and the purpose of storytelling in different cultures should be examined by students at all grade levels.

To demonstrate the similarities among cultures, students should be encouraged to identify recurring archetypes, themes, or motifs that are evident in storytelling. For example, creation stories found in nearly all cultures provide an excellent opportunity to compare and contrast religious beliefs, special ceremonies, and rituals, and they can be used to introduce the concept of cultural diversity. (See Appendix B for resources containing creation stories.) Many myths demonstrate mankind's attempt to explain the various influences on the struggle for a day-to-day existence. Students are especially intrigued with different versions of familiar myths, legends, and folk literature found in a variety of cultures.

In addition to the study of the mythology of various cultures, students find it interesting to investigate the explanations outlined in even the simplest myth or *pourquoi* tale. For example, during a study of oceanography, Sandy's students were intrigued with the explanation of why the sea is salty. As an extension of a science lesson, several stories were shared related to the topic of oceans. One of the stories shared was "Why the Sea Is Salt" (*Best-loved Folktales of the World*, 1982). This story, a Norwegian tale of two brothers, described a bargain in which the poor brother had to travel to visit with the Devil. While visiting the Devil, he gained possession of a magic hand-mill that had the capability to produce anything, including gold. The poor brother eventually gained wealth and sold the mill to the captain of a ship who commanded the mill to produce salt. The mill ground so much salt that it sank the ship and continues to grind salt from the bottom of the ocean. For comparison, the students also listened to a Pacific Island folktale, "Why the Ocean Is Salty" (*Once In the First Times: Folk Tales From the Philippines*, 1969). This story is a tale of an island giant who built a bridge out of snow-white bricks and bamboo in an attempt to release a goddess from her place of darkness. The goddess instructed the giant to use snow-white bricks in the construction of the bridge. The giant knew that the only white thing on earth was salt. After locating the salt, he built bamboo supports and, with the help of men, began to carry the bricks across. The tranquil ocean became disturbed by all the commotion and sent up huge waves that knocked down the bridges and swallowed the men and salt bricks. The bricks dissolved and changed the fresh water into the salt water we know today. Following the stories, the students discussed the explanations and compared similarities, such as the importance of the sea in both cultures. They recognized how the people in both locations would be interested and curious about the composition of such a valuable part of their day-to-day existence. The students contrasted the plots of the stories. They suggested the story format from the Philippines appeared more like a Greek or Roman myth, with the goddess and giant characters; whereas the Norwegian tale seemed more like a folktale, with the element of magic and adventure.

The "trickster," such as Coyote from Native American folklore in the story that opens this chapter, is a popular character archetype evident in storytelling. Anansi (or Ananse) the Spider, a central character found in many African folktales; the character Jack, with his European and American influences; and Brer Rabbit, reflecting characteristics from African and American backgrounds, are often trickster/heroes who overcome adversity in ways which do not usually reflect superior physical strength. (See Appendix B for resources containing trickster stories.) Sometimes the trickster is portrayed as a foolish character who humorously humiliates himself and ends up the object of the lesson. Even though Native American versions vary greatly from tribe to tribe, many of the trickster characters are animals. Coyote is often found in tales from the western tribes and is the embodiment of all positive and negative human traits (Mourning Dove, 1990). Many times the trickster character is used to teach special messages or lessons, much as Coyote in Tyler's bedtime choice featured at the beginning and end of this chapter does.

"Nearly every culture has trickster tales in which a character uses wit, pranks, lies, deceit, and mischief to triumph over more powerful creatures" (Young & Ferguson, 1995, p. 490). Trickster tales are very popular ones to use with students and can be particularly helpful in emphasizing a society's value structure and the specific characteristics of a community of people or culture. They can generate valuable discussion of dishonesty and the need to be alert to real life tricksters who could take advantage of us. Students especially enjoy the humor found in trickster tales, which sometimes appears to transcend existing cultural barriers.

The trickster tale is an excellent way for students at all levels to observe their own wealth of original personal stories. Students can be encouraged to ask a family member to tell a story about the time that someone in their family played a trick on someone else. "Anna Joyce and Shelby" found in Chapter 4 is an example of a family story that contains an element of the trickster in it, as does the following story, "The Trick That Worked."

✿

The Trick that Worked

As Told by Jane Crooks

He had always been a trickster. He was always up to some kind of foolishness. But he had such an innocent face, people fell for his shenanigans nearly every time. He would pull your leg, even under the most serious circumstances, even when he got engaged to Cora and took her home to meet Aunt Lyla, the family matriarch. Not a single young person in Merle's family ever went to college, or took a job, or got married, or made any serious decision without talking it over with this formidable lady. She was well-loved, authoritative, overbearing, and wise. And it didn't hurt that she had a right healthy sum of money saved up with no offspring to leave it to. But none of that kept Merle from having some fun, because he knew that under her crusty exterior, Aunt Lyla had a sense of humor.

When it came time to introduce Cora to the family, Aunt Lyla would be the first to meet this lovely girl who had said "yes;" and Merle wanted these two very special women to become good friends. "Now Cora, I think you'll like Aunt Lyla," he said. "But there's just one problem."

"What is that?" asked Cora. The old woman is probably going to be very difficult, and Merle is going to tell me that I have to watch my p's and q's, she thought.

"Well, Aunt Lyla is a fine woman. But she is very hard of hearing. And she refuses to admit it. Won't wear a hearing aid. Doesn't want anyone to know that she can't hear it thunder. We just talk as loud as we can, and pretend that nothing is wrong. So when I introduce you, be sure to speak up as much as you can."

"I think I can do that," said Cora. She did not notice the slight smile that came over Merle's face as he shared this important piece of information. She was simply relieved that the problem was not something worse.

That evening Merle called Aunt Lyla on the phone to tell her that he was going to bring his fiancée home to meet the family. "Now, Aunt Lyla," he said in a normal tone of voice, "Cora is a wonderful girl, and I am really in love with her. I think you will like her, but she does have one problem."

"What is that problem, nephew?" asked Aunt Lyla, who heard every word he said as clear as a bell. I wonder if this poor girl comes from a bad family or has a bunch of unruly children, she thought. I certainly hope not.

"Well," said Merle, as serious as he could be, "Cora is a fine woman. But she is very hard of hearing. And she refuses to admit it. Won't wear a hearing aid. Doesn't want anyone to know that she can't hear it thunder. I just talk as loud as I can, and pretend that nothing is wrong. So when I introduce you, be sure to speak up as much as you can."

"Poor child," said Aunt Lyla, who felt grateful that with advancing age she had been spared the kind of hearing impairment that afflicted so many of her contemporaries. She felt sorry that Merle's sweetheart should have to struggle with such a handicap at a young age.

Soon the day arrived. Merle brought Cora home to meet the family. And he upheld the old tradition of making sure that Aunt Lyla was the first family member to meet his beautiful fiancée.

"Aunt Lyla," he shouted. "This is Cora Matthews. Cora, this is my aunt, Miss Lyla Womack."

Mercy! thought Aunt Lyla. She must really have a hearing problem.

Heavens! thought Cora. She must really have a hearing problem.

Neither woman had ever heard Merle talk so loudly before. And, eager to make a good impression and to communicate with this new person, each woman did as she was advised to do. She spoke at a very high volume.

"I'm very pleased to meet you, young woman," shouted Lyla.

"I am very pleased to meet you, too, Ms. Womack," shouted Cora.

"Won't you sit down and have a cup of tea?" asked Aunt Lyla. Her voice was loud and strong.

And so the conversation went, each woman shouting politely to the other. They were both so intent on making themselves heard that they did not notice the grin that began to spread across Merle's face. It began with a slight smile that rapidly grew wider and wider. No one knows how long they would have gone on like that, shouting at each other, as they were cautioned to do, but soon they were mercifully interrupted by an enormous explosion of laughter. Unable to contain himself any longer, Merle had completely lost control, and had begun to laugh. Both women were shocked that Merle, who had always been a sensitive man, would laugh so disrespectfully and so uproariously at someone with such a handicap.

"Merle! I've never known you to be so rude!" exclaimed Aunt Lyla.

"I can't help it," he said, hardly able to get his breath in the midst of such hilarity.

"I cannot keep a straight face any longer," he said. "Aunt Lyla, Cora is not hard of hearing. Cora, Aunt Lyla can hear as well now as she could 20 years ago. I told each of you that the other woman was hard of hearing just to get a big laugh. And I was not disappointed. It was hilarious to sit here and watch two perfectly able women yelling their heads off at each other for no reason at all."

"Well! How could you play such a mean trick on such a nice person?" huffed Cora and Aunt Lyla, in a unified reaction of embarrassment and disgust. And then they, too, broke into great explosions of laughter that was even heartier than Merle's.

And of course the trick worked. The women took an instant liking to one another. Now, these two strangers had something in common that created a bond between them. They had been duped by a gentle trickster whom they both loved in spite of himself.

Merle and Cora got married. Cora and Lyla remained good friends from that day to this. Neither of them ever fell for any more of Merle's tricks. And neither woman ever shouted at the other one again.

When telling a trickster tale, the storyteller should tell not only about the joke or prank but also about the consequences. For example, in "The Trick That Worked," Cora and Lyla developed a bond because they had both been duped by Merle. Also, students should discuss the differences between harmless tricks and dangerous or cruel ones that cause pain or harm to others. Many families can fondly recall incidents in which one person played a trick or a joke on other members of the family. Pranks, tricks, or jokes can be a rich vein to mine in family stories for helping to reflect the family's cultural influences.

Little people also abound in folklore. The Hawaiian dwarf creatures who can accomplish great feats in little time are known as the menehunes (Ehlers, 1958). Irish and Scottish stories feature fairy creatures and leprechauns. European variants also include pixies, elves, and dwarfs. Jinns are woven into

Arabian folklore and, like their Celtic and European counterparts, they live underground and have unique powers to control animals and humans (Sutherland, 1997).

There are parallel versions of stories originating in different cultures in addition to creation stories, trickster tales, and stories of little people. Similar story theme archetypes are found in different cultures, although the stories are told with different characters and in very different settings. For example, "Hardy Hardhead" (*The Jack Tales*, 1943), retold by Richard Chase, is an Appalachian version of the same story that is the basis for the Russian tale, *The Fool of the World and the Flying Ship* (1968), retold by Arthur Ransome; and the culture represented by the story is evident through language and some characteristics of characters and setting. For example, *The Fool of the World and the Flying Ship* features Russian peasants, a czar, a princess, and a magic flying ship while, "Hardy Hardhead" features Appalachian mountain characters, a king (probably due to the British ancestry of many Appalachian settlers) and his daughter, as well as a magic flying ship. While some characters and details are different, the story plot is the same. The main character is a simple fellow who undertakes a series of adventures in an attempt to win the heart and hand of the princess or break the witch's spell on the king's daughter. The similarity of the plots is easily recognized even though the stories are influenced by their respective cultures.

The Jack Tales (Chase, 1943) provide a rich source of comparison with many parallel European story versions. During European immigration to the American colonies, many stories traveled with the immigrants to their new world. Over time, as the stories were told, changes began to develop, and the stories began to reflect the people's new surroundings or present culture. As the country grew and developed, many colonists moved westward, locating in the Blue Ridge and Appalachian Mountains. Collected by Richard Chase, *The Jack Tales* (Chase, 1943) and *Grandfather Tales* (Chase, 1948) contain stories of the simple mountain people of America, which show evidences of their European origins. One example is a parallel story plot of talking animals who band together and eventually find wealth and happiness. "Jack and the Robbers" (*The Jack Tales*, 1943) is the story of a boy named Jack, who through a series of meetings acquired a donkey, a dog, a cat, and a rooster as traveling companions. Jack had run away from home and met each of the animals who were to be killed soon by his or her master. The group traveled together and stumbled upon an isolated cabin in the woods inhabited by robbers. Through a carefully coordinated plan, the animals and Jack outwitted the robbers, found the stolen treasure, and decided to live together in the cabin. A European parallel story is "The Bremen Town Musicians" (Cole, 1982). In this story from Germany, a donkey, a dog, a cat, and a rooster traveled together to Bremen to become musicians. The talking animals came upon a cabin inhabited by robbers. They contrived a plan to chase away the robbers, and, in much the same fashion as in the American version, they succeeded and moved into the cabin.

Stories with numerous variants, such as "Cinderella," "Jason and the Golden Fleece," "Rumpelstiltskin," and many stories included in a Brothers Grimm anthology can be found in a variety of cultures (Maguire, 1985). The "Cinderella" motif provides an excellent opportunity to compare and contrast themes. "Cinderella" stories exist in numerous cultures worldwide, with more than five hundred variants identified (Dundes, 1982). As the story traveled among cultures, the different versions took on characteristics of particular

Figure 11.1 Story Element Comparison Chart

	Story 1	Story 2
TITLE	*Cinderella* by Charles Perrault	*The Korean Cinderella* by Shirley Climo
CHARACTERS	Cinderella Stepmother Stepsisters Prince Fairy Godmother	Pear Blossom Omoni, wicked stepmother Peony Magistrate Frog, Sparrows, Black Ox
SETTING	Country home Castle in Europe	Korea Tile-roofed cottage
PLOT	Cinderella is mistreated by her stepmother and stepsisters. A fairy Godmother uses magic and helps Cinderella attend a ball and meet a handsome prince.	Pear Blossom is mistreated by her wicked stepmother and stepsister. Magical animals help her with her duties and make it possible for the handsome magistrate to see and fall in love with her.
THEME	Good triumphs over evil.	Good triumphs over evil.

cultures. Sharing different versions of "Cinderella" provides an opportunity for students to compare and contrast. (See Appendix B for various "Cinderella" stories.) Figure 11.1 shows a comparison of two such stories. These stories with parallel themes provide the listener an opportunity to gain a sense of "what the people value; what they laugh at; what they scorn, fear, or desire; and how they see themselves" (Young & Ferguson, 1995, p. 491).

Figure 11.2 Comparison of stories featuring Brer Rabbit and Ananse

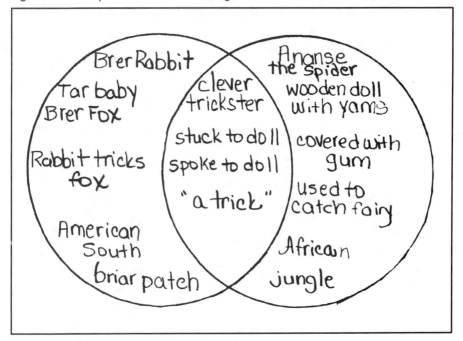

A comparison of Brer Rabbit stories and Ananse the Spider stories demonstrates the elements of similar story structure evident in folktales from different cultures. Stories of African origin traveled to different parts of the world during a time in history when many African people were traded and used as slaves. The oral tradition of the African culture was kept alive and, for generations, stories were told and retold, often reflecting the individual's new surroundings. Anansi, the African trickster featured in "Spider Stories," has counterparts in many areas including the West Indies and the southern United States (Chocolate, 1993). African-American stories, many featuring the trickster Brer Rabbit, were collected and published by Joel Chandler Harris who grew up in the American South listening to these tales (Lester, 1987). He called them Uncle Remus stories. Figure 11.2 graphically compares details of stories featuring Brer Rabbit and Anansi. This diagram can help to demonstrate the effect of surroundings and encourage students to evaluate the influence of culture in the development of oral narration.

Folktales also present the opportunity to contrast the different structures of stories. Folktales offer the opportunity to compare and contrast beginning and ending phrases as well as plot development and sequence of events.

Many folktales open with standard beginnings that capture the attention of the listener and establish the time and mood. Sometimes these beginning phrases vary in folktales from different cultures. "Once upon a time" is a recognizable opening for many English variants, while folktales from the Philippines open with "In the first times," and many African storytellers begin with "A story, a story, let it come, let it go." These phrases not only help to place the listener in a "dream world where anything is possible" (Sutherland, 1997) but also provide a hint at the culture the story may reflect.

In addition to standard beginnings and endings such as "and they lived happily ever after," the internal structure of folktale variants representing different cultures can be compared and contrasted. Many English variants depict a plot involving a sequence of three events or tasks while many Native American stories may involve a sequence of four. In most folktales, however, the plot develops rapidly and is of primary importance (Sutherland, 1997).

When telling stories from other cultures, the storyteller must understand and respect the culture from which his/her stories come. Instead of just locating stories for retelling from a book, author and storyteller Bruchac (Dailey, 1994) suggests that tellers should learn stories from the people through visits and/or attempts to discover as much as possible about their day-to-day lives and languages. He also cautions storytellers to find out as much as possible about the story. Gathering information concerning the type of story you wish to tell may result in the discovery that the story is to be told only during certain times of the year or under specific circumstances. Hirschfelder (1995, p. 133) says this about Native American storytelling: "Stories are told during designated periods, usually winter, when snakes and stinging insects are asleep. Ancient traditions forbid summer storytelling....Listening to good stories would make animals forget their place in nature and wander dazed through the forests. Likewise, plants would forget to grow, birds would forget to fly south when winter came, and people would become lazy." Native American people recognize the importance of working during the summer; therefore, stories are used for entertainment and teaching during the winter season. Telling stories during restricted times of the year would upset nature. Efforts to tell stories from other cultures are encouraged; however, storytellers should recognize the importance of telling stories responsibly with appropriate respect for their cultural origins.

How Can Stories Expand the Understanding Students Have of the World in Which They Live?

Storytelling provides students an opportunity to recognize a myriad of cultures. The act of comparing and contrasting stories helps students to recognize and identify those characteristics that describe their own personal cultures. Students should be encouraged to celebrate their diversity and share stories based upon their own personal experiences, special events, or celebrations that might reflect different cultural influences and demonstrate knowledge and pride in their own personal heritages.

A classroom project that illustrates this type of story collection and sharing is described in Chapter 4. Students were encouraged to locate and share stories of local origin. During the sharing of the stories, one featured character began to reappear in many of the stories. These stories became recognized as "Jake Bridgewater" stories, and they bound the rural East Tennessee students together with their common knowledge and the specific sense of humor exhibited in the stories.

Pellowski (1987, p. 1) states, "For centuries and centuries, stories have been the best means of explaining and passing on the moral values a family or people wishes to retain. Stories can show that there are others in the world who have different values and that toleration of these does not have to diminish one's own sense of right or wrong." Who we are, what we have been, and what we are to become are all reflected and expressed through a culture's art. Storytelling is an art that embodies such expression. Storytelling captures all that makes us human and provides a vehicle for the development of understanding and tolerance.

"No matter who you are, you have a tradition of storytelling as your heritage" (Bruchac, 1991, p. x). Storytelling can provide an avenue for students to develop a better understanding of world events and social issues, both past and current. For example, Aunt Lovie's story, in Chapter 12, creates a visual image of the contrasting roles of women over time. It enables the young listener to compare what life was like in the rural South for women during a time about which young people may have very little knowledge. Her story also paints a picture of a remote geographic area experiencing tremendous change because of progress and governmental interventions. These changes affected the lives of the area's people in many ways. Lovie's story is only a fleeting glimpse of that changing everyday life, yet it demonstrates how looking at day-to-day experiences provides insight into the characteristics of a community or culture. In an effort to understand other cultures better, many students may first need to observe their own and then describe the similarities and differences between their cultures and the cultures of others.

Storytelling can provide a documentary of a people from their early beginnings to their most current event. From day-to-day experiences to worldwide news events, storytelling provides the opportunity to experience life in any culture. "Storytelling is a way of keeping alive the cultural heritage of a people. It is akin to the folk dance and folk song in preserving the traditions of a country for the foreign-born child and of building appreciation of another culture for the native-born child" (Baker & Green, 1977, p. 23).

As Tyler's bedtime story continued, Tyler settled deeper into the bed, smiling smugly. He knew Coyote was headed for trouble.

Coyote became quite boastful. He began to dance, but he danced out of step. He began to sing, but he sang off-key. The blackbirds were no longer having fun with Coyote. They began their slow, steady chant. Coyote hopped along, flapping his feathered legs and singing. Just then the graceful bird dancers spread their wings and took flight. Soon they were flying high over the canyon. Coyote tried to keep up, but couldn't. He cried out to the birds, "Carry me!"

The blackbirds encircled Coyote but did not carry him. Instead, they watched and laughed as the feathers began to fall from Coyote's legs. Coyote began to sink through the air and fall to the earth. He fell so fast, his tail caught fire. Still to this day Coyote's tail has a burnt black tip.

And during the time of the year when birds fly south for the winter, if you listen carefully you can still hear them laughing about how Coyote tried to act like someone else and ended up in trouble, as usual.

"I could have told him not to try that!" murmured Tyler as he drifted off to sleep. The story had achieved its purpose. It provided the listener an opportunity to laugh and enjoy the antics of the featured character, Coyote, while also teaching a valuable lesson about nature.

  Suggested Activities for Use with Students

1. Develop a pen pal or a computer electronic mail key pal project between your students and students from another culture. Encourage the students to share personal stories that reflect some aspect of their culture and ask their pen pals or key pals to do the same.

2. Have pen pals or key pals from different cultures exchange traditional stories from their own cultures.

3. Guide the students in a research project searching for stories depicting ethnic or cultural differences. Encourage the students to use a variety of possible sources, including the Internet, the local public library, and the school library. Revise and update web site locations, as they may change frequently.

    Suggested World Wide Web Sites for Multicultural Studies
    (Compiled by Pam Petty and Kandy Smith, 1996.)

    http://curry.edschool.virginia.edu/go/multicultural/teachers.html

    http://curry.edschool.virginia.edu/go/multicultural/sites/education.html

    http://www.mapquest.com

    http://www.wfi.fr/blair/(multicultural awareness in the classroom)

    http://www.fau.edu:80/library/kids.htm (just for kids)

4. Schedule a field trip to a local Import/Export business to provide the students an opportunity to study objects associated with specific cultures. Identify items that have connections with stories.

5. Invite guest speakers or resource persons to your class to demonstrate different languages, to discuss different customs, or to share personal stories as a result of traveling or living in another culture.

6. a. Share different versions of stories with the class. For example: collect a variety of "Rumpelstiltskin" versions, creation stories, or trickster stories.

    b. Divide the class into groups, assign one version to each group.

    c. Instruct each group to review its version and work cooperatively to prepare a retelling of the version to the remaining class members.

    d. Have the groups work cooperatively to present the retelling of the assigned version.

    e. Have the students complete a story element comparison chart, such as the one that follows, using the Raven story found in Chapter 9 (Cherokee) and the one found in Chapter 10 (Pacific Northwest Tribe).

STORY ELEMENT COMPARISON CHART

	Story #1	Story #2
TITLE		
CHARACTERS		
SETTING		
PLOT		
THEME		

f. Discuss the specific influences of the culture while comparing and contrasting the narrative story elements of specific stories. Students are often intrigued by the comparison of character names. Using the comparison chart provided, students are encouraged to discuss the differences in the names of the central characters as well as the variations in setting, plot summary, and theme. During this comparison, students should be encouraged to discuss the similarities and differences of specific objects, styles of dress, family structures, daily life routines, and the roles of each of the characters.

References

Baker, A., & Greene, E. (1977). *Storytelling: Art and technique*. New York: R.R.

Bruchac, J. (1991). *Native American stories*. Golden, CO: Fulcrum.

Caduto, M. J., & Bruchac, J. (1988). *Keepers of the earth: Native American stories and environmental activities*. Golden, CO: Fulcrum.

Chase, R. (1943). *The Jack tales*. Houghton Mifflin.

Chase, R. (1948). *Grandfather tales*. Houghton Mifflin.

Chavez, L. (1993). Should America foster cultural diversity? Special Report Number 66. Grove City, PA: Public Policy Education Fund, Inc., January.

Chocolate, D. M. N. (1993). *Spider and the Sky God: An Akan legend*. New York: Troll Associates.

Climo, S. (1993). *The Korean Cinderella*. Mexico: HarperCollins.

Cole, J. (1982). *Best-loved folktales of the world*. Garden City, NY: Doubleday & Company.

Dailey, S. (1994). *Putting the world in a nutshell: The art of the formula tale*. New York: H. W. Wilson Company.

Dundes, A. (1982). *Cinderella: A casebook*. Madison, WI: The University of Wisconsin Press.

Ehlers, S. (1958). *Hawaiian stories for boys and girls*. Honolulu, HI: Hawaiian Service, Inc.

Griffin, B. B. (1989). *Students as storytellers: The long and the short of learning a story. Book 1*. Medford, OR: Griffin McKay Publishers.

Hamilton, M., & Weiss, M. (1990). *Children tell stories: A teaching guide*. Katonah, NY: Richard C. Owen.

Hayes, J. (1983). *Coyote &: Native American folktales*. Santa Fe, NM: Mariposa Publishing.

Hirschfelder, A. (Ed.). (1995). *Native heritage: Personal accounts by American Indians 1790 to the present*. New York: Macmillan.

Lester, J. (1987). *The tales of Uncle Remus: The adventures of Brer Rabbit*. New York: Dial Books.

Maguire, J. (1985). *Creative storytelling: Choosing, inventing, and sharing tales for children*. Cambridge, MA: Yellow Moon Press.

McDermott, G. (1994). *Coyote: A trickster tale from the American Southwest*. New York: Harcourt, Brace, and Company.

Mourning Dove. (1990). *Coyote stories*. Lincoln, NE: University of Nebraska Press.

National Storytelling Press, The. (1994). *Tales as tools*. Jonesborough, Tennessee: The National Storytelling Press.

Pellowski, A. (1987). *The family storytelling handbook: How to use stories, anecdotes, rhymes, handkerchiefs, paper, and other objects to enrich your family traditions*. New York: Macmillan.

Perrault, C. (1984). Cinderella. In *Junior Great Books* (pp. 18-31). Chicago, IL: The Great Books Foundation.

Petty, P., & Kandy S. (1996). World tour. A presentation given at the Tennessee Reading Association Fall Conference, Gatlinburg, TN, December.

Ransome, A. (1968). *The fool of the world and the flying ship*. New York: Farrar, Straus, & Giroux.

Sawyer, R. (1987). *The way of the storyteller*. New York: Viking Press.

Sechrist, E. H. (1969). *Once in the first times: Folk tales from the Philippines*. Philadelphia, PA: Macrae Smith.

Sutherland, Z. (1997). *Children & books* (9th ed.). New York: Addison-Wesley.

Young, T. A., & Ferguson, P. M. (1995). From annoyance to Zomo: Trickster tales in the classroom. *The Reading Teacher*, (March), pp. 490-503.

Chapter 12
Using Storytelling to Help Understand Self and Others

⚜

The first eight years of my life were spent living on a farm right next door to my grandparents. It was a great place to spend the first few years of life—a farm on a powdery dirt road with cows, pigs, chickens, mules, and a pony.

Both my parents worked when I was very young, and I spent my days with my grandmother. Every morning I'd go into her house all sleepy and bundled. Her house would smell like bacon and coffee. There would always be fresh homemade biscuits left over from my grandfather's breakfast. Nowadays, if I take the time to make home-made biscuits, my family shows respect with a moment of silence and sometimes we even have a marching band! But my grandmother made scratch biscuits twice a day, every day.

Busiest woman I ever saw. Ran everywhere she went. Ran from room to room, from front yard to garden to pasture. My grandfather would leave for work, and the running of the farm would be up to us. We would settle into our day. I remember being so glad to have her all to myself.

After she made the beds, washed all the breakfast dishes, swept and mopped the kitchen floor, she would take off her apron and put her bonnet on. That was a good sign that the day was taking a turn for the better.

Once outside, we moved the cows. I can remember thinking how odd it was that no matter where cows were, they were supposed to be somewhere else. And it seemed to me that cows did the same thing no matter where you put them, but I went along with the process.

My grandfather, even when he had a fairly good sized number of cattle, always seemed to have a name for every one of them. They were like large pets to him. He could walk out into the pasture and call a few names and, like old friends, they would migrate slowly toward him. They would gently nudge him as they went by, and then he would walk them to where he wanted them to be.

My grandmother used an entirely different strategy. She would walk to the edge of the pasture, plant her feet squarely toward those cows, give one loud high pitched call and point toward the barn. Cow heads popped up like popcorn out of the pasture; and those cows would form a neat, orderly line and march toward where that finger was pointing. It was a sight to see. I'd stand there and act real proud to be on her side. Cows would bawl, stomp and try to stare her down—but I don't recall one ever stopping to directly argue the point.

Then there were eggs to gather. "Aigs," my grandmother called them. A routine job for her, mission impossible for me. The idea is that you are going to reach your hand in under a chicken, into that nice warm nest, and get that egg she has just worked so hard to put there.

I decided early on in life that chickens were very fickle creatures. Passive and submissive one minute and possessed the next. My grandmother would grab that empty egg basket in one hand and me in the other and into that hen house we would go. Now even the smell of a hen house should tell you it's not a good place to be, but my grandmother would forge ahead.

There was always one chicken appointed to sound the alarm; then the others would join in, and chaos would break out. There would be flapping and feathers, birds going up and birds coming down. I would hold my ears and think to myself—it's just not worth it! And by the time I had said the quickest and best prayer I knew, "Now I lay me down to sleep"—which didn't fit the occasion but just somehow made me feel better—it would all be over, and we would be back outside in the sunlight with a basket full of warm, brown eggs. My grandmother would head straight to the house just like nothing happened, but I always glanced behind us a few times to make sure they weren't fol- lowing us—I just never did trust chickens (Petty, 1996).

The class of college students responded to Pam's personal story. Smiles appeared on their faces as they searched for and visualized those special char- acters in their lives, past or present, who fit the vivid descriptions Pam pro- vided. With her story, Pam tapped into memories and observations with which many of the students identified. She demonstrated how her own nostalgic memories, crafted into a personal family story, provided insight into under- standing herself, as well as the characters in her story.

How Can Stories Help Us Understand Ourselves?

Days are filled with people not only telling their stories, but living them. Storytelling is a natural form of communication that allows us to share our experiences and learn from others. Teachers are continually searching for strategies or techniques that will enhance student learning. Personal storytelling is such a strategy; however, it is so much more. It is an avenue that leads to self-awareness. It is also a creative product resulting from the need for self-expression.

Even when children are very young, storytelling skills can be observed. Small children spontaneously narrate their actions at play while often developing a story pattern that includes characters, plot, setting, and resolution. Some children create imaginary characters that can be called upon to fill an empty space when an actual friend or playmate is absent. Others pick up an object, such as a stick or rock, and weave a story of magnificent proportions involving this simple, yet critical prop.

Striving for self-awareness involves introspection and the ability to analyze feelings, thoughts, and interests. Many times this process of self-examination requires the consideration of the past, present, and future. Reflecting on past events and experiences often clarifies or helps to explain elements of the present. Analyzing previous experiences and current events also provides guidance for future plans.

For many, storytelling provides a special link to the past. Stories have been used for centuries to share information that is unique to a specific culture or group of people. "Through the telling of stories the wisdom, strength and values of a people are expressed and passed to new generations" (Crosson & Stailey, 1988, p. 3).

Stories provide excellent resources for the development of morals and virtues. Bennett (1993) outlined specific virtues and included in his anthology, *The Book of Virtues*, stories that provide "reference points" and "anchors" for the moral development of children. Storyteller Bonnie Fussell (1996) recommends "The Magic Thread," a story from Bennett's anthology, not only to entertain, but also to reinforce the importance of patience and acceptance; virtues valued in our culture, as well as in many others.

When students compare what they hear in stories to important aspects of their own lives, storytelling offers opportunities for them to identify and clarify values—a fundamental step toward analyzing personal feelings and thoughts. Schram (1987, p. 13) described the influence of Jewish stories on her moral development: "My parents did not just lecture on principles . . . they used the power of stories to...lead me to discern the values they upheld." The stories taught her that not only should she do certain things as a result of her own personal values, but also because she was part of a larger community.

For many, the knowledge of ancestors and cultural heritage provides

insight into personally held values and beliefs. Stories are gifts that are presented from one generation to another in the hope that the cultural legacy
might continue. Personal and family stories are examples of these gifts; they
are treasures that exist in all cultures.

Donald Davis is one of many widely known storytellers who emphasizes the importance of telling family stories. Many of his stories are based
on personal and family experiences. Davis suggests that family stories "help
a family define their identity and stay in touch with who they are" (Davis,
1993, p. 6).

As people get older, they continuously accumulate material for stories.
With each life experience, a new story can be created. This continual renew-
al of possibilities exists for everyone and provides the common link that binds
us together as a people. Storytelling makes the sharing possible.

Numerous teachers have discovered that one successful way to introduce storytelling is through the sharing of personal stories. The classroom is
a treasury of sources. Each individual, including the teacher, has stories to
tell. Some individuals are more reluctant than others to share; but, with
encouragement and support, even the most reticent student will discover the
joy of storytelling.

To introduce personal stories, teachers often begin by sharing examples
of their own. Sometimes the examples involve recent experiences, while others may be childhood memories. Stories of a parent's or another older individual's childhood fascinate children (Keeshan, 1996). They often find these
stories humorous and entertaining. This modeling of self-expression provides
an introduction that encourages the students to tell and join in the fun. The
teacher can also take advantage of the opportunity by demonstrating effective
storytelling techniques, such as appropriate use of voice and gestures and the
establishment of eye contact with the audience.

When first asked to share personal stories, many novice tellers will
respond by indicating that nothing ever happens to them. Their life is not
exciting; therefore, they don't have stories to share. One of the first steps to
successful storytelling is to acknowledge that stories are all around.
Sometimes stories are activated memories that must be crafted and shaped
into a format that can be retold or shared.

Boyd Ray (1996) invites the listener to join him in a story based upon a
memory from his past:

To raise vegetables for the produce market a person needed some
sort of a truck to run about in to supply various needs, as well as haul
workhands from one place to another. Also, if you could not sell to the

local buyers and needed to sell to the local area markets, you needed a truck.

That year, in 1939, Daddy and I decided to try raising some vegetables other than beans, that sold for a lot more money than beans: like cauliflower, yellow crook-necked squash, fresh garden peas, broccoli and celery. We figured that since these were new crops to the area, and the supply would be small, the buyers who were buying our beans would think we were more or less captive, and try to buy these new products much too cheap. I needed to be in a position to haul them to the larger stores in the area. Places like Elizabethton, Johnson City, Kingsport, Bristol and Abingdon.

So I started out to buy an old truck that would serve both purposes as needed. In 1939 money was hard to come by and I was looking for something cheap, yet usable. Any truck on a used car lot was priced much too high. Any truck that was offered by the owner was also too high for me. I didn't have much money, but needed a pretty good old truck.

There was a fellow who operated a garage at the edge of town who also dealt in used cars and trucks. His name was Brown, and he was a long, lanky, thin man who spoke just as slow and deliberate as he looked. He was a good mechanic and a very interesting man.

When I got to his place I found him with his head under the hood of an old truck working on it. "Hello, Mr. Brown, do you have an old truck you would sell?" I asked.

Without looking up he said, "Why sure, I'll sell you this one I'm working on."

"Fine," I said, "and how much is this truck costing today?"

Again, without looking up or stopping work, "Oh, I guess I'll have to have about two hundred dollars for this good truck."

"Well, now, that's a bit rich for my blood, I need something cheaper. What else do you have?"

"Come to think of it," he said with his head still under the hood. "I do have one here I'll sell you for a lot less than that."

I looked around, all over the place, inside and out, and saw no truck. All I saw was a great scattering of what seemed to be junk parts and pieces of cars. Going back to him I said, "Aw come on now, don't kid me, there's only one truck in the place, and that's the one you're working on."

As he raised up from under the hood wiping his hands on a rag, he said, pointing as he talked, "You just don't recognize it. Right over there is the motor, and in the corner is the transmission." He was pointing at what looked like piles of junk as he continued. "Out back is the chassis, and the cab is beside that pile of tires on the upper side of the building. Up home I have a good radiator and differential that will fit it. That's the major parts." Then, after stepping to the window and spitting a large stream of amber through a broken glass, he turned to me and with a wave of his hand said, "I'll get the rest of the parts from this pile of junk you see laying around here." Then picking up his wrench, he put his head back under the hood of the truck.

I was amazed. "And what kind of truck is this going to be, and what will it cost me?"

"It's a three-quarter-ton Chevy, without a bed." As he backed out of the hood, he added, "I'll put it all together, with good used tires, and guarantee it to run for fifty dollars."

At that point I could raise fifty dollars, and I needed an old truck mighty bad. "Mr. Brown, you have made a deal," I said pleased as I could be. For the first time in my young life I was going to own a truck. All I needed to do was put a bed on it. And I knew a lot of places where I could get some pretty good junk lumber.

That old truck did a good job for me that summer. I hauled needed material and workhands to help in the production and harvesting of the crops. Also, I used it to haul several loads to the outlying area stores. The only trouble I had with it was that it used a tremendous amount of oil. But I soon learned to carry a gallon can full of used oil in the cab so I could stop ever few miles and pour in some more oil.

That fall I sold it for sixty-five dollars. When I put that with the ten I had left from selling vegetables, there was enough to enroll for one quarter of my senior year in East Tennessee State University (Ray, 1996, pp. 67-69).

⊱≺◦≻⊰

This story gives insight into the character of a person who is goal oriented and resourceful. He is a person who knows how to make do with what is available. He also is a person who values education, since his hard-earned money was spent for college tuition.

Teachers integrating storytelling into the curriculum often encourage students to question or interview family members about specific events, traditions, or special memories. "Oral history...serves to 'connect' a child to family and its various components..." (Keeshan, 1996, p. 7). This collection of information often yields stories that can be shared in the classroom. It may be necessary to provide the students with a specific list of questions to serve as an outline for gathering their information and conducting their interviews. The following questions, designed for interviews of parents, guardians, and other family members, provide prompts that help reveal information that could be developed by students into personal stories:

1. Am I named for someone in our family? If so, who was this individual, and why was I named for him or her? Has there ever been anyone else in our family who had my name? If so, who? If you had named me some thing else, what would you have chosen? Did you consider other names when I was born, or was my name the only one you had thought about? Why was I given this particular name?

2. Do you remember any stories about yourself when you were my age? Did you go to a school like mine? What did you eat for lunch? Did you ride a bus? What class was your favorite? What class was your least favorite? What is your best memory of school? What games did you play when you were my age? What books did you read? What stories did you listen to or tell when you were my age?

Interview questions vary and can be composed by the teacher, by the student, or as a collaborative effort. When students are collecting or gathering information for personal or family stories, it is helpful to create a document for recording the responses to the questions. Students may be interested in tape recording the interviews to be replayed as needed. Another possibility is that the student may videotape the interviews, which would provide, not only the auditory element, but the visual as well.

In order to collect information for a retelling activity for a fifth grade social studies classroom assignment, Dusty Smith was instructed to interview his maternal great-grandmother. The purpose of the activity was to compare and contrast his educational experiences with hers and to share this information with the class in the form of a story. Dusty was first required to outline the characteristics of his community, school facility, and current educational program. This activity provided the basis for comparison with the information from his great-grandmother.

During the interview, Dusty discovered that his great-grandmother had repeated the eighth grade three times, a revelation that truly astonished him! Upon further investigation, however, he discovered that she had willingly repeated the eighth grade because she did not want to attend the "local" high school, which was a long way from her home. As an alternative, she chose to remain at home and continue her education by repeating the eighth grade for three years! Thus, what initially seemed a weakness—repeating the eighth grade—turned out to be a strength reflecting his great-grandmother's overwhelming desire to learn.

The interview assignment not only provided a wonderful storytelling opportunity, but it also prompted Dusty to reflect upon cultural changes that have taken place in rural areas in the Upper Cumberland region of Tennessee. Dusty could easily compare the structure of the communities and educational programs; moreover, he developed a more realistic understanding for how much change had taken place between the educational practices of today and those of days gone by. Perhaps he even gained a greater appreciation for his own educational opportunities that were not available to his great-grand-mother, who would have enjoyed them.

Storytelling provides the opportunity for sharing personal experiences and offers the tools that enable individuals to investigate those experiences. The powerful impact of storytelling on an individual's ability to investigate himself or herself may result in personal stories that reveal private problems or troubling issues. Gillard's (1996) analogy, comparing the story of Pandora's box to the sharing of personal stories in the classroom, suggests that even though a student may reveal more than you, as the teacher, may want to know, the insight gained from the process provides the hope for healing. If a student shares a personal story revealing problems of a serious nature, you should resist interacting by questioning or trying to resolve the story, accord-ing to Gillard (1996). If the information warrants, you may need to engage support from outside sources. However, Gillard contends that the sharing of personal stories promotes understanding and helps to organize the chaos prevalent in life experiences. The process of sharing can also bring the teller and the listener to the realization that others have similar problems or chal-lenges.

Jeff Huddleston (1996), in response to the death of his maternal grand-mother, created an original story that summarized memories of his special rel-ative. The sharing of his memories eased his grief and helped him to under-stand better one of life's difficult experiences. The following is the family story based upon his memories:

❧✻❧

I remember, as far back as I can, visiting Granny Ollie. This visit usually involved an hour's drive around a curved road on Sunday afternoon. Now, no one ever described my Granny as a neat house-keeper. To me, her house was like a museum filled with treasures and artifacts just waiting to be explored and investigated. The trinkets on the dressers and mantle held a particular appeal for me. My most favorite treasures were the snow globes. Granny would take them down and shake them up while I watched the snowflakes swirl around and around inside the magical space. Sometimes she would give me a special one to bring home. I love and cherish them to this very day!

Even though Granny had an outside bathroom, she didn't lack for other modern conveniences. She had a television for watching "As the World Turns" (she never missed it and would always tell you how much she hated that old Lisa Shea) and her radio for listening to the news and "The Grand Ole Opry" on Saturday Night. She had an old crank telephone that was located beside her bed, and for a long time the only person she could talk to was my uncle who lived nearby. Her phone was hooked up to his but not through the telephone company. This was always a mystery to me, but she let me play on it; and I didn't really care if I had service or not.

Once I had talked on the phone, it was always tempting to climb up onto the quilt-covered bed in her living room and jump to pull the string attached to the bare light bulb that shone on the old coal stove in front of the boarded up fireplace. I would have to wait to do that when she and my parents took their walk outside to look at Granny's flowers and vegetable garden. (This was a routine that took place toward the end of each family visit.)

Granny's house was surrounded by huge boxwood shrubs and lots of flowers, plants and trees. The clapboard two-story house was old and gray, with a porch in front and a well in the back. When thinking about that well, my mouth always waters; water has never tasted any cooler or sweeter than it did when she gave me a drink from that old metal dipper that usually hung on the post by the well. I can close my eyes and hear the creaking metal of the pulley as she lowered the bucket into the water and pulled it up, while my dad held me up to look down into that deep hole. I was fascinated.

Even though my Granny is no longer here, the part of her 95 years I shared has given me more than a few memories. I will never forget the Moon Pies always kept on top of her refrigerator, just waiting until my next visit. Or the image of her wooden walking cane or the jar of snuff on the small table beside her chair. It's amazing the images I have of her and her life. I wonder what legacy I will leave behind for my grandchildren. I do know one thing: I have a few special snow globes to pass along!

Storytelling can be therapeutic. Sharing personal stories encourages the analysis of internal emotions through external means and listening to personal stories develops empathy and establishes a bond that can lead to greater acceptance and understanding (O'Toole, 1995). O'Toole's life experiences have led her to sharing stories as a therapeutic process. Her personal story is one of grief and loss in which storytelling has had a tremendous impact.

How Can Stories Help Us Understand Others?

Aunt Lovie settled back into the comfortable old rocker, closed her eyes, and smiled as she began her story:

❧

"When Redd and I got married, he was working at the lock, and we moved into the house that was built near the lake. Redd would help take the ferry back and forth across the lake. Of course, I didn't work anywhere at the time; I just kept house. We lived close enough that most of the time Redd would walk from our house to the lock and back home again for dinner at night.

Now, our house was built near the lake and was built up on tall poles so that the floor was off the ground, just in case the lake got up and flooded the area. Redd always parked the car under those poles that supported the house so that it was sort of like a garage like people have today.

One day I decided that I didn't have a lot to do, and I had been yearning to learn to drive. I had watched Redd, and I didn't think it looked too hard; so I decided that I could do it! I could teach myself to drive the car while Redd was at work, and I wouldn't tell him anything about it until I could surprise him with my new skill. I made my mind up that I would sneak out to the car and try my hand at it once Redd left for the ferry that very afternoon.

Everything went just like I had planned. I put the key in, like I had seen him do, and I started the car! I put it in gear (first gear, I remember), and I took off around the house real slow. I did just fine! I pulled the car back up under the house and got out and looked to make sure I had parked it in exactly the same spot where Redd had parked it before. After that, I went on into the kitchen to start Redd's dinner.

Redd came home for dinner, and I never said a word. I tried real hard not to let on that I had been up to something. Soon Redd finished eating and went back to work. I went out and tried it again! I drove the car around the house real easy and pulled up under those poles just like before.

That evening, Redd come home and didn't come right on into the house. I went out to check on him and he was at the car doing something. I thought to myself, Oh, no! But he just said something about a flat tire. He changed the tire and took the flat one with him the next day to have it patched at the garage in town.

Well, that day, while he was gone, I tried my hand at driving that little car again. (I was getting better and better, or at least I thought I was!) That night, Redd come home and said he couldn't believe it, but he thought that he noticed another flat tire on the car. (Now, the first flat didn't alarm me. I couldn't imagine that I could have been responsible for the flats, but just maybe—I bit my tongue and still didn't say a word!) Redd changed that second flat and replaced it *with the tire he got fixed at the garage. He planned to carry the second flat and get it fixed the next day.*

I was nervous about trying it again after the two flat tires, but I did it anyway! I was real proud, 'cause I was changing those gears easier and faster and was able to get my speed up some, too. After I drove around the yard, parked the car and checked the tires, I was satisfied that everything was all right. I vowed right then and there that I wouldn't give up until I learned to drive as good as Redd.

Redd come on home for dinner a little while later, and sure enough he found another flat tire! This one had a nail in it!

Aunt Lovie continued her story while her listeners laughed and tried to imagine how Redd would react if only he had known what she had been doing!

After Redd had checked the tire and found another nail, he came into the house and looked at me. Well, I just started to cry and tell him all about my sneaking to drive the car while he was at work. When I got to the part about where I had been driving, Redd listened and then he started to laugh and laugh! See, I didn't know it, but before we had got married, Redd had torn down an old chicken house out behind the main house and my driving path went right through where that old chicken house had been. Redd explained that more than likely there were still several nails lying around on the ground and I was just lucky enough to pick them up.

After that, Redd took me out on Sunday afternoon and let me try my hand at driving. At first, I just drove on the back roads. After a while Redd decided that I was ready, and he let me drive out on the blacktop. It wasn't long before I went and took my driving test and got my license. Then you couldn't have tied me down. I drove pretty much anywhere I wanted to; I even drove to Nashville once to see a doctor. The only place Redd would not let me drive was through the yard where that old chicken house had been, but that was all right with me."

Aunt Lovie visited Granny Smith every summer for at least two weeks at a time. During those two weeks, she and Granny reminisced, retelling personal stories about growing up in rural Tennessee, such as the one about her learning to drive. They wove their tales, describing their lives before the Tennessee Valley Authority (TVA) and modern technology drastically changed the geographic face of their world. Their personal anecdotes and stories gave the listeners a glimpse of how the building of TVA dams throughout Tennessee and Kentucky affected the lives of the people in those areas. With their unique expressions and authentic language of Appalachia, they not only could entertain with their stories, but they could also provide insight into the culture of the people in the Upper Cumberland region of Tennessee. Listeners were invited to travel through time and to experience the range of emotions and reactions to the changes taking place all around; moreover, individuals could identify with the characters and settings so vividly described. They could share the agony and worry of moving to a new home and leaving behind what had been their heritage, as Lovie and Granny remembered with such feeling and candor. A link was established between the listeners and who they were today with how they came to be. Through their ability to share personal stories, language, and values, many of the characteristics that made up the unique culture of early 20th-century Appalachia were poignantly brought to life with each retelling.

Storytelling helps us to understand the characteristics and complexities of human behavior. Many times listening to a story is like looking at oneself in a mirror. Stories engage the imagination and interest of the listener. While actively involved, the listener may create visual images of characters that display familiar characteristics. The characters' reactions to events may be easily predicted by the listener. Some of the story elements may even parallel the listener's true-life experiences.

Children and adults view life from their own perspectives. These views are influenced by numerous factors. Young children often echo the attitudes and beliefs of their parents. Many voice opinions and react to events in the same way as their peers. Role models have a great deal of influence on a child's behavior patterns and developing attitudes. It is difficult and challenging for such complex beings to change behaviors and attitudes. Storytelling, however, is a medium that can guide the development of character and influence the child's point of view.

The development of empathy is important in the process of understanding others. "The ability to see and feel things as others see and feel them is the key that unlocks our prison house of self-absorption" (Kilpatrick, Wolfe & Wolfe, 1994, p. 39). One way to broaden students' views is to introduce them to characters and events through storytelling. Stories such as "The Ugly Duckling" create empathy and reinforce the importance of showing compassion.

Stories may provide role models through fictional characters as well as through real-life individuals from biographical, personal or family stories (Malone, 1994). Interacting with these characters, sharing their experiences, and evaluating their reactions and attitudes provide the student with examples he or she can emulate.

Being able to identify with story characters is extremely powerful. Sandy discovered the impact of this identification for one special needs student during a puppet show performance utilizing a storytelling format. The show featured a puppet wearing leg braces. During the introduction of the cast of characters, one student exclaimed, "Hey, she's just like me!" The student who excitedly made this observation did indeed wear leg braces as a result of spina bifida, the same disability that the puppet supposedly had. This identification with the puppet character enhanced the interest of not only the one student, but the entire group of students. Each member of the audience established a connection with the story character who, in turn, not only promoted the understanding of a disability; but, more importantly, influenced the acceptance of one individual.

There are numerous stories that can be used by teachers to promote understanding of oneself and others. Motifs evident in folklore provide opportunities to explore themes, character types, character actions, and circumstances (Livo & Rietz, 1991). Fables often explicitly teach by summarizing the theme of the story in the form of a moral. Much like proverbs and parables, fables often depict contrasting behaviors, reinforcing the power of the most desirable trait when contrasted with the least desirable. For example, in Aesop's fable, "The Goose with the Golden Eggs," the hazard of greed versus contentment is illustrated in the moral: "Greed often overreaches itself" (Aesop, 1982, p. 179).

Fairy tales often provide an effective source for contrasting obvious character types or motifs. Many characters featured in fairy tales are portrayed with exaggerated behavioral characteristics. For example, Red Riding Hood is good-natured and helpful, while the opposing character, Wolf, is sinister and clever. To explore characterization fully and its influence on developing the understanding of others, teachers should use a variety of story sources and not limit selections to only a few genres.

Stories also provide the opportunity for the listener to vicariously experience things that, otherwise, he or she would never dream of doing in real life. This is one of the features of the trickster tales that makes them so popular and appealing. Along with these enchanting characters, the listener is transported through the sequence of events and engages in outrageous and mischievous behavior. Maguire (1985, p. 64.) states, "The trickster represents the best and the worst in all of us." Many times we can identify with the trickster character and support him in his antics even though he may not always follow the rules to accomplish the deed.

Storytelling helps to create a sense of community in the classroom. It supports self-discovery and encourages self-expression. Through the use of stories, teachers can create a climate of acceptance and tolerance where students acquire lifelong values and beliefs resulting from their understanding of themselves and others.

The sights and smells of the setting featured in Pam's story about her grandmother were vivid. The expressions evident on the faces of the adult listeners were very childlike. Even though they physically remained within the boundaries of the university classroom, through the portals of their own memories, the students had joined Pam and her grandmother on their trip to gather eggs.

There was one chicken I liked though. My grandfather had an old shed just behind the house. Leaning up against that shed was a huge black iron pot that we used when we killed hogs. Now this one chicken had built a nest under the pot, and it delighted me so to catch that chicken away from her nest! I would slip my arm in behind that pot and feel around until I touched something warm and smooth and come out with a perfect brown egg. I'd go running in the house with it and proudly give it to my grandmother. It was like my little victory over the world of poultry!

One day I saw this particular chicken in the side yard, and I knew I could make my move. I knelt down beside the black pot, reached my whole arm in behind it, felt something warm and smooth and brought it out. Much to my surprise I had a whole handful of snake. I froze. The snake froze. One of us screamed. Later I decided that it must have been me because my grandmother came out of that back door at lightning speed with her apron flapping in the wind. Without hesitation, she grabbed a hoe that was leaning against the shed and went to work on that snake. One quick chop and that snake and its head were two separate beings—each with its own idea of which way to go. It reminded me of when my grandmother would wring a chicken's neck and the body would parade around the yard for a while before it gave up (reinforcing my idea that any critter that could run around without its head could probably do other things too that I just didn't want to think about).

I must have been about 5 years old when I had the scariest dream of my whole life. I remember it just as vividly as if I had dreamed it last night. In my dream I was standing on my grandparents' glassed-in back porch, looking up that big hill behind their house. And there, on top of the hill, right in the middle of the garden, was a huge, white polar bear. In my dream I called my grandmother, who walked directly out that back door, grabbed that hoe that was leaning against the shed and started up that hill to kill that bear.

Not before or since, awake or asleep, have I known such pure, paralyzing fear. Fear that something would happen and my grandmother would never come back from the top of that hill.

Now, my grandmother has never fought a bear with a hoe, but even though it was a dream, I believe if the situation had ever occurred, she would have given it her best shot—and I wouldn't have been betting on the bear.

My grandparents still live on that same old farm today. My grandfather still names his cattle, but my grandmother has a little trouble with names, dates and places. Her world is a mixture of real and not-so-real. Her answers don't always exactly match the questions, and her questions have no answers. I know it's scary where she is now, and I long to take her hand and lead her out into the safety of the sunlight.

But when I look into those soft, hard brown eyes, I see the never-ending love of a faithful wife and mother. And more than that, I see the peace that comes from having lived a good life.

I don't leave her feeling sad, only saying, "What a beautiful spirit!"

 ## Suggested Activities for the Teacher

1. Establish and maintain a story time for your classroom. Be sure to include personal and family stories as possible sources for selections to share.

2. Create a climate that encourages the investigation of family stories. Prepare displays or bulletin boards that feature personal artifacts such as photos, utensils, clothing, books, and any items that offer information about an individual. Students can refer to the display when researching their families' oral histories.

3. Create a list of questions for students to use as an outline when interviewing family members. Encourage the students to audio- and/or video-tape the interview.

4. Prepare a personal experience and/or family story of your own to share with students. When telling your story, be sure to model effective communication skills and storytelling techniques.

Suggested Activities for Use With Students

1. Ask students to bring a souvenir or cherished object to class. Have students create personal stories, explaining why the objects are significant

to them. An example might include a seashell from a memorable family vacation.

2. After sharing stories that feature embarrassing or humorous situations, ask the students to think about their most embarrassing moments or the funniest things that ever happened to them. The students should then create personal stories to share orally based upon their memories of the events. Remind the students to include characters, setting, plot, and resolution when creating their personal stories.

3. Ask students to create time lines of their lives as visual displays. The displays should include pictures, important dates, and drawings. Once the time lines are completed and displayed, ask the students to compose biographical stories, following the time-line displays. Students should share the stories orally with the class, using the time lines as visual aids.

4. Encourage the students to maintain journals on a regular basis. Use the journals with students as opportunities for their self-expression, but also scan the journals for possible personal story ideas.

5. Review and discuss the components of fairy tales. Ask the students to write their personal stories as if they were fairy tales. Students can follow up their personal fairy tales with bookmaking and illustrating activities. The fairy tales can be familiar or original stories.

6. Ask students to identify characters from literature with whom they share traits. Have them complete comparison charts and outline the traits and behaviors of themselves and their chosen characters. To follow up, suggest they share their personal comparisons with stories that begin, "I am most like _____ because...."

7. Ask students to interview family members to collect stories that tell about particular members or events that involve family oral history. Develop a coat-of-arms to share, accompanied by information about family names, creeds, legends, origins, and accomplishments. Display the coat-of-arms and compile a class book of the different family histories collected and shared by the students.

8. Have students interview each other, using a list of questions brainstormed by the class. Once the information is collected, ask the students to write articles based on their interviews with their very important people. The stories, accompanied by pictures, should be written appropriately for publication in a newspaper. Discuss the expository style as compared to a narrative style. The articles and pictures might be scanned and pasted onto a desktop publishing program, which would then create a classroom newspaper of interviews and other articles that might also be added.

9. Ask students to create songs or ballads that chronicle the events of their personal lives or those of special family members, using the tune to a familiar ballad or folk song. Examples of ballads or folk songs that might be used include "Bonny Barbara Allen," "Tom Dooley," and "Clementine."

10. Ask students to create personal experience poems that describe significant events in their personal lives or in the lives of particular family members using the rhyme and meter of a familiar narrative poem. Examples of narrative poems that might be used include "Casey at the Bat," "The Highwayman," and "Paul Revere's Ride."

References

Aesop. (1982). The goose with the golden eggs. In *Best-loved folktales of the world,* selected by Joanna Cole (pp. 178-179). Garden City, NY: Doubleday & Company, Inc., .

Bennett, W. J. (Ed.). (1993). *The book of virtues*. New York: Simon & Schuster.

Crosson, V. L., & Stailey, J. C. (1988). *Spinning stories: An introduction to storytelling skills*. Austin, TX: Library Development Division of the Texas State Library.

Davis, D. (1993). *Telling your own stories*. Little Rock, AR: August House.

Fussell, B. (1996). Informal storytelling session. Tennessee Reading Association Conference, Gatlinburg, TN, December.

Gillard, M. (1996). *Storyteller, storyteacher.* York, ME: Stenhouse.

Huddleston, J. (1996). Personal conversation. Byrdstown, TN.

Keeshan, B. (1996). *Books to grow by*. Minneapolis, MN: Fairview Press.

Kilpatrick, W., Wolfe, G., & Wolfe, S. M. (1994). *Books that build character*. New York: Simon & Schuster.

Livo, N. J., & Rietz, S. A. (1991). *Storytelling folklore sourcebook*. Englewood, CO: Libraries Unlimited.

Maguire, J. (1985). *Creative storytelling*. Cambridge, MA: Yellow Moon Press.

Malone, S. (1994). Therapeutic storytelling in the school setting. In *Tales as tools* (pp. 149-153). Jonesborough, TN: National Storytelling Press.

O'Toole, D. (1995). Re-storying brokenness. *Storytelling World* (Summer/Fall), *4*, 2, 21-23.

Petty, P. W. (1997). My story. Unpublished manuscript. Cookeville, TN.

Ray, B. S. (1996). *Blue mountains & green valleys: Stories from Upper East Tennessee*. Kearney, NE: Morris Publishing.

Schram, P. (1987). Jewish stories one generation tells another. *The National Storytelling Journal* (Summer), *4*, 3, 12-14.

Appendix A
Suggested Storytelling References

Akert, R. U. (1991). *Family tales, family wisdom: How to gather the stories of a lifetime and share them with your family*. New York: Henry Holt. Akert's description of his success in motivating elderly people to share the stories of their lives can be a helpful resource for students who want to interview parents and grandparents about family stories.

Baker, A., & Greene, E. (1987). *Storytelling: Art and technique* (2nd ed.). New York: R. R. Bowker.
Chapter 5 contains advice about how to tell whether children are enjoying a story and what to do if students are not in the mood to listen. Chapter 6 contains information on telling stories to children with special needs, such as those with visual and/or hearing impairments, learning disabilities, and emotional difficulties.

Breneman, L. N., & Breneman, B. (1983). *Once upon a time: A storytelling handbook*. Chicago, IL: Nelson-Hall.
A collection of practical ideas for helping tellers develop fluency, characterization, and unity in their stories. The authors also include a chapter entitled "Anticipating a Real Audience" and stories that can be used as models for all ages.

Cooper, P. (1993). *When stories come to school: Telling, writing, and performing stories in the early childhood classroom*. New York: Teachers and Writers Collaborative.
Chapter Four contains information on helping young children dictate their own stories. Chapter Six provides a straightforward guide to weaving storytelling into the daily schedule.

Cooper, P. J., & Collins, R. (1992). *Look what happened to frog*. Scottsdale, Arizona: Gorsuch Scarisbrick.
Chapter 5 provides helpful ideas for determining your own storytelling style

and voice. Chapter 6 discusses six steps involved in dramatizing stories.

Crosson, V. L., & Stailey, J. C. (1988). *Spinning stories: An introduction to storytelling skills*. Austin: Texas State Library.
Crosson and Stailey include a list of kinds of stories to avoid. Similarly, they include elements to avoid in the telling of a story. For example, they advise against apologizing for your lack of skill or other problems with the telling or the environment.

Dailey, S. (1994). *Putting the world in a nutshell: The art of the formula tale*. New York: H. W. Wilson.
Dailey explores the structure and appeal of formula tales, provides a rationale for teaching and telling them, shows several categories of formula tales, and gives examples of stories that fall in each category. She asserts that the simplicity of formula tales makes them very appropriate for teaching storytelling to neophytes.

Dyson, A. H., & Genishi, C. (Eds.). (1994). *The need for story: Cultural diversity in classroom and community*. Urbana, IL: National Council of Teachers of English.
A very theoretical book, *Cultural Diversity* is a collection of essays on the theory and the application of storytelling in a number of settings. For example, Jerome Bruner's constructivist approach views narrative as an ongoing interpretation of what happens in our lives; and Shirley Bryce Heath's study of inner-city youth shows that adolescents use personal stories to explore their own identities and those of their peers.

Farrell, C. (1991). *Storytelling: A guide for teachers*. New York: Scholastic Professional Books.
Farrell's chapter on six hints for telling is very helpful. She also includes eight tellable stories.

Greene, B., & Fulford, D. G. (1993). *To our children's children: Preserving family histories for generations to come*. New York: Doubleday.
This book contains a comprehensive list of thought-provoking questions that can prompt family members to share their stories about everything from elementary school to favorite vehicles. If you are puzzled about how to start collecting family stories, the questions in this book will give you some ideas about where to start.

Griffith, K. (1990). *Writing essays about literature: A guide and style sheet*. San Diego: Harcourt Brace Jovanovich.
While this book is designed primarily for college instructors, Chapter 4 contains helpful information on the plot structure and other major elements of fiction. Writing in a clear, accessible style, Griffith discusses the Freytag Pyramid, the elements of plot, characterization, setting, and point of view. It is a resource for teachers who want to help storytelling students work effectively with the elements of fiction.

Harris, S. G. (1994). *Getting started in storytelling*. Indianapolis: Stonework.
Chapter 5 is helpful for learning how to arrange the room and the audience for an effective storytelling performance.

Hedberg, N. L., & Westby, C. E. (1993). *Analyzing storytelling skills: Theory to practice*. Tucson, AZ: Communication Skill Builders.
This book contains a complex discussion of the relationship of narrative discourse to literacy development. Chapter 8 is an exploration of children's narrative development between the ages of 2 and 10.

Kinghorn, H., & Pelton, M. H. (1991). *Every child a storyteller: A handbook of ideas*. Englewood, CO: Libraries Unlimited.
In this practical resource, the authors have provided a wealth of ideas and activities for the classroom teacher.

Landor, L. (1990). *Children's own stories: A literature-based language arts program*. San Francisco: Zellerbach Family Fund.
Landor provides a description of *The Children's Own Stories* language arts program for students in grades K-4, along with models of stories for teachers who wish to emphasize the importance of encouraging children to share stories from their personal experience.

Ledoux, D. (1993). *Turning memories into memoirs: A handbook for writing life stories*. Lisbon Falls, ME: Soleil Press.
Ledoux offers a number of practical ideas for collecting, researching, telling, writing, and sustaining personal and family stories.

Livo, N. J. (Ed.). (1988). *Joining in: An anthology of audience participation stories and how to tell them*. Cambridge, MA: Yellow Moon Press.
This book not only provides a collection of audience participation stories, but it includes with each story marginal notes almost like stage directions to help the storyteller elicit audience participation at key points in the story. With some stories, the tellers have included the scores of songs appropriate to the story. After each story, readers will find notes that tell the story behind the story.

Livo, N. J., & Rietz, S. A. (1991). *Storytelling folklore sourcebook*. Englewood, CO: Libraries Unlimited.
This sentence from the introduction says it best: "*Storytelling Folklore Sourcebook* aims to bring understanding to how folklore of ancient times still influences us in our speech and actions today" (p. xiii).

MacDonald, M. R. (1993). *The storyteller's start-up book: Finding, learning, performing and using folktales including twelve tellable tales*. Little Rock, AR: August House.
For busy teachers, one chapter contains nine tips for learning stories quickly. While the tips were written for teachers who tell stories to their children, these tips would work well with students in middle school and high school.

Mellon, N. (1992). *Storytelling and the art of imagination*. Rockport, MA: Element.

While Mellon's primary audience is adults from all walks of life, her ideas for helping people develop the stories locked within them can be easily adapted for a storytelling class on the secondary school level.

Mooney, B., & Holt, D. (Eds.). (1996). *The storyteller's guide*. Little Rock, AR: August House.

This book provides numerous ideas of use to storytellers. The chapter entitled "How Do I Control Stage Fright?" contains advice from a number of experienced storytellers on avoiding stage fright and on controlling it when it does overtake you.

Moore, R. (1991). *Awakening the hidden storyteller: How to build a storytelling tradition in your family*. Boston: Shambala.

Moore effectively weaves together interesting personal stories with unusual and appealing activities, called "voyages," to help tellers unlock their imaginations. The ideas in this book would work well with secondary school students.

National Storytelling Association. (1994). *Tales as tools: The power of story in the classroom*. Jonesborough, TN: The National Storytelling Press.

This resource contains a collection of stories and methods for telling them across the curriculum.

Niles, J. J. (1961). *The ballad book of John Jacob Niles*. New York: Bramhall House.

This resource for teachers who wish to teach the ballad in depth provides more than one version of a given ballad and stories about the singers and tellers.

Rosen, B.(1988). *And none of it was nonsense: The power of storytelling in school*. Portsmouth, NH: Heinemann.

This is an account of one teacher's effective use of storytelling as a way of teaching literature to reluctant adolescents.

Sherman, J. (1994). *Once upon a galaxy*. Little Rock: August House.

This book contains a collection of essays that explain the ancient mythology behind such current "myths" as *Star Wars, Star Trek, Superman*, and *The Lord of the Rings*. "Trekkies" and students who are "into" other current fantasy stories will find this book an interesting introduction to ancient myths from all over the world. It is a motivator for teachers who want to incorporate storytelling into the teaching of world literature.

Stone, E. (1989). *Black sheep and kissing cousins: How family stories shape us*. New York: Penguin.

Stone shares a number of ideas about telling family stories. One of her most interesting chapters, entitled "Going Against the Grain," discusses family stories that illustrate a kind of morality that values tolerance, dependability, and honesty, especially when these virtues may be in short supply among others in the community. It would be an interesting springboard for encouraging students to tell their own family stories that illustrate such virtues.

Trousdale, A. M., Woestehoff, S. A., & Schwartz, M. (Eds.). (1994). *Give a listen*. Urbana, IL: National Council of Teachers of English.
The book is a collection of essays arranged in three major categories: How Storytellers Get Started, The Power of Storytelling in the Classroom, and A Community of Listeners and Learners. Marni Schwartz's essay, "The Journal of One Storyteller," provides ideas on using learning logs as a "pre-telling" strategy.

Wanner, S. (1994). *On with the story: Adolescents learning through narrative*. Portsmouth, NH: Boynton/Cook.
Wanner discusses the decline of oral culture and laments the loss of shared experience because a vast number of Americans no longer tell personal stories in a group that is eager to listen. Wanner emphasizes the value of teaching students to tell their own stories with a sense of respect for themselves and for the ancient traditions that they are upholding.

Wason-Ellam, L. (1991). *Start with a story: Literature and learning in your classroom*. Portsmouth, NH: Heinemann.
Wason-Ellam asserts that students "must hear language and...use it themselves in order to grow linguistically" (p. 9). She provides ideas for telling and listening in the primary grades.

Watts, I. N. (1992). *Making stories*. Portsmouth, NH: Heinemann.
Chapter 5, "Getting Started," provides incremental steps for young children to ease into storytelling a step at a time.

Appendix B
Sources of Stories for Tellers

Aardema, V. (1991). *Borreguita and the coyote*. New York: Alfred A. Knopf.

This is an example of a coyote story from Mexico. Aardema presents this tale of conflict between Coyote and Borreguita, or the little lamb. The author provides a glossary that contains words or phrases in Spanish that are used throughout the story.

Andersen, J. C. (1995). *Myths and legends of the Polynesians*. New York: Dover.

Andersen shares a narrative history of the Polynesian people that provides insight into their culture through legends and stories of their arts and beliefs.

Appiah, P. (1967). *Tales of an Ashanti father*. Boston: Beacon Press.

This book is dedicated to the Ashanti people. Appiah shares a collection of folktales which include the West African trickster, Ananse the Spider.

Aurandt, P. (1980). *More of Paul Harvey's the rest of the story*. New York: Bantam Books.

Aurandt has compiled a number of stories based upon the radio show performances of author and public speaker, Paul Harvey. This collection presents unique stories of individuals such as Elvis Presley and Walt Disney and significant events such as the sinking of the *Titanic*.

Balsamo, K. (1987). *Exploring the lives of gifted people in the sciences*. Carthage, IL: Good Apple.

A number of biographical sketches are provided in this resource, featuring outstanding individuals who have contributed significantly in the field of science. Examples of the individuals featured in this book include Dr. Sally Ride, U.S. astronaut, and Dr. Isaac Asimov, nonfiction and science fiction author.

Baltuck, N. (1993). *Crazy gibberish and other story hour stretches*. Hamden, CT: Linnet.

Suggested for ages 5-14, this is a collection of the author's favorite silly, call-and-response, and echo songs, in addition to chants, riddles, tongue twisters, participation games, and stories.

Beckwith, M. (1971). *Hawaiian mythology*. Honolulu: University of Hawaii Press.
The mythology of the Hawaiian people is chronicled in this collection of oral narratives. The stories tell of the gods, children of the gods, the chiefs, Hawaiian mythology, heroes, and lovers.

Bennett, W. J. (Ed.). (1993). *The book of virtues: A treasury of great moral stories*. New York: Simon & Schuster.
Bennett provides an overview of traits essential for the development of moral character and an anthology of stories and books that illustrate the ideals outlined.

Bruchac, J. (1994). *The great ball game: A Muskogee story*. New York: Dial.
This story from the Muskogee or Creek Indian Nation describes a method used to settle a disagreement between the animals and the birds. A game was played and the winner was allowed to issue the penalty. This tale provides an explanation of why birds must fly south for the winter and why the bat is considered an animal. This selection is an interesting resource for teachers who wish to integrate storytelling into their science curriculum.

Buehner, C. (1996). *Fanny's dream*. New York: Dial.
Buehner's retelling is a homespun Cinderella story set in the farmland of Wyoming. Fanny Agnes is the central character, who has always wished to marry a prince. This Cinderella variant ends with a twist that makes it an interesting story to contrast with other variants.

Buffett, J., & Buffett, S. J. (1988). *The jolly mon*. San Diego: Harcourt Brace.
A magic guitar, a lucky man, and a dolphin are all featured in this book that combines the art of storytelling with music.

Burke, J. (1978) *Connections*. Boston, MA: Little, Brown.
A written companion to the Public Broadcasting Service series, the book is a review of stories leading to eight major inventions that helped to usher in the current age of technological advancements.

Caduto, M. J., & Bruchac, J. (1989). *Keepers of the earth: Native American stories and environmental activities for children*. Golden, CO: Fulcrum.
A collection of North American Indian stories and a wealth of environmental activities that encourage interdisciplinary studies are found in this resource.

Caney, S. (1985). *Steven Caney's invention book*. New York: Workman Publishing.
In this book filled with stories of creative thinking and inventions, Caney provides students a workbook approach to the world of the inventor.

Chase, R. (1943). *The Jack tales: Folk tales from the Southern Appalachians*. Boston: Houghton Mifflin.
"Jack Tales" are storytelling treasures that probably traveled to the Appalachian Mountains with the early settlers and have been told and retold for many generations.

Chase, R. (1948). *Grandfather tales*. Boston: Houghton Mifflin.
These stories are examples of the rich oral tradition prevalent in the culture of the Appalachian region of the United States.

Chocolate, D. M. N. (1993). *Spider and the Sky God: An Akan legend*. New York: Troll Associates.
Chocolate retells this story of Ananse the Spider that is a legend of the Akan people of West Africa that explains the origin of stories. It is an example of the trickster motif.

Cohen, D. (1978). *Young ghosts*. New York: Scholastic.
In this selection, Cohen shares interesting ghost stories from a number of areas. Stories include the "Bell Witch of Tennessee," "The Radiant Boys," "Christmas Ghosts," and other tales where children are ghosts or are witnesses to the appearances of ghosts.

Cohen, D. (1983). *Southern fried rat & other gruesome tales*. New York: Avon Flare.
Cohen shares numerous stories that may be described as gross or gruesome. They are the type of stories told at camps and slumber parties. Many are examples of urban legends.

Cohn, A. L. (1993). *From sea to shining sea: A treasury of American folklore and folksong*. New York: Scholastic.
Arranged in a chronology of United States history, this is a real treasure of stories and songs that have been told and sung by a variety of ethnic groups in the nation. It is a rich resource for teachers who wish to use storytelling in the history classroom.

Cole, J. (1982). *Best-loved folktales of the world*. Garden City, NY: Doubleday.
Cole provides an anthology of stories representing numerous cultures and peoples. The tales are organized under the following categories: West Europe, British Isles, Scandinavia, Northern Europe, East Europe, the Middle East, Asia, the Pacific, Africa, North America, the Caribbean and West Indies, and Central and South America. A number of trickster tales are included.

Colman, P. (1995). *Rosie the riveter: Women working on the home front in WWII*. New York: Crown.
Colman shares accounts of the roles of women during World War II and the time period that followed.

Climo, S. (1989). *The Egyptian Cinderella*. New York: HarperCollins.
The author shares a Cinderella variant set in ancient Egypt with illustrations provided by Ruth Heller.

Climo, S. (1993). *The Korean Cinderella*. New York: HarperCollins.
The author shares a Cinderella variant set in ancient Korea with illustrations provided by Ruth Heller.

Climo, S. (1996). *The Irish Cinderlad*. New York: HarperCollins.
This tale features a male character named Becan who eventually is fitted with the boot that helps to win the hand of the princess. A Cinderella story with a different gender perspective, this story is a popular one to share with students.

Compton, J. (1994). *Ashpet*. New York: Holiday House.
In Compton's retelling, Ashpet is a servant girl who eventually marries the doctor's son. Set in Appalachia, *Ashpet* is a Cinderella variant that was first published by Richard Chase in the *Grandfather Tales*.

Cooney, B. (1958). *Chanticleer and the fox*. New York: Thomas Y. Crowell.
This story is adapted from Chaucer's *The Canterbury Tales*. Cooney retells the "Nun's Priest's Tale" and shares this story of the sly fox; Chanticleer, the rooster; and the fair hen, Partlet.

Dailey, S. (1994). *Putting the world in a nutshell: The art of the formula tale*. New York: H. W. Wilson.
The author shares a collection of 38 stories with suggestions on how to ease into storytelling using formula tales.

Davis, D. (1990). *Listening for the crack of dawn*. Little Rock: August House.
This book presents a collection of stories woven together by the author to share experiences of growing up.

Dayrell, E. (1968). *Why the sun and the moon live in the sky*. Boston: Houghton Mifflin.
Dayrell retells this *pourquoi* tale from Africa that explains why the sun and moon are located where they are today.

Durrell, A. (1989). *The Diane Goode book of American folk tales & songs*. New York: Dutton.
Stories for telling and songs for singing are included in this collection. Songs such as "Clementine" and "Yankee Doodle" are folk song favorites that children will be sure to recognize. Stories such as "The Talking Mule" and "The Coyote and the Bear" are examples of the multicultural stories also presented in this collection by Durrell.

Ehlers, S. (1958). *Hawaiian stories for boys and girls*. Honolulu: Hawaiian Service.
This book offers a collection of stories reflecting the legends of giants, ogres, and menehunes from the Hawaiian Islands of Kauai and Niihau.

Erdoes, R., & Ortiz, A. (1984). *American Indian myths and legends*. New York: Pantheon.
This book includes creation stories, hero stories, animal stories, ghost stories, and stories of war and love. It also offers a separate chapter on trickster tales,

including ones about Coyote, Beaver, Raven, and Rabbit.

Ewing, J. (1985). *A treasury of Tennessee tales.* Nashville, TN: Rutledge Hill Press.

A collection of unique and interesting stories of Tennessee's people and places are found in this resource. Stories are arranged thematically and include colorful characters, strange bedfellows, historic places, Indian tales, military adventures, and law and disorder.

Fairman, T. (1991). *Bury my bones but keep my words: African tales for retelling.* New York: Puffin.

Fairman presents 13 stories in an interesting format that helps to maintain the oral tradition of the African culture.

Feldmann, S. (Ed.). (1965). *The storytelling stone: Traditional Native American myths and tales.* New York: Dell.

This anthology of literature includes mythology and folktales from numerous Native American sources. For example, the book includes creation stories, trickster tales, folktales, and hero tales.

Fitzgerald, B. S. (1962). *World tales for creative dramatics and storytelling.* Englewood Cliffs, NJ: Prentice Hall.

Written over 35 years ago, this book is a timeless treasure of stories from various cultures and age groups. A glossary of unusual names and places is included.

Fleischman, P. (1990). *Shadow play.* New York: Harper & Row.

Integrating the folktale of "Beauty and the Beast," Fleischman creates the story of a brother and a sister visiting a carnival and watching a special production involving shadow puppets. The book is illustrated by Eric Beddows.

Foster, J. R. (Ed.). (1994). *The world's great folktales: A collection of 172 of the best stories from world folklore.* New York: Galahad.

Classic folktales are included in this comprehensive anthology of 172 folktales from all over the world. Tales are categorized under the following topics: otherworld and transformed lovers, birth, adventures of the soul, fairies, ogres and the like, more ghosts, witches and wizards, saints and sinners, the power of the name and magic words, the evil eye and things charged with magic, and maladies and remedies.

Gatti, A. (1994). *Tales from the African plains.* New York: Dutton Children's Books.

Gatti includes 12 stories in this resource of traditional African tales. The tales range from the fantastic to the mundane. Some tales include tribal customs, and many involve animal characters.

Grimm, J., & Grimm, W. (Eds.). (1974). *The complete Grimms' fairy tales.* New York: Pantheon.

This valuable resource contains folklore collected by Wilhelm and Jacob Grimm. The Grimm brothers, who were extremely interested in the development of the German language, began their research as a study of language origins. Their scholarly endeavor resulted in a collection of stories with universal appeal that has endured through time and is still accepted with as much enthusiasm as it was originally received.

Hague, M. (1970). *Aesop's fables*. New York: Henry Holt.
This collection contains thirteen of Aesop's fables. Hague presents a sample of popular favorites, including "The Town Mouse and the Country Mouse," "The Lion and the Mouse," and "The Fox and the Grapes."

Haley, G. E. (1970). *A story—a story*. New York: Simon & Schuster.
Haley retells and also illustrates the popular African "Spider Story" in this Caldecott Medal Award book.

Hamilton, V. (1985). *The people could fly: American Black folktales*. New York: Alfred A. Knopf.
Storyteller and writer Hamilton has compiled an anthology of tales prevalent in the African-American culture.

Hautzig, D. (1983). *The story of the Nutcracker Ballet*. New York: Random House.
In this book, illustrated by Diane Goode, Hautzig shares the story of the popular ballet. Students may enjoy reading this book before they watch the ballet itself.

Hayes, J. (1983). *Coyote &: Native American folktales*. Santa Fe: Mariposa Publishing.
Numerous stories featuring Coyote, the trickster, are retold by Hayes in this collection of North American folktales.

Helprin, M. (1989). *Swan Lake*. Boston: Houghton Mifflin.
Helprin presents an original fable while the illustrations by Chris Van Allsburg provide the dimensions to the characters necessary to bring the story of the famous ballet to life.

Higgs, R. J., & Manning, A. N. (Eds.). (1975). *Voices from the hills*. New York: Frederick Ungar (Co-published with Appalachian Consortium Press, Boone, NC).

Higgs, R. J., Manning, A. N., & Miller, J. W. (Eds.). (1995). *Appalachia inside out*. 2 vols. Knoxville: University of Tennessee Press.
Voices From the Hills and *Appalachia Inside Out* are collections of Southern Appalachian literature. They are valuable resources for middle and high school teachers interested in teaching literature from the Appalachian region.

Hirschfelder, A. (Ed.). (1995). *Native heritage: Personal accounts by American Indians 1790 to the present*. New York: Macmillan.
Hirschfelder has compiled a rich and varied anthology representing the oral tradition of the Native American culture, reflecting centuries of Native American history.

Huck, C. (1989). *Princess Furball*. New York: Scholastic.
Huck retells this Russian variant of the Cinderella story.

Huffstetler, E. W. (1996). *Myths of the world: Tales of native America*. New York: Michael Friedman Publishing Group.
Huffstetler provides an overview of Native American mythology, including creation stories and a special chapter featuring the mischievous trickster.

Jones, L., & Wheeler, B. E. (1991). *Hometown humor, U.S.A.* Little Rock: August House.
The authors share their collection of jokes and stories filled with "down-home" humor from different areas of the United States.

Justice, J. (Ed.). (1992). *The ghost & I: Scary stories for participatory telling*. Cambridge, MA: Yellow Moon Press.
Justice presents a variety of ghost stories and also includes suggestions on how to tell them using the audience participation format.

Keeshan, B. (1996). *Books to grow by*. Minneapolis, MN: Fairview Press.
This resource includes a listing of recommended books for teaching and reinforcing values. The books were selected by TV's "Captain Kangaroo."

Kilpatrick, W., Wolfe, G., & Wolfe, S. M. (1994). *Books that build character*. New York: Simon & Schuster.
The authors provide a source for numerous stories to be used in the development of character through the sharing of literature.

Kimmel, E. A. (1992). *Anansi goes fishing*. New York: Holiday House.
Kimmel offers a retelling of an African folktale featuring the trickster, Anansi. In this particular tale, the origin of the spider web is revealed.

Lester, J. (1987). *The tales of Uncle Remus: The adventures of Brer Rabbit*. New York: Dial.
In this selection, Lester retells the popular adventures of the African-American trickster, Brer Rabbit. Some of the popular Brer Rabbit adventures in the book are "Brer Rabbit Tricks Brer Bear," "Brer Rabbit's Riddle," and "Brer Rabbit and the Tar Baby."

London, J. (1993). *Fire race: A Karuk Coyote tale*. New York: Scholastic.
This Karuk tale, often told during the winter months, relates one version of the myth describing how Coyote, the trickster, brought fire to the people.

Loriot, reteller, & Muller, J. (1978). *Peter and the wolf: A musical fairy tale by Sergei Prokofiev*. New York: Schirmer.
This book illustrates the development of the famous musical fairy tale with pictures and text. Illustrations reveal the characters as they introduce the various instruments of the orchestra. They also depict the plot of the tale.

Louie, A. (1982). *Yeh-Shen: A Cinderella story from China*. New York: Philomel.
Retold by Louie and illustrated by Ed Young, this Cinderella story is based upon one from the T'ang dynasty. The author notes that evidence of this version predates the first recorded European Cinderella tale and offers the sug-

gestion that the variant possibly traveled to Europe from Asia.

Martin, C. (1982). *Swann Street*. McMinnville, TN: Womack Printing.
The author shares his personal accounts of growing up in a small rural middle Tennessee community.

Martin, R. (1993). *The rough-face girl*. New York: Scholastic.
Set in a village on the banks of Lake Ontario, this Algonquin Indian retelling of the traditional Cinderella story presents a brief portion of a longer and more complex story. Rough-face Girl, scarred as a result of the mistreatment received from her two sisters, sees the Invisible Being and becomes eligible to marry him, according to a tribal legend. In traditional Cinderella style, the story has a happy ending; Rough-face Girl and the Invisible Being marry and are never parted.

Martin, R. (1996). *Mysterious tales of Japan*. New York: G. P. Putnam's Sons.
Martin shares a variety of traditional Japanese stories and also includes story notes that provide additional information about parallel versions and related stories.

McCaughrean, G. (1985). *The Canterbury tales*. Chicago: Rand McNally.
McCaughrean presents Chaucer's tales in a version that is organized by story titles that reflect the content or theme rather than the storyteller. For example, "The Nun's Priest's Tale is entitled "The Nightmare Beast of the Firebrand Tail."

McDermott, G. (1992). *Zomo the Rabbit: A trickster tale from West Africa*. New York: Harcourt Brace.
This humorous West African trickster tale features Zomo the Rabbit. Like his United States variant, Brer Rabbit, Zomo is always into mischief. This is the story of Zomo's quest for wisdom in which he must accomplish three difficult tasks outlined by the sky god.

McDermott, G. (1993). *Raven: A trickster tale from the Pacific Northwest*. Harcourt, Brace.
McDermott retells and illustrates a story with the trickster motif found in Native American folklore from the Pacific Northwestern region of the United States. In this version, Raven discovers the origin of light. After Raven changes himself into a pine needle, the daughter of the Sky Chief swallows him when she takes a drink. Later, the daughter gives birth to a child who looks like Raven. Eventually the child is given the light source, and he immediately flies into the sky and places the light source where it remains today.

McDermott, G. (1994). *Coyote: A trickster tale from the American Southwest*. New York: Harcourt Brace.
McDermott retells and illustrates a story with the trickster motif found in Native American folklore. In this version, Blue Coyote discovers that it is not wise to try to be something that you are not.

McDonald, M. (1996). *Tales of the constellations: The myths and legends of the night sky*. New York: Smithmark.
This collection contains stories related to 27 of the major star constellations.

McKissack, P. (1992). *The dark-thirty: Southern tales of the supernatural*. New York: Alfred A. Knopf.
Dark-thirty, described by McKissack, is a specific time of day just before night falls. During that thirty minutes, it is neither day nor night and shadows begin to cast a eerie spell. It is the perfect time for sharing the original stories presented in the book. The 10 suspenseful stories included in this selection were inspired by the author's rich oral storytelling tradition and African-American history.

McNeil, N., & Squibb, J. (1989). *A Southern Appalachian reader*. Boone, NC: Appalachian Consortium Press.
These stories from Southern Appalachia were collected by teachers interested in integrating stories of Appalachia into the high school English curriculum.

Miller, T. (1988). *Joining in: An anthology of audience participation stories & how to tell them*. Cambridge, MA: Yellow Moon Press.
Miller presents an anthology of audience participation stories, as well as offering suggestions on how to tell them effectively.

Milnes, G. (1990). *Granny will your dog bite and other mountain rhymes*. New York: Alfred A. Knopf.
This book is filled with rhymes, riddles, and songs that have been preserved and shared orally for generations. "Old Dan Tucker," and "What're We Gonna Do with the Baby-O?" are examples of some of the rhymes that are included in this collection of traditional mountain lore.

National Storytelling Association, The. (1991). *Best-loved stories told at the National Storytelling Festival*. Jonesborough, TN: National Storytelling Press.
This anthology contains a number of stories which have been told at the annual National Storytelling Festival held each Fall in Jonesborough, Tennessee. This valuable source of stories features professional storytellers such as Jackie Torrence, Jay O'Callahan, Kathryn Windham, Donald Davis, J. J. Reneaux, David Holt, Elizabeth Ellis, and many others.

National Storytelling Association, The. (1995). *Many voices: True tales from America's past*. Jonesborough, TN: National Storytelling Press.
Accompanied by a Teacher's Guide, this source of 36 biographical stories also includes curricular and activity suggestions.

Nelson, P. (1993). *Magic minutes: Quick read-alouds for every day*. Englewood, CO: Libraries Unlimited.
This book offers a number of very short stories for teachers who need those quick transition or filler activities. A variety of multicultural selections is presented and organized by months, beginning with September and ending with

May, with an additional section for summer. The stories include trickster
tales, creation stories, and math related selections.

Opie, I., & Opie, P. (Eds.). (1974). *The classic fairy tales*. New York:
Oxford University Press.
In this anthology, the editors include folklore selections, but also offer histor-
ical information and indicate cultural variants of the tales.

Pollock, P. (1996). *The turkey girl: A Zuni Cinderella story*. Boston:
Little, Brown.
Illustrated by Caldecott Award-winner Ed Young, this variant of the
Cinderella story is retold by Pollock from the folklore of the Zuni Indians of
the Southwestern region of the United States.

Raboff, E. (1986). *Art for children*. New York: Harper & Row.
This series highlights 16 painters and includes illustrations and background
information about the artists' most famous works.

Ransome, A. (1968). *The fool of the world and the flying ship*. New York:
Farrar, Straus and Giroux.
In this Caldecott Medal book illustrated by Uri Shulevitz, Ransome retells a
popular Russian folk tale.

Ray, B. S. (1996). *Blue mountains & green valleys: Stories from Upper
East Tennessee*. Kearney, NE: Morris Publishing.
Ray shares his unique personal experiences of growing up in East Tennessee
in this collection of family stories and anecdotes.

Reader's Digest Association, Inc., The. (1976). *Strange stories, amazing
facts*. Pleasantville, NY: Reader's Digest Association..
Offering an assortment of subject areas, this entertaining collection provides
a variety of unusual and informative stories. Stories are arranged thematically and include wonders of the natural world, the marvels of science, man's
amazing inventions, popular facts and fallacies, intriguing and unsolved mysteries, legendary lands and beasts, curious and bizarre beginnings, and the
world of tomorrow.

Regier, W. G. (Ed.). (1993). *Masterpieces of American Indian literature*.
New York: MJF Books.
Reiger provides an anthology of numerous classic Native American stories,
including stories featuring the trickster, Coyote.

Ringgold, F. (1991). *Tar Beach*. New York: Crown.
A Caldecott Honor Book, Tar Beach is based on a story quilt, combining
autobiography, fiction, painting, and quilting into one art form.

Ringgold, F. (1993). *Dinner at Aunt Connie's house*. New York:
Hyperion.
This children's book features a story of two children who discover the influence of African-Americans in American history and culture through portraits
hanging on Aunt Connie's wall.

Ross, S. (1994). *Shakespeare and Macbeth: The story behind the play*. New York: Viking Press.

The book provides background information about Shakespeare and the development of the play Macbeth.

San Souci, R. D. (1994). *Sootface: An Ojibwa Cinderella story*. New York: Doubleday.

A native tale of Canada's Micmac tribes, this variant embraces the traditional Cinderella story line. Sootface sees the invisible warrior and is chosen to become his bride. Later her name is changed to Dawn-Light, in order to reflect her true beauty.

Sawyer, R. (1970). *The way of the storyteller*. New York: Penguin.

Eleven of Sawyer's favorite stories are included in this respected storyteller's resource book.

Schroeder, A. (1997). *Smoky Mountain Rose: An Appalachian Cinderella*. New York: Dial.

This Cinderella adaptation is set in Appalachia and features the character Rose. Retold in Appalachian dialect, the story begins, "Now lis'en," and continues to tell about a magic pig, a shindig, a man named Seb, and the traditional glass slipper.

Schwartz, A. (1981). *Scary stories to tell in the dark*. New York: Harper & Row.

Schwartz retells a number of stories in this collection of horror favorites.

Sechrist, E. H. (1969). *Once in the first times: Folk tales from the Philippines*. Philadelphia: Macrae Smith.

Sechrist provides folklore samples from the Philippines that include legends and myths, describing customs and beliefs of the island people.

Shannon, G. (1985). *Stories to solve: Folktales from around the world*. New York: Scholastic.

Shannon has collected stories from around the world that appear in the form of puzzles or problems that must be solved. Answers are provided following each clever mystery or story.

Shepherd, S. (1995). *Myths and legends from around the world*. New York: Simon & Schuster/Macmillan.

This collection includes thematically organized stories representing numerous cultures. This book provides a rich multicultural resource of stories for retelling.

Sherman, J. (1992). *A sampler of Jewish-American folklore*. Little Rock: August House.

Sherman explores the wisdom of Jewish-American folklore in this collection of folktales, proverbs, and riddles.

Sherman, J. (1993). *Rachel the Clever and other Jewish folktales*. Little Rock: August House.

The author shares a variety of Jewish-American stories that reflect multicultural origins in the 46 tales of this collection.

    Smith, J. N. (Ed.). (1988). *Homespun: Tales from America's favorite storytellers*. New York: Crown.

This comprehensive resource includes more than thirty stories by professional storytellers who have appeared at the National Storytelling Festival held each October in Jonesborough, Tennessee. In addition to the popular stories, the book also presents information about the individual tellers and offers storytelling tips and suggestions for developing effective storytelling skills. Stories are thematically organized and include stories of Southern Appalachian Mountains, Humor and Wit, Faraway Times and Places, Supernatural, American Traditions, Family and Friends, People from Truth and Fantasy, and Contemporary Life.

    Spier, P. (Illus.). (1961). *The fox*. New York: Dell.

This Caldecott Honor book combines art and music as effective companions to this folksong.

    Steptoe, J. (1987). *Mufaro's beautiful daughters*. New York: Scholastic.

Steptoe retells this African variant of the Cinderella story.

    Stille, D. (1995). *Extraordinary women scientists*. Danbury, CT: Children's Press.

Stille provides stories of 50 great women in the field of science.

    Stock, C. (1984). *Emma's dragon hunt*. New York: Lothrop, Lee & Shepard.

When Emma's grandfather visits from China, Emma is given explanations of numerous natural phenomena, based upon stories from Chinese dragon legends.

    Tashjian, V. (1995). *Juba this and Juba that*. Boston: Little, Brown.

Tashjian has compiled a variety of songs, chants, and poems in this resource.

    Taylor, C. F., & Sturtevant, W. C. (Consultants.) (1996). *The Native Americans: The indigenous people of North America*. New York: Smithmark.

The authors provide an overview of the people indigenous to the North American continent. The book is written in a historical essay style with photographs and graphics.

    Thompson, S. (1995). *Folk tales of the North American Indians*. North Dighton, MA: JG Press.

Thompson provides a resource of folklore from the Native American culture, including tales that Native Americans have borrowed from Europeans. This book includes a section on trickster tales.

    Thompson, V. L. (1966). *Hawaiian myths of earth, sea, and sky*. Honolulu: University of Hawaii Press.

Thompson shares a collection of twelve Hawaiian myths that explain natural phenomena. Stories of particular interest are "The lost Sun, Moon, and Stars" and "The Woman in the Moon."

Thompson, V. L. (1969). *Hawaiian legends of tricksters and riddlers.* Honolulu: University of Hawaii Press.
Thompson shares a collection of 12 Hawaiian trickster and riddle stories. "Maui-the-trickster" and "The Riddling Chief of Puna" are two of the stories included in this selection.

Warren, J. (1984). *"Cut & tell:" Scissor stories for fall.* Everett, WA: Warren Publishing House.

Warren, J. (1984). *"Cut & tell:" Scissor stories for winter.* Everett, WA: Warren Publishing House.
In both *"Cut & Tell"* books, Warren presents original stories to accompany the featured cutout patterns. The books are recommended for preschool, kindergarten, and first and second grades and provide explicit details on how to tell the stories and deliver the instructions for the paper plate cutouts. As students listen to the stories, they follow directions and cut out patterns using paper plates. The completed cutout will relate to the theme or content of the story told. For example, in "The Apple Tree," students listen and cut out the shapes of two apples and one tree.

Williams, M. (1996). *The Iliad and the Odyssey.* Cambridge MA: Candlewick Press.
Williams retells the classic epics with modern appeal.

Winter, J. (1988). *Follow the drinking gourd.* New York: Alfred A. Knopf.
The story of Peg Leg Joe and the Underground Railroad illustrates the historical significance of music and storytelling for purposes beyond entertainment and education.

Winthrop, E. (1991). *Valissa the beautiful.* New York: HarperCollins.
Winthrop presents this retelling of a Russian folktale with a plot similar to the plot of Cinderella. Valissa, the central character, is mistreated and sent into the forest where she must deal with the horrible witch, Baba Yaga. With the help of her magic doll and her weaving skills, she impresses the Tzar, whom she later marries.

Yeats, W. B. (Ed.). (no date). *Irish fairy and folk tales.* New York: Random House.
This collection of fairy and folktales presents imaginative storytelling material about fairies, changelings, ghosts, witches, giants, kings, queens, princes, and robbers.

Yolen, J. (1995). *A sip of Aesop.* New York: Blue Sky Press.
In this collection, the author shares a number of Aesop's fables, including "The Fox and the Grapes."

Young, E. (1989). *Lon Po Po: A Red-Riding Hood story from China.* New York: Philomel.
In this Caldecott Medal-winning book, Young retells and illustrates the Red-Riding Hood Story variant from Chinese folklore.

Young, R., & Young, J. (Eds.). (1993). *African-American folktales for young readers*. Little Rock: August House.
This collection features stories told by popular African and African-American storytellers. The stories are organized by sections and many are introduced with story notes to aid in the understanding of the narratives.

Young, R., & Young, J. (Eds.). (1990). *Favorite scary stories of American children*. Little Rock: August House.
In this collection, the authors have compiled a variety of scary stories specifically designed for children, ages 5 to 10.

Young, R., & Young, J. (Eds.). (1992). *Stories from days of Christopher Columbus*. Little Rock: August House.
This collection offers stories told in the 1400s, during the time of the famous explorer. These stories do not feature Columbus; instead, they provide the reader with a glimpse of the people whose lives he impacted.

Index

Title Index

Subject Index

Biographical Information

Betty D. Roe, a Professor of Education at Tennessee Technological University in Cookeville, is author or coauthor of 29 college textbooks and numerous professional articles, many about storytelling. She developed and taught a storytelling course at the University. Her storytelling presentations across the United States and in Canada include being a Featured Teller at the International Reading Association's Informal Gathering several times and giving storytelling informational sessions at the IRA Annual Convention, the IRA World Congress on Reading, and the National Council of Teachers of English Convention. She chaired the IRA Storytellers' Special Interest Group and served as the editor of *Once-Upon-*  *A Times*. She has been profiled in *The Tennessee Storytelling Journal* and was featured on the cover of the June, 1991, issue. She currently serves on the editorial review board for *Storytelling World*.

Suellen Alfred, Associate Professor of Education at Tennessee Technological University in Cookeville, incorporates the use of storytelling in her English Education classes. She is the Associate Editor of the *Tennessee English Journal*. Before moving to Tennessee Tech, she taught secondary English and used story-telling extensively with her students. She was invited by the president of National Council of Teachers of English to present a storytelling session at the convention in Orlando in 1994. She has made story-telling presentations in other cities across the United States.

Sandy Smith is currently an Instructor in the Department of Curriculum and Instruction at Tennessee Technological University in Cookeville, Tennessee. Sandy often presents workshops and staff development programs, a great many of which feature storytelling. Active in a number of professional organizations, she has presented at the International Reading Association and National Council of Teachers of English annual conferences. Before joining the University full time, Sandy taught special education and gifted education classes in the public schools as well as university courses as an adjunct instructor. Sandy has observed the power of storytelling both professionally with her students and personally with her family.